A Matter of Justice

A Matter of Justice

Lesbians and Gay Men in Law Enforcement

Robin A. Buhrke, Ph. D.

Routledge

New York and London

Published in 1996 by
Routledge
29 West 35th Street
New York, NY 10001

Published in Great Britain by
Routledge
11 New Fetter Lane
London EC4P 4EE

Library of Congress Cataloging-in-Publication Data

Cataloging-in-Publication Data may be obtained by writing the Library of Congress

To my father, Paul Buhrke and the memory of my mother, Marguerite Buhrke, and to lesbians, gay men, and bisexuals everywhere for whom homophobia makes their workplaces unsafe

Contents

Preface

With a handful of names, several boxes of blank cassette tapes, a concept for a book, and a megadose of optimism, I began a journey that took me to the four corners of the country, and places in between. It took me to small towns and large metropolitan areas. It took me into the hearts and souls of a group of courageous individuals—people who were willing to share their triumphs, their sadness, and their everyday lives with me.

I sought answers to such questions as:

What are the experiences of lesbians and gay men working in the criminal justice system?

What is it like to be an openly gay criminal justice worker in such places as rural West Virginia, North Dakota, or Dallas, Texas?

What is it like being a gay police officer in need of backup when no one comes to the aid of the "fag?"

What makes some openly gay and lesbian criminal justice workers flourish and grow in their jobs while others falter and stumble?

What is it like to be an outsider in a traditionally heterosexual, White, male-dominated, able-bodied, "macho" profession?

What is it like to be forced to choose between self-disclosure and safety?

I learned the answers to these questions and many others I had not even imagined. I met and spoke with criminal justice professionals across the country and conducted in-depth interviews. The people I met were amazing; the experiences they shared were poignant and riveting.

Rather than distill all the information I gathered into small bits and pieces to present to the reader, I wanted to convey not only the incidents that occurred to these people, but their characters and personalities—their essence, if you will—as well. In sharing our humanity we can see that our similarities transcend many of our differences, and that our differences need not be feared.

Approach

Over the course of a two year period beginning in June of 1993, I interviewed seventy-two lesbians and gay men employed in various criminal justice positions. I was unable to interview any self-identified *bi*sexual criminal justice personnel, and therefore any conclusions based on these stories may not relate to their experiences. The stories presented here do not represent a random sample of lesbian and gay criminal justice professionals—there's no way they could. What I attempted to do was discover and present the "diversity" of experience rather than the "average" experience.

I gathered my sample in two ways: about 10 percent came via public notices through the internet and 90 precent were derived by snowball sampling—the people I talked with and interviewed provided me with the names and phone numbers of other contacts. The data is almost entirely qualitative, coming from semi-structured interviews which lasted anywhere from an hour to four and a half hours. Each interview consisted of three parts. The first section focused on developmental history—when and how did they know they wanted to enter criminal justice, and how did being lesbian or gay affect the decision to pursue a criminal justice career. The second section focused on experiences as lesbians or gay men in criminal justice—what is it like to be lesbian or gay in criminal justice; if they weren't out, how did they manage to keep closeted; and if they were out, how did they come out, and what were the reactions of fellow officers. The third section focused on experiences as law enforcement personnel in the lesbian and gay community.

Most of those interviewed gave permission to be fully identified, while a few wished for (and received) varying degrees of anonymity. The stories recounted here represent twenty-one males and twenty-two females from sixteen states, the District of Columbia, and Canada. Thirty-one are White, U.S. born; five are African-American; two are Hispanic; two are White, U.S. immigrants; one is Native American; and one is Canadian. One has a disability. Ages range from twenty-seven to fifty-two, and they have spent anywhere from less than a year to twenty years in criminal justice. Education levels range from high school level to graduate work. Many have bachelor's degrees, several have master's, one has a Ph.D., and a few have law degrees. One was in medical school and another was in the last year of coursework for a Ph.D. when they both dropped out to become cops. Thirty-three departments are represented, ranging in size from the more than eight thousand officers in the Los Angeles Police Department to the eight officer department in Pineville, WV. Twenty four are with police departments, five are with sheriff's departments, four are with state departments of corrections, four are with campus police and security departments, three are judges, one is a state trooper, one is a deputy district attorney, and one is a former FBI agent. There were nine sergeants, one lieutenant, and one chief. Most of them were still on the job when I interviewed them, but one had retired, two had been fired for being gay, one had resigned, and three were on medical leave.

Each interview was audiotaped. After transcribing the tapes, I edited the transcripts for clarity, redundancy, and grammar. Where possible, each person reviewed his or her own story, corrected any errors, and approved the editing. The stories were organized around the functions of the criminal justice system: apprehension, detention, adjudication, and incarceration of those who break the law, as well as "special forces." Because the functions of detention and incarceration are so similar, the categories were collapsed.

The words and the stories are theirs. Each story has a rhythm and a melody of its own. Individual perspectives corroborate as well as contradict one another, yet collectively they provide a view of the world of criminal justice and its attitudes regarding its lesbian and gay members.

Acknowledgments

It has been said so often that it seems cliche: No project of this magnitude could have been completed without the help of countless others. Yet it is unalterably true. First and foremost, I am grateful to those individuals who participated in this project. Without their generosity of time and spirit, this book would not exist. Nor would it have been possible had people not opened their address books and connected me with potential participants: There are no telephone directories of lesbian and gay criminal justice workers. I apologize to those whose words do not appear here. There were many more stories to tell than space permitted. Many old friends, and some new friends, fed and sheltered me during my travels. They patiently listened to my tales, soothed my frustrations, and propped me up when I had conducted one too many interviews for the day. This book is as much theirs as it is mine.

I am grateful to my editor, Philip Rappaport, formerly of Routledge Press for his encouragement, nudging, and belief in this project, and to Charles Hames who shepherded it through production. My colleagues at Duke University's Counseling and Psychological Services, and in particular Co-Directors, John Barrow and Libby Webb, were extremely understanding and supportive of my efforts. Their excitement for and interest in the project made juggling work and "the book" that much easier. Transcribers Steven Koes, Linda McGee, Michele Lechman, Diana Swancutt, Charles Carson, and Holly Hyland translated hundreds of hours of audiotapes into written text. Without them, I would still be sitting at my computer listening to audiotapes, and the book would not be ready during this century. Katherine Hufstetler combed the local libraries searching for reference materials and provided me with a twelve-inch stack of articles to review. My research team members and editors extrodinaire, Lydia Buki and Stephanie Jenal, provided ongoing support, hand-holding, and gentle critiques. Holly Hyland edited the entire manuscript, and kept reminding me that it was possible to maintain the integrity of the text while making the transcripts readable. All of these people helped make the process of bringing this book to fruition easier and more enjoyable.

I am grateful to the many friends who, perhaps long after they had heard enough stories, continued to ask, "How's the book?" I especially appreciate the patience of friends who didn't wince when I brought my computer along on vacation and worked while they soaked up the rays on the beach.

Finally, I am indebted to my partner, Holly Hyland, for her patience, wisdom, love, and support for me and this project. My life is sweeter because of her. After two long years of travel, transcribing, and, "I have to work on the book," we are both ready for it to be completed.

Introduction

In 1991, I was Chair-Elect of Dade ActionPAC, a political action committee formed in Dade County, FL to address the concerns of the lesbian, gay, and bisexual community. Members of the gay community had lodged numerous complaints against two Miami Beach police officers who were allegedly entrapping gay men by going off to a secluded spot on the boardwalk, pretending to engage in oral sex, inviting men to join them, and then arresting them for lewd and lascivious behavior. As a result, several of us went to visit the chief to discuss our concerns. That was the beginning of an ongoing relationship between the lesbian and gay community and the Miami Beach Police Department. Members of Dade ActionPAC were invited to conduct sensitivity training sessions with the three hundred-plus officers over the course of the next year and a half. During that time we also helped the department write a non-discrimination policy that included sexual orientation. The chief appointed a lesbian and gay liaison team that consisted of an openly gay patrol officer and a heterosexual major who was commander of the patrol division. And several officers—gay and straight alike—marched in uniform in the 1992 gay pride parade and recruited reserve officers at the pride festival.

In May of 1992, then-President Bush came to the Miami Beach Convention Center to speak at a commencement ceremony, and police intelligence sources learned that several bus-loads of members of ACT UP (AIDS Coalition To Unleash Power), an organization known for its radical protests, were planning to demonstrate. The department asked me to work as a liaison between the protesters and the police. Several events that day sparked this project.

The department had set up a row of barricades with spots for each of the many protesting groups. Although the department supported the rights of the protesters to demonstrate, they didn't want anyone to get hurt, and they wanted to avoid arrests. Because it was Miami Beach, numerous groups were demonstrating against U.S. foreign policies in Central and South America. The sky was clear, the sun was hot, and the air was full of chants, protestations, and indictments in English and Spanish.

I was stationed on the police side of the barricade. When I walked up to the ACT UP protestors—most of whom I knew from my work in the community—one taunted, "Traitor! What are you doing over there?" That allegation provided my first taste of the dilemma faced by lesbian and gay officers.

The demonstrators began their protests, shouting complaints at the President—who, of course, was nowhere near earshot. At some incalculable point, the target of the shouting and cursing shifted from the President to the police officers who were lined up between the protestors and the building. The jeers were ironic in that the officers facing the ACT UP protestors and taking the brunt of this cop-bashing were themselves lesbian and gay. In that moment, the dilemma of the lesbian and gay officer became crystal clear to me: these officers all too often are not accepted by their police community because they are gay or lesbian, and because they are cops, they are rejected by the lesbian and gay community. As you will see in the stories that follow, in the world of law enforcement, many are faced with being "fags" and "dykes" in the eyes of their fellow officers, and "pigs" to their gay and lesbian brothers and sisters. I wondered what it was that led these officers to choose to stay in such a potentially conflict-ridden career. I received part of my answer a year later, at the 1993 March on Washington.

The march was envisioned to be, and was, the largest civil rights demonstration to date in the history of the United States. Plans for the march, the accompanying events, and the anticipated million-plus participants began more than a year before the first marchers stepped off the curb near the Washington Monument. The week was filled with dances; protests and demonstrations around such issues as governmental AIDS/HIV policies, gays in the military, and the lack of civil rights protections; religious observations; lobbying on Capitol Hill; a display of the AIDS quilt; and a huge outdoor wedding ceremony where same-sex couples declared their love and commitment to one another and the world. It was a week of affirmation, celebration, and pride, as well as a time of remembrance and sadness for the losses, of anger and frustration over sometimes excruciatingly slow progress, and of hope for the future. It was a time when lesbians, gay men, and bisexuals flooded the Metro and the Mall, and where because of the sheer numbers, same-sex couples could, for once, walk hand in hand down the streets of the nation's capital without fear of harassment or violence.

Lesbians, gays, bisexuals, transgendered, and their allies arrived from all over the country to participate in the march. Among them was a handful of Miami Beach police officers—most of whom I had seen vilified by members of the gay and lesbian community a year earlier. After standing in the warm, April sun for more than four hours, the Miami Beach Police Department contingent, made up of lesbian, gay, and heterosexual officers, their spouses, and their friends, began what would turn out to be the walk of a lifetime. Instead of the curses and profanity they had received the year before, they were met with an uproar of applause and boisterous cheers all along the march route, not to mention photographers and journalists wanting to document this historic event. That one mile journey had the power to wipe away years of abuse and harassment at the hands of the gay and lesbian community. For once, these officers were truly comrades with the gay and lesbian community.

Experiencing these extreme reactions to lesbian and gay law enforcement personnel was the catalyst for this project. I hoped that members of the lesbian and gay community might see how they were excluding, harassing, and sometimes oppressing members of their community because of their work in criminal justice. I hoped members of the criminal justice community might see how they, too, were excluding, harassing, and sometimes oppressing other criminal justice workers because of their sexual orientation. I hoped that both communities might better understand, develop compassion for, and begin to respect lesbian and gay criminal justice workers. I hoped that each group might see that we are a lot more similar than different.

Lesbians, Gay Men and Law Enforcement

For most of the lesbian and gay community, the words "law enforcement" conjure images of bar raids, police harassment and abuse, and victimization by the criminal justice system rather than "brothers and sisters in blue." And for good reason. Legal sanctions against homosexual behavior date back to Colonial times when death was the punishment for the offense of sodomy (D'Emilio, 1983). Although most states had abolished the death penalty for sodomy by the mid 1800s, in 1950 all but two states still classified sodomy as a felony, and in New York, "homosexual behavior" was a felony punishable by twenty years in jail. Simply talking suggestively about same-gender sex was grounds for arrest, and plainclothes officers entrapped gay men by initiating such conversations (Marotta, 1981). In 1971, 110 men were sentenced to fifteen years to life for "sodomy and oral copulation" (Shilts, 1982). Although relatively few have been punished to the full extent possible, these laws served to label and stigmatize same-gender eroticism as criminal.

As D'Emilio explained, although the penalties have lessened, the stigma remains:

> As a gay subculture took root in twentieth-century American cities, police invoked laws against disorderly conduct, vagrancy, public lewdness, assault, and solicitation in order to haul in their victims. Gay men who made assignations in public places, lesbians and homosexuals who patronized gay bars, and occasionally even guests at gay parties in private homes risked arrest. Vice squad officers, confident that their targets did not dare to challenge their authority, were free to engage in entrapment. Anxious to avoid additional notoriety, gay women and men often pleaded guilty even when the police lacked sufficient evidence to secure convictions. (pp. 14, 15)

Numerous writers have provided a detailed history of police entrapment and harassment of gay men and lesbians; the interested reader should refer to D'Emilio (1983), Marotta (1981), Kennedy and Davis (1993), Chauncey (1994), Rosen (1980), or Dodge (1993). The following are some of the more notorious examples of this abuse.

In 1948, police attempted to shut down the Black Cat, a San Francisco bar frequented by gay men and lesbians, because they served liquor to lesbians and gay men (Shilts, 1982).

> Paddywagons routinely rolled up to the doors of gay bars and police bused all the patrons to jail....charges were dismissed most times, but usually after the city's newspapers printed not only the arrested person's name, but his address and place of employment. Police also followed up these arrests with calls to the victim's employer and family, even if charges were dropped within hours. (p. 54)

It took another fifteen years of harassment, but the police finally succeeded in closing the Black Cat.

When, in the mid '50s, contrary to the desires of management, New York's King Cole Bar began to get a gay clientele, it was visited by a private detective and his assistants who walked through the crowd making insulting comments. When that strategy failed, he began taking fingerprints from glasses and shooting photographs of patrons; the bar emptied (Duberman, 1991).

It was not unusual for newspaper editors in the '50s to print the names, addresses, and places of employment of those arrested in bar raids, for police to park squad cars in front of bars to intimidate patrons, and for police to resort to entrapment to arrest gay men (D'Emilio, 1983).

Labelling them "obscene," the Post Office refused to deliver early gay publications (Sullivan, 1990).

In 1964, at a San Francisco New Year's Eve dance, the police trained floodlights on the entrance and filmed everyone entering the establishment. In spite of paddy wagons waiting in the background, more than five hundred lesbians and gay men attended the event (Shilts, 1982).

The 1940s and '50s were characterized by witch hunts against gay men and lesbians (Katz, 1976) designed to remove homosexuals from employment in Federal government. The police department in the District of Columbia had an office in its vice squad whose sole function was to root out "homosexuals." In the nearly four years from the beginning of 1947 to the end of 1950, 4,954 cases were processed—4,380 in the military and 574 on Federal civilian payrolls (Katz, 1976). Reputedly one of the most infamous and virulent homophobes of the time, J. Edgar Hoover was also rumored to be a gay man (Turner, 1993); he was said to have had a long affair with his assistant director, Clyde Tolson. Hoover fired any agent suspected of being (or known to be) gay; the private living quarters at the FBI Academy were "bugged," allegedly in efforts to detect "latent homosexuals" (Turner, 1993).

One of the most famous cases of police harassment of the gay community is known as the beginning of the modern day gay liberation movement. During the early and mid '60s, New York's Stonewall Inn was a popular gathering place for gays and lesbians, particularly among young Puerto Rican and Black gay men and drag queens. Because of frequent raids by the police, a lighting system had been installed to warn patrons of police presence. If any suspicious types entered, the light would flash and dancing would stop (Duberman, 1991). On Friday, June 27, 1969, when police raided the Stonewall Inn once again, they presented the manager with a warrant charging that liquor was being sold without a license and attempted to make arrests. Those who had identification were allowed to leave; those who did not were to be taken to the station for questioning. Those who left assembled across the street to watch the proceedings (Marotta, 1981). A crowd gathered as the police attempted to load patrons into the paddy wagons. Witnessing the last patron's struggle against the police, the crowd exploded in anger and protest, pelting the officers with beer cans, bottles, and coins. The police were forced to retreat into the bar and had to be rescued by reinforcements. Rioting continued into the night and for the next several nights by crowds estimated at more than two thousand (D'Emilio, 1983).

Although the frequency of bar raids may have diminished over the years, lesbians and gay men are still the target of witch-hunts and banned from employment in some arenas (Shilts, 1993). Moreover, abuse at the hands of those whose job is to "protect and serve" is not uncommon, and conflict between the gay community and law enforcement is not a thing of the past.

> As recently as 1991, riots broke out between the gay community and the police in Los Angeles (Serrano, 1991) at a demonstration protesting Governor Pete Wilson's veto of gay rights bill AB 101. Gay leaders claimed that mounted police officers provoked the fracas (Ferrell, 1991). Multiple arrests were made and numerous injuries resulted. Protestors were subjected to beatings and anti-gay slurs. The American Civil Liberties Union filed suit against the LAPD charging that police officers forcibly broke up

the crowd of protesters with the purpose of discouraging any further demonstrations (Boxall, 1992A).

After suggesting to subordinates that they seize copies of the gay and lesbian newspaper, the *Bay Times*, for publishing an unflattering photo and criticizing his manner of dealing with "heavy-handed" arrests during a recent demonstration, the head of San Francisco's police department, Richard Hongisto, was removed from office for abuse of power (Gallagher, 1992; "San Francisco," 1992).

A Duxbury, MA officer was charged with felonious assault and battery with a dangerous weapon for allegedly breaking a beer bottle over the head of a woman while yelling anti-lesbian remarks (Batten, 1994).

Events such as these result in a wide-spread condemnation of and a lack of trust in law enforcement's willingness or ability to serve the lesbian and gay community. The courts have offered little protection for lesbians and gay men, as well. Police tend to ignore gay-bashing, may assault lesbians or gay men themselves, and even if a basher is brought to trial, the defendant's behavior is often excused by the court (Dodge, 1993). "All law enforcement efforts that touch on issues of sexual orientation take place against a background of hostility and mistrust. There is a long history of antagonism between the police and the gay and lesbian community" (Dodge, 1993, p. 302). It is not an uncommon belief in the gay community that if gay-bashers are arrested, prosecutors often fail to file charges against them and some judges give vastly reduced sentences because the victims of the attacks were "queers."

Despite this long and bleak history of conflict between criminal justice and the lesbian and gay community, there are some glimmers of hope. Top officials in many major cities have begun holding meetings with gay and lesbian leaders promising positive changes and increased sensitivity to the way police departments treat members of the lesbian and gay community (e.g., Boxall, 1992B; Griffin, 1992, Morris, 1991). Many departments have instituted sensitivity training programs for officers and new recruits, more and more members of the lesbian and gay community are actively recruited to become officers, and liaisons between the lesbian and gay community and various police departments have been appointed. Some departments, in fact, are actively cracking down on perpetrators of anti-gay violence in attempts to curb hate crimes (Bardwell, 1991).

This shift in police conduct from harassing and abusing to more positive collaboration is attributable, in large part, to the increasing power of the gay community. Physical resistance (i.e., as demonstrated by Stonewall), political resistance (i.e., voting power), and community pressure have shown the police that the gay community is no longer willing to be passively victimized (Rosen, 1980). Positive change may also be augmented by officers' increased exposure to lesbians and gay men as more and more law enforcement and criminal justice personnel come out of the closet.

Many would argue that law enforcement and criminal justice is still closed to lesbian and gay officers and is antiquated in its views. Although this may be true, the field has come a long way since its origins.

The Criminal Justice System: Then and Now

Laws, Courts, and Punishment

At the root of the criminal justice system is the law. The criminal justice system is designed to enforce the law and to apprehend and punish violators. In the 1600s, each colony devised its own set of laws and its own legal system; all colonial law was subordinate to English law (Friedman, 1985). Colonial law, however, was not widely read or distributed; reports of court decisions did not become readily accessible until after the War of Independence.

In formulating their laws, colonists used various combinations of (1) "folk law"—English law, typically local customs and local law, brought over by early settlers, (2) laws developed to cope with new and unique situations in the colonies such as dealing with hostile native tribes, and (3) ideological principles of the Puritans (laws developed because of the values and beliefs of the colonists). The colonies began with relatively simple structures which became more complex and specialized over the course of years. "In the beginning...the same people made laws, enforced them, decided cases, and ran the colony. A special court system grew and divided into parts, only when there were enough people, problems, and territory to make this sensible" (Friedman, 1985, pp. 37, 38).

By 1639, Massachusetts Bay had a full system of courts consisting of a general court which acted as the legislature and as the highest court; a court of assistants, which was primarily, but not exclusively, an appeals court; and a county court, more an administrative body than a court by today's standards, although it did handle some criminal cases (Friedman, 1985). Beneath the county courts were individual magistrates.

The colonial criminal justice was much more efficient than today's:

> [The] process began when a magistrate learned or heard that someone
> had committed an offense. He would send out the marshal or a deputy
> to haul in the offender. The magistrate would examine the suspect pri-
> vately, often in his own home, but with other magistrates or deputies
> present....There were no lawyers present, on either side. If the magis-
> trate felt the man was innocent, or the proof too weak, he could dismiss
> the case; if there was good evidence, or if the suspect confessed, the case
> was scheduled for trial. Until trial, the defendant was mostly free to go
> about daily life...The trial itself took place soon, quickly, and without
> jurymen or lawyers. Witnesses appeared and gave whatever evidence
> they had. The magistrate was in firm control. Of course, the magistrate
> felt fairly sure of guilt before the trial even started. (Marcus, as cited in
> Friedman, 1993, p. 25)

Seventeenth-century criminal justice workers were laymen, and not professionals as they are today. The sheriff was in charge of law enforcement,
arrests were made by constables, and patrolling was done by night watchmen,
most of whom were "ordinary" citizens (Friedman, 1993). Lawyers were not in
great numbers as the belief was that people should tell their own stories to the
court—an early form of self-representation. This was not the case, however,
for the prosecution. Contrary to England's method of individuals prosecuting
their own cases at their own expense, the colonies developed a position that
came to be known as the district attorney that was responsible for prosecuting
crime on behalf of the state.

Colonial laws were shaped in large part by religious beliefs, particularly in the
Puritan North (Friedman, 1993). As a result, much of the punishment meted out
entailed shaming and fines. Whipping, branding, letter-wearing, and mutilation
were alternate forms of punishment less frequently invoked. Banishment and
death, the ultimate forms of punishment, were relatively rare, and imprison-
ment was uncommon. Colonial jails housed debtors and prisoners awaiting
trial, whereas "houses of correction" held "vagrants, idlers, and paupers."

The federal system was established when the Constitution was ratified in
1787. At this time, a national criminal justice system was placed above the existing state (former colonial) systems. In the late 1700s and early 1800s, prisons of a
sort were developed where inmates experienced silence, isolation, discipline,
and regimentation. The first federal prison was established at Fort
Leavenworth, Kansas in 1891, about a century later. Prior to that, federal prisoners were boarded in state and local jails.

Policing

When the first police officer was appointed in 1634, law enforcement and policing bore little resemblance to more recent times (Fosdick, 1920). The Constable for Plymouth not only served as constable, jailer, and "executor of punishment and penalties," but also "gave warning of marriages" (Fosdick, 1920, p. 58). He had the powers of a police officer, deputy sheriff/jailer, corrections officer/prison guard, and judge.

The first "night watch" was established in Boston in 1636 (Fosdick, 1920), and by the early eighteenth century, the notion of the night watch—patrolling the streets at night and, in some locations, caring for the street lamps—had become well established. In the 1830s and '40s, many major cities established day watches to supplement night watches. Boston's first day police force consisted of six men, and in 1844, New York's day watch consisted of sixteen. Soon after day watches were established, it was found that two separate systems—a day watch and a night watch—didn't work. Friction and conflict between the systems proved untenable, and a series of riots—the Irish in Boston in 1837, the Philadelphia "Negro riots" of 1838 and 1842, the 1844 "Native American riots," and similar turmoil in Baltimore and New York—proved too volatile for police forces to handle and the militia had to be mobilized. Consequently, New York passed legislation in 1844 creating "day and night police"—an organization of eight hundred men reporting to a chief of police. This action provided the foundation for modern police organizations. Other major cities followed suit over the next twenty years. The first police departments were not uniformed because uniforms were deemed "un-American," "undemocratic," and too reminiscent of military rule. Instead, New York officers were identified by medals worn around their necks. The first police uniforms were adopted in 1856 in New York; however, they were not standard across wards.

By 1920, police department organizations were fairly standardized, and in many respects, the basic structures remain in place today. In larger cities, the police chief reported to a civilian commissioner or board, while in smaller municipalities, the chief was responsible to the mayor. Departments were organized into two main branches—uniformed patrol and detectives. Cities were divided into precincts or districts presided over by a captain, and individual precincts were subdivided into "beats." The hierarchical reporting arrangement—from patrolmen to sergeants to lieutenants to captains to the chief—solidified and clarified rules, regulations, duties, and responsibilities. From these seeds grew the modern criminal justice system.

Modern Criminal Justice

Today, laws are established through one of four methods: as stated in federal and state constitutions; as prescribed by legislative bodies such as the U.S. Congress, state legislatures, and city or county councils; by ballot initiatives voted upon by the general population; and in the courts as a result of judges' interpretations of statutes. Although court systems vary from state to state, they are quite similar (Lewis, Bundy, & Hague, 1978). Trial courts are the "port of entry" for most defendants in the system. Depending on the offense, the trial court may be a municipal, county, state, or federal court. The next level is the intermediate appellate court, where trial court decisions may be appealed. The "court of last resort" is at the apex of the judicial system. This court is typically, but not always referred to as the "Supreme Court;" for example, New York's top court is the "Court of Appeals," and its "Supreme Court" is the trial court of general jurisdiction. The federal judicial system resembles that of many states. The Supreme Court is the court of last resort, there are eleven intermediate courts of appeal—the U.S. Courts of Appeals—and the lowest level, the trial courts, are known as the U.S. District Courts.

Criminal justice professions can be organized according to their function within the criminal justice process. Generally speaking, criminal justice work focuses on *apprehension, detention, adjudication,* and *incarceration* of people who break the law, as well as *"special forces."* A wide variety of criminal justice workers such as police officers, deputy sheriffs, state troopers, FBI agents, and detectives typically apprehend and take into custody individuals who are suspected of breaking the law. After arrest, the accused have to be housed and protected in jails until arraignment and/or trial. Jails are typically run or supervised by sheriffs and their deputies. During adjudication, the government first decides if the case against the accused is sufficient to take to trial (decisions made by prosecutors, district attorneys, and their assistants or deputies). If there is sufficient evidence, the case is presented by the prosecution at a trial. A judge or a jury weighs the evidence, passes judgment as to guilt or innocence, and sentences those found guilty. Individuals convicted of misdemeanors and felonies may be sentenced to jails or prisons, respectively. Prison inmates are cared for by corrections workers. Finally, there are criminal justice workers who are involved in special capacities separate from the above categories, such as recruitment, training, background investigation, and personnel administration; community liaisons and services; and dispatchers. Although the delineations of roles are often clearer in theory than in practice, the system is still much more clearly defined and articulated now than it was in Colonial America.

Until 1960, police departments were composed almost entirely of White, male heterosexuals (Bouza, 1990). During the 1960s and 1970s, physical requirements that denied women access to police jobs were removed, and more women entered the profession. Similarly, a series of court decisions with regard to race, changing demographics of cities, and the civil rights movement, led to the employment of greater numbers of African-Americans. Although it is likely that lesbians and gay men have worked in criminal justice for a long time, because sexual orientation has been stigmatized and its invisibility makes it possible to hide, little is known about the presence and experiences of lesbians and gay men in criminal justice. The White, male, heterosexual ranks were broken first by race and later by gender. Therefore, it is important to examine the experiences as people of color and women integrated into the criminal justice profession to provide a context for integrating lesbians and gay men.

African-Americans and Criminal Justice

Many African-Americans view the criminal justice system with skepticism, and for good reason. Whites in the U.S. hold more positive attitudes toward the police than African-Americans or other racial minorities (Law Enforcement Assistance Administration, 1977, as cited in Yarmey, 1990). Research has shown that African-Americans are treated more harshly than Whites by the police and the criminal justice system, and that they attribute this to racism (Yarmey, 1990). Ghetto African-Americans are more likely than poor Whites to have negative interactions with the police (Yarmey, 1990). During the civil rights movement, Southern police departments sympathized with White supremacists and denied protection to civil rights activists. Those who have less power and privilege are more often the recipients of violence; police officers are more likely to show restraint to those of the middle and upper classes (Alex, 1969). Although police-community relations are improving in many communities, many African-American leaders continue to experience police departments as biased.

This conflict between the African-American and criminal justice communities has placed many African-American criminal justice workers in an awkward position *vis à vis* the African-American community. As Alex (1969) has pointed out

> The Negro who enters into the police role is subject to all the tensions
> and conflicts that arise from police work. Moreover, the conflict is com-
> pounded for the Negro: he is much more than a Negro to his ethnic
> group because he represents the guardian of White society, yet he is not

quite a policeman to his working companions because he is stereotyped as a member of an "inferior" racial category. He may find it necessary to defend his serving as a police officer....Often he feels that he is subject to criticism by his ethnic peers derived from premises inapplicable to his situation—that is, they may consider him a traitor to his race because his race does not benefit from the protection that he offers. Yet he may defend his race because he is a Negro and inextricably bound up in the current struggle for civil rights and the demands of Negroes for social and legal equality. It is difficult for him to play both roles. To be a Negro and a policeman is to be subject to double marginality, and gives rise to some special problems. (pp. 13, 14)

Historically, White immigrants and their children have entered police work as a way to establish themselves in American society. White officers have resisted integrating African-American officers into the ranks (Alex, 1969), resulting in African-Americans being underrepresented in criminal justice professions (Friedman, 1993).

Although there is evidence to suggest that there was an African-American officer in a New York police department as early as 1865, it wasn't until some twenty-five years later that African-Americans as a group began entering the department (Alexander, 1978). The first African-American sergeant was not appointed until 1926, and the first African-American captain was not appointed until twenty-five years later (Leinen, 1984). Initially, most African-Americans were assigned to precincts as doormen, although many later moved up the promotional ladder. The next African-American officer to serve in the greater New York area was Wiley G. Overton who was appointed to a footpost in Brooklyn's police department. Alienated and isolated by his White counterparts, denied the opportunity to learn from his colleagues, and subjected to considerable hostility, Overton resigned after less than two years of service. Three more African-American officers at the time threatened to file a law suit in order to get their fully earned promotions (Alexander, 1978). Although African-Americans moved into the patrol ranks, other forms of discrimination held them back from advancing.

Treatment of African-American officers in the 1910s and '20s was anything but collegial. For two full years, one African-American officer reported that his White colleagues in New York refused to speak to him—not one word. For the first half of the twentieth century, White officers could work anywhere, whereas their African-American counterparts were usually restricted to African-

American communities. Moreover, African-American officers were not assigned to work with White partners, and they often received the least desirable work assignments, all of which resulted in resentment toward White officers (Alexander, 1978). Even into the 1960s, African-Americans were not assigned to work in radio cars as were their White counterparts (Alex, 1969). Because most police work was conducted out of radio cars, African-Americans were not able to acquire the experience that White officers acquired. This restriction placed them at a disadvantage when applying for other positions and promotions. In some cities, African-American officers had no legal authority to arrest White suspects (Grimes, as cited in Leinen, 1984). Only in 1965 did a police commissioner issue a statement warning that police officers should resign if they could not respect the rights of minority groups (Alexander, 1978). Many White officers charged that the policy represented "special treatment" for African-Americans, and African-American-White relationships became increasingly polarized.

Progress was spurred on by the Federal Civil Rights Act of 1964, which was designed to assure access to jobs in the private sector for African-Americans, women, and certain other minority groups. The Civil Rights Act established the legal precedence for the 1972 Federal Equal Employment Opportunities Act, which extended protections to cover employment practices in the public as well as the private sector. In addition, the federal courts began to rule against traditional practices which limited the ability of African-American applicants to be hired, and in some cases established racial quotas for new hires. In cities across the country during the '70s, the courts mandated the hiring of African-American applicants in an effort to increase minority representation within police forces. Many other cities began instituting voluntary programs to recruit minority candidates in order to avoid legal battles. Discriminatory hiring policies and arbitrary criteria were struck down in the courts. As the numbers of African-American officers grew, so did their influence. A number of organizations developed with the goal of promoting and protecting African-American officers' special interests (Leinen, 1984).

By the end of the '70s, a number of cities had significantly increased their proportion of African-American officers—Detroit had 35 percent, Washington, D.C. had 42 percent, and Baltimore, Chicago, Memphis, Philadelphia, and San Francisco all had about 20 percent (Leinen, 1984). New York City lagged behind, and in 1980 it lost a law suit filed by the Guardians, an organization of African-American officers. As a result, racial quota systems were instituted in NYPD, and by 1982, 17 percent of the NYPD were people of color.

Gains continued to be made, and by 1988, 130 U.S. police departments were headed by African-Americans, including six of the country's ten largest cities (Narine, 1988). African-American officers made up more than half of Atlanta's police department (Hudson, 1990). In spite of these advances, problems persist.

During his forty-eight year tenure, former FBI Director J. Edgar Hoover hired no African-American agents, and even sixteen years after his death African-Americans still only comprised 4 percent of agents ("A black," 1988). Of the approximately half million law enforcement officers in 1985, fewer than 10 percent were African-American; of the officers in the country's fifty largest cities where African-Americans make up on average 26 percent of the population, only 14 percent of the officers are African-American (Serrill, 1985). For those African-American officers on the force, the environment is far from equitable. Lawsuits continue to be filed on behalf of African-American officers alleging discrimination in hiring and on the job (e.g., Gest, 1987; Lewis, 1992; Marks, 1995) and in most locations, the proportion of minority officers does not match the proportion of minorities in the communities they police (Hudson, 1990; Kaminski, 1993; Marks, 1995). Minority officers are more likely than their White counterparts to be seriously wounded or killed in the line of duty (Alexander, 1978). Obviously there is still a long way to go.

Women and Criminal Justice

Even when compared with African-Americans, women are relative newcomers to the ranks of criminal justice. No women lawyers existed before the 1870s, and practically no women performed as judges or jurors until the 1900s. During that same time, policewomen were uncommon, and although a small percentage of criminals were women, most women in the criminal justice system were victims (Friedman, 1993). New York City hired its first female prison matron in 1845. Los Angeles waited until 1910 to hire Alice S. Wells as the first sworn policewoman in the country. By 1915, at least twenty-five U.S. cities had followed suit. Most women were assigned to work with women or children, and not to patrol (Martin, 1980). By 1950, women made up 1 percent of all officers, and over the next twenty years their proportion doubled, but their roles within police forces were generally circumscribed to secretarial or juvenile work. For example, from 1918 to 1967, all women officers in the District of Columbia were assigned to the Women's Bureau; when the Women's Bureau was disbanded the officers were reassigned to the Youth Division. Many departments refused to hire women, and training and promotions for women were restricted. Clearly women were not accepted as equals to men.

Spurred on by the Civil Rights Act of 1964, the Equal Employment Act in 1972, and a series of resulting lawsuits in the 1970s, women began to be incorporated into police departments. This change did not occur without some pitfalls. For example, in 1972, Washington D.C. became the first city to make extensive use of female patrol officers; however, they were still required to wear skirts and medium height heels and to carry their guns in their purses. By 1975, although women made up 7 percent of the D.C. force, some stations did not have adequate locker room or bathroom facilities for female officers (Martin, 1980).

Legislative changes and lawsuits, the 1973 change in the height requirements for officers from 5´7´´ down to 5´0´´, and the strengthening of the women's movement all contributed to a number of "firsts" for women: the first women were admitted to the Secret Service in 1971, to the FBI in 1972, and to various state highway patrol troops in the early '70s. By 1974, more than a third of the departments had women assigned to patrol (Martin, 1980). However, even after women received their patrol assignments, they were less likely to be placed in choice duties and more often relegated to the precinct house and footbeats than to patrol cars.

Women have lagged far behind men in becoming fully integrated into their criminal justice positions. Even in the 1990s, women have difficulty breaking into some aspects of policing (Heidenshon, 1992). Most positions of power in police departments continue to be dominated by heterosexual, White men (Bouza, 1990). As Martin (1980) noted, "Policing has been and remains a male-dominated occupation, closely associated with masculinity" (p. 19). Integrating women into policing has been routinely opposed and resisted. Most men oppose assigning women to patrol, and some oppose hiring women in the first place (Bell, 1982). The concerns they offer to support their bias include claims that women in the ranks weaken the camaraderie among the men and pose a threat to their wives (Vincent, 1990), worries about women's smaller and weaker physiques, questions about women's ability to defend themselves on the street, complaints about having to inhibit their language and conversations around women, and fears that as more women enter the profession, the status of the job will decrease (Martin, 1980).

Despite clear empirical evidence that women do the job as well as men (Bartol, Bergen, Volckens, & Knoras, 1992; Charles, 1981; Grennan 1987), male police officers generally believe that women can not do the job (Balkin, 1988). Not only are women sufficiently strong to do the work (Charles, 1982), they are more likely than men to defuse a potentially violent situation without anyone getting hurt (Grennan, 1987). In addition, women receive fewer citizen complaints, and men are much more likely to be cited for excessive use of force (McDowell, 1992). Yet the most common source of stress for women officers stems not from dealing with perpetrators on the streets but from coping with the repercussions of being women—being ignored, harassed, watched, and viewed as sex objects (Wexler & Logan, 1983). Even in the 1990s, female officers not only lack the respect of most of their male colleagues (Daum & Johns, 1994), but also must deal, in many cases, with males who are openly hostile to them (Brown, 1994). Women have to work harder to be accepted, and most experience sexual harassment on the job (Daum & Johns, 1994). There continues to be a strong undercurrent of bias, discrimination, harassment, and abuse of women officers by their male colleagues and superiors (Heidenshon, 1992).

Despite the improvements that took place in the 1980s and '90s, criminal justice continues to be a harsh environment and "uneven playing field" for women. For example:

> Penny Harrington was appointed Chief of Portland, Oregon's Police
> Department only after having won a series of forty sex discrimination
> complaints in the course of her twenty-one-year career (Wilhelm, 1985).

> Royal Canadian Mounted Police officer Alice Clark quit the force in 1987
> as a result of experiencing repeated incidents of sexual harassment,
> being grabbed and propositioned by male colleagues, being publicly
> humiliated by her supervisor, and finding life-sized plastic breasts
> attached to her desk. She was awarded ninety-three thousand dollars in
> 1994 after winning her lawsuit which named twenty-six separate
> incidents. A number of other women have since come forward
> describing similar experiences (Corelli, 1995).

> Uniforms specifically tailored for women, including bulletproof vests,
> have been available only since the late 1980s (House, 1993).

> Although women constitute 9 percent of the nation's 523,262 police
> officers, only 3 percent are above the rank of sergeant (McDowell, 1992).

> Women have had to put up with lewd jokes over the radio, uniforms
> designed for men, sexist comments in the hallways, and condoms and
> nude centerfolds in mailboxes (McDowell, 1992).

> Two-thirds of the female officers in a 1993 study reported incidents of
> sexual harassment and saw sexist and suggestive comments as "part of
> the job" (Corelli, 1995).

> The major problems reported by female police officers are dealing with
> negative and sexist attitudes of male colleagues and supervisors,
> believing that they have to be exceptional to gain minimal acceptance,
> feeling that they are labelled as troublemakers when they are aggressive
> about their job opportunities, and experiencing a "constant subtle, often
> crude, sexist atmosphere in which they must work daily" (Timmins &
> Hainsworth, 1989, p. 201).

By the late 1980s, 40 percent of female officers were African-American or
Hispanic (Heidenshon, 1992). In some departments, African-American women
outnumber White women. In 1988 in the Metropolitan Police Department of
Washington, D.C., 82 percent of the female officers were African-American. For
women of color, the difficulties are compounded. As Haynes (1993) has noted, in
addition to fighting crime in the streets, women of color also are fighting sexism
and racism within their departments. African-American women do not advance
as quickly as White women (Townsey, 1982), they are not as trusted as their
White and male counterparts, and they are not as protected as White women
(Martin, 1994). Perhaps this is because

> in comparing the discrimination experienced by female and minority
> male officers, Pike (1991) suggests that minority men do not challenge the
> "quintessential" police officer role in the same way women do.
> Stereotypes of Black men fit into the traditional police model since they
> are seen as physically strong, street-wise, and masculine; their integration
> did not require organizational changes. In contrast, the integration of
> women required changes in facilities, uniforms, and physical training
> programs" (Martin, 1994, p. 385).

By 1990, 28,335 women in policing represented only 8.3 percent of the force
(House, 1993). Equal opportunity had not yet been achieved.

Lesbians, Gay Men, and Criminal Justice

The newest group to break in to criminal justice professions are open lesbians
and gay men. As with any field, it is likely that lesbians and gay men have been

serving in these professions for many years, in many cases hiding and unde-tected, in some cases with a tacit agreement of silence, and in a few cases open-ly. African-Americans started entering policing in larger numbers in the late 1960s (Leinen, 1993), the ranks of women swelled in the '70s, and in the '80s and '90s, open lesbians and gay men began applying for criminal justice positions, and increasing numbers of those already employed in criminal justice began coming out. The first law officer to publicly acknowledge his sexual orientation did so a year after he left the job (Suraci, 1992). A year later, Sergeant Charles Cochrane became the first gay officer to come out while serving on the NYPD (Griffin, 1993). Since then, more and more lesbian and gay officers have begun to shake the closet door.

Although initially the experiences of lesbians and gay men are similar to those of ethnic minority and female officers, once on the job, they encounter some differences (Leinen, 1993). Lesbian and gay officers can choose to hide their sexual orientation, and this hiding creates a number of stresses. Fears of perse-cution and harassment are often well founded. "Being gay or lesbian is not acceptable in the eyes of the majority of our law enforcers" (Burke, 1993, p. vii). Lesbians and gays are among the most disliked categories of people by the police (Burke, 1993), in spite of empirical evidence that there is no difference between lesbian and gay applicants' and heterosexual applicants' suitability for hire or in performance ratings once on the job (Hiatt & Hargrave, 1994).

As a result, lesbians and gay men historically have been excluded from the ranks of policing usually on moral and religious grounds; concerns have been raised about unit cohesiveness, trust, and morale; and in some cases, legal argu-ments against lesbian and gay officers have been put forth (Leinen, 1993). In states where same-sex behavior is illegal, it has been argued that gay and lesbian officers are criminals. Most lesbian and gay criminal justice officers do not come out on the job due to fears of rejection, of being the butt of jokes and pranks, of being victims of overt harassment and discrimination, and of not being backed up on calls (Leinen, 1993). Some officers create fictional relationships to hide their identities and thus "protect" themselves. Many lead double lives; they hide their lesbian or gay identity from fellow officers and their police identity from the les-bian and gay community (Burke, 1993).

Although the lesbian and gay rights movement has parallelled the civil rights and women's movements, sexual orientation remains an unprotected class. That is, it is still legal to deny employment on the basis of sexual orienta-tion in all but a handful of jurisdictions. In many cases, lesbians, gay men, and their allies in criminal justice fear for their jobs and sometimes their lives.

Gay officers have been blackmailed, beaten, and forced out of their jobs. Some have committed suicide, and others live in fear of being found out (Campbell, 1993).

Portland, OR Police Chief Tom Potter received death threats after marching in a gay pride march in support of the gay community and his daughter, an out lesbian officer in his department (Egan, 1992). A few years later, Nominee Potter was encouraged to withdraw from consideration for a post in the Justice Department because of his strong and visible support for gay rights ("Strange justice," 1994).

New York's Gay Officers Action League members were harassed by Puerto Rican police during the group's convention in San Juan ("Puerto Rico," 1995).

The good news is that things are gradually changing. In some departments and in some agencies across the country, the climate is improving for lesbians and gay men. And in some cases, in spite of the absence of federal civil rights legislation, the courts are paving the way.

In 1992, Mica England won the right to apply to become a Dallas police officer when a state judge ruled that the Dallas Police Department cannot ban employment of lesbian and gay officers (Gallagher, 1992).

In 1993, Maryland State Police dropped its policy barring lesbians and gay men in part because of a lawsuit filed by a lesbian attempting to become a trooper (Valentine, 1993).

In 1993, former agent Frank Buttino's lawsuit against the FBI was settled, and Attorney General Janet Reno approved a new policy that forbids Justice Department divisions from firing or refusing to hire solely on the basis of sexual orientation ("Fired gay," 1993).

In February, 1993, Mitch Grobeson settled a five million dollar million lawsuit against the Los Angeles Police Department (LAPD) in which he alleged that he had been harassed for being gay, subjected to continuing derogatory comments, and frequently was not backed up in potentially dangerous situations. The city agreed to numerous changes in policy

regarding gays and lesbians, namely hiring a "sexual orientation counselor," providing training for recruits, and actively recruiting gay and lesbian officers (Boxall & Torres, 1993).

For the first time in the history of New York Police Department (NYPD),
in June of 1994, lesbian and gay officers of the Gay Officers Action League
displayed a banner entitled, "Lesbian and Gay Pride in Policing" for gay
pride at police headquarters, One Police Plaza (James, 1994).

News item sound bites and court decisions do not tell the whole story any
more than a final score of 3–2 tells the whole story of a baseball game. The fact
that one officer is promoted after coming out whereas another is fired, reveals
little of the content of their experiences. Although traditional quantitative
research is useful in describing the common elements of the experiences of a
large number of people, qualitative approaches are more valuable for understanding individual experiences in depth (Dey, 1993; Patton, 1990). Using a quantitative approach is much like designing a multiple choice test: it requires
knowing specific facts but does not allow for detailed explanations or explo-
rations of what those facts might mean. Little room is left for the humanity and
diversity of experience to emerge. Employing the narrative approach allows the
reader to know not only the experiences of the speakers, but their personalities
as well. If, as Herek (1984) has stated, individuals who know someone who is lesbian or gay are less likely to hold homophobic views, then perhaps encounter-
ing these lesbians and gay men through their stories can facilitate an improve-
ment in attitudes about lesbians and gay men in criminal justice.

This book takes you beyond the "bottom line" reported facts and statistics and
into the lives and hearts of current and former criminal justice professionals.
Much like a patchwork quilt, each story is unique and self-sufficient; yet common threads run among the narratives. Using their own words, these men and
women describe their experiences—the good and the bad—that have come
from choosing the life of a criminal justice professional.

Part One:
Apprehension

C riminal justice workers who *apprehend* law breakers do so in
  many ways. They may patrol a given area by way of
walking or driving through neighborhoods, precincts, counties,
or highways; respond to emergency and non-emergency
requests for assistance from the public or other agencies; or
conduct investigations into crimes and criminal activity
culminating, one hopes, in an arrest. Typically, municipal
police officers have jurisdiction over municipalities, deputy
sheriffs over counties, state troopers over highways, and FBI
agents over certain federal matters. These criminal justice
workers represent the first point of contact for those accused of
breaking the law. Perhaps in the most dangerous jobs, these
personnel never know what their next call may bring.
Teamwork, trust in and reliance upon one's partner, and
backup are all critical components of safe and effective
apprehension of criminals.

Mitch Grobeson

Department: Los Angeles (CA) Police Department
Age: 35
Rank: Sergeant
Job: Field Supervisor
Years in Law Enforcement: 13

After years of harassment and death threats at the hands of his fellow officers, Mitch left the LAPD *and filed a law suit. Over brunch at a cafe in West Hollywood, he talked about his landmark victory over the* LAPD.

While I was still in high school they began the very first police-explorer program; I joined up and went through a very rigorous academy. I was fifteen at the time. We were the largest separate agency of police explorers they'd ever had. It was a pretty amazing experience; your first day they had you standing at attention, and they walked down the lines saying, "We want all the Blacks here, the spics over here, and if you're fags, you should leave now." We lost half the people that were there on the first day. After I graduated I went to college and majored in criminal justice. I did very well in college and graduated with every award the college offered.

There was only one real police academy in my mind, and that was LAPD. Having grown up there, they were the only major police department. They were the essence of professionalism. As I saw it, there was no other. My goal was to join the FBI—the Federal Bureau of Investigation—and someone had told me that if you graduated number one from the Los Angeles Police Academy the FBI sought after you. So I graduated college, put an application in, and pretty much broke the record. Within three months I was in the police academy.

I had worked in law enforcement since I was fifteen. Policemen talked about two things: they talked about pussy, and they talked about fags. They talked about getting laid, their girlfriends, their wives, or their wives and their girl-friends. When they weren't talking about that they talked about fags, making it clear that homosexuality wasn't acceptable. It was legal in California to be gay, and what I did was in the privacy of my own home, so I truly believed I would be accepted regardless of my sexual orientation. I believed I'd be accept-ed by my ability to serve the public, by my ability to throw serious criminals in jail, and by my ability to help out my fellow officers rather than what I did off duty. I was wrong.

There were no openly gay officers in LAPD. At that time there were no open-ly gay officers in southern California. Every single gay or lesbian that was on the LAPD was either married to a heterosexual partner to conceal it; was alco-holic 'cause they were so scared of being found out, so upset about what was going on, and so demeaned by having to conceal it that they were often suici-dal; had left the department ashamed about not standing up for themselves; or had already committed suicide. It was a horrible environment.

Seventy-five percent of the officers in the LAPD don't engage in major mis-conduct. They are professional police officers; they don't care about your sexu-al orientation, your race, your gender, or anything. They do their job. But a small number—up to 25 percent—engage in harassment and do so without any fear of retribution. At that time they acted with the complete knowledge and support of management.

When I joined LAPD I was twenty-three years old, had graduated college, and still hadn't had sex. Even though I knew I was homosexual I wasn't "practic-ing." When I joined the police department, they asked you, "Have you ever had sex with another man?" If you said, "Yes," you were disqualified.

At the time I entered the LA Police Academy it was a very hostile environ-ment. It was one of the last major stress academies; the instructors were very aggressive, very demeaning, and physically abusive. They had just been forced to start recruitment efforts for women by a court consent decree and were very hostile toward women. In fact, they instructed a group of the male offi-cers including myself that it was our duty to ensure that none of the women graduated; when we began combat wrestling we were to ensure that they became injured and did not graduate; "recycled" was the term. They did not want women in there.

Out of our class of eighty-one people we wound up with thirty-five. I pulled one of the women aside and worked with her; she didn't understand that her own classmates were out to get her. I worked with her to convince her that, "They're after your job; even though it's a classmate you have to defend yourself. You have to scream, yell, and swing your baton like you mean it or they'll fail you." They failed every single woman except her. They wanted to drum out one guy that they thought was gay, so they had us goose-step and chant directing our hostility at this poor guy. We'd yell his name, and then we'd go, "NO GOOD. WON'T CONFORM." They got rid of him that way. The goose-stepping was really shocking to me. It was chilling. It was scary to see this paramilitary, Nazi-like atmosphere. They drilled into you an unwritten code that what goes on in the police car stays in the police car; what goes on with you and your partner stays with you and your partner; "I lie and you swear to it." A code of silence.

I was so stunned by everything that went on that I wanted to beat them at their own game, and I did. I graduated number one in the police academy. I was the top overall in physical fitness, self-defense, academics, and shooting. I was their honor cadet. I was also elected by my peers as class president. When I graduated the chief shook my hand and stated how I exemplified the ideal Los Angeles police officer. He didn't know I was gay.

I promoted faster than any of my peers. Right off of probation I took the exam to become a training officer, and I worked a large variety of assignments. Around December of 1984, I was in West Hollywood, and at that time the sheriff's department was actively harassing gays. A deputy stopped me, and he talked about how he didn't like gays out on the streets—they were ruining the neighborhoods and all this sort of stuff. He recognized that I was a cop, contacted my supervisors, and told them I was a "fruit." Then he contacted the operations headquarters bureau and told them that I was a fruit and they should fire me. From then on the harassment started.

I transferred to Rampart Division; it was the highest gang area of the city at the time. It was one of the most violent areas of the city. At that time the officers were encouraged by LAPD to raid gay bars on a regular basis. They would brag that when they'd get a gay-bashing case, they'd say to the gay-basher, "Did this guy defend himself? Did this guy push you or try to get away? Did he hit you? Did he have any kind of contact with you? You have the right to make a private person's arrest of him for battery on you." They'd say to the victim, "If you arrest him for gay-bashing, he's going to arrest you for battery." They'd brag about how they put them both in the back seat of a police car. The gay victim would be so scared that he'd say, "Forget it." So the gay community knew, "If you get gay-bashed, don't tell LAPD" I've had people tell me, "I've been victimized once, I'm not going to be victimized twice by going to LAPD."

There were four separate stages to what they did because they were so astounded that I didn't resign. First they were in awe 'cause I didn't resign, so I'd be in the locker room and somebody would come in and say to one of the officers, "Is it true you've got a fruit?" Then he'd bring them over and point me out: "Yeah. That's him." Or I'd be on a call and officers from my division would go to officers from other divisions and say, "That guy's the fag we heard about." Not only didn't I leave, I was also the number one officer in the division. I was one of the only ones working on gang enforcement, I organized the largest community watch groups in the city, and I developed a graffiti paint-over project later adopted by the city attorney. So I was a major threat to the macho culture because if a fag could do their job and do it as good or better than they did, what could these big, macho gun-fighters say about themselves? I was throwing more serious criminals in jail. I was taking apart gangs. I was out there protecting my community.

The second phase was when they thought they could intimidate me. I'd come to work in time to get ready for roll call, my locker would be super-glued shut, and they'd write me up if I was late. When Rock Hudson died of AIDS they wrote, "To Mitch, Love, Rock Baby," and glued his picture on my locker. In the men's restroom in the locker room they had one bathroom stall where officers would write dozens of insults to me on a daily basis.

When that didn't work they began the next phase; nobody would work with me 'cause I was a homosexual. I was in the highest gang area in the city without a partner. Every single person refused to work with me 'cause I was a fag. They refused to back me up. The first time I documented it was in 1985 when I went to a robbery alarm call. In California that was the second highest call where officers were killed or seriously injured, so you always got backup. I was alone, I went to the call, and I was sitting in the middle of Sunset Boulevard with my shotgun over the hood of the car. Usually when there's a robbery you have a car waiting to take the perpetrators away. I kept waiting and waiting, and not one officer in the entire city of Los Angeles backed me up.

The second time was on October 6, 1985. There were two gang members who had stolen a moped, and I went in foot pursuit. I caught the first gang member, handcuffed him, and went in pursuit of the second one. When I caught him I'd already used my handcuffs on the first guy. I didn't have a second set of hand-cuffs, and I was surrounded by thirty gang members. Fifteen minutes into the call and not one of the eight thousand officers in LAPD backed me up. The dispatcher was screaming in the radio, "What the hell is going on here? Where the hell is his backup?" I got back to the police station and went down to the locker room before I wrote all my reports. I went to take off my bullet-proof vest, and the officer who had a locker right across from me turned to me and said, "What happened out there?" I said, "What do you mean?" He said, "You didn't get any backup out there, did you?" I said, "No." He said, "They're trying to teach you a lesson. Get the hell out of Rampart Division before you get killed."

After that it became real severe. The captain would call me into his office every Friday and harass me, telling me, "Get out of my division." They'd threaten me in roll call. One of the officers sat behind me, dropped his flashlight right behind me, leaned over, and whispered in my ear, "Oops. Missed." This was the norm. It was a horrible environment, and I was barely staying alive. By that point I believed there was no way out; I was so miserable that every night I'd go home and say, "I don't want to go to work tomorrow morning. If I kill myself, I won't have to."

I transferred out of Rampart Division and became a detective trainee. I was a real good detective. Then I was promoted and went down to Seventy-seventh Division   South Central Los Angeles. They did all kinds of things there, too. I transferred back to Pacific Division where both my captains—the two highest ranking people in the division—were fundamentalists. They assigned a lieutenant to harass me out of the department, and he assigned ten officers to get complaints against me. It was a horrible situation. They had taken my photograph from my personnel file and put it up for all the officers and arrestees to see. It said, "Would you buy a used dildo from this man?" The lieutenant started doing interrogation sessions with me. He'd call me into the station, make me give up my gun, take me to a jail interrogation cell, and interrogate me. He'd accuse me of all kinds of misconduct and ask me about my sexual orientation. He'd say, "We're going to get rid of you."

Finally I confronted one officer and said, "What the hell are you doing saying these things?" He said, "I didn't say anything." I said, "I'm going to write it down but I'm going to let you go. If you do it again, you're going to be disciplined." He bragged to everybody, "I'm going to set him up." One day he arrested a cocaine addict, brought him in, and said, "This guy wants to make a complaint against Grobeson." The Los Angeles Police Department charged me with sending subliminal messages that I was a closet homosexual to this cocaine addict. It cost me two thousand five hundred dollars for an attorney. In the middle of the trial board, the cocaine addict admitted under oath that he had been approached by no less than ten officers who told him I was a fag. He was told he'd be given immunity to use or sell drugs as he pleased because of his complaint against me.

At that point, I decided I had no choice; I had to come out of the closet. So I went to the president of the Police Commission, he reviewed my personnel package, and he said, "You're an outstanding police officer. We'll set up a meeting with Chief Gates to get this stopped." Chief [Daryl] Gates said, "No way. I'm not meeting with him." So I went to two city councilmen, and one said, "Chief Gates is so bad there's nothing I can do. You've got to file a lawsuit; that's the only way you're going to make a change." I said, "No, I'm not filing a lawsuit. My parents don't know I'm gay. I want to make changes in a positive way. Lawsuits are negative. I want to work within the system to make changes." He said, "There's nothing you can do." I contacted three state agencies and two federal agencies, but they told me straight-out, "There's nothing we can do for you because it's a sexual orientation issue."

I got a phone call warning me that a sergeant who I had made a complaint against was going to call Internal Affairs and tell them I was selling drugs so they'd do a search warrant on my home. I knew that when they kicked in my door to do the search warrant, they'd blow me away; they'd kill me. The sergeant felt that that way they'd find evidence such as gay magazines, and once and for all determine if I was a homosexual. When you do a search warrant, one of the officers carries a shot gun and the others use their automatics. I'd be in bed and pull out my little snub-nosed, five-shot revolver from under my pillow, not knowing it was the police kicking in my door, and they'd blow me away and kill me. I knew I wouldn't live through it.

I wouldn't leave until I was vindicated, until they proved there was no misconduct on my part. At that time I beat most of LAPD's records, having saved seven lives in one year, received 135 letters of commendation from the public I served, and been awarded three meritorious service citations by City Council members.

I found out about the search warrant on Wednesday. On Friday, my trial board finished, and they found me not guilty of any misconduct. On Sunday I concluded a seminar I organized working with five hundred deaf community members, finished all my paperwork, cleaned out my locker, put all my possessions in my car, walked in to the lieutenant, and said, "I'm leaving. I'm resigning." Within three days I was in San Francisco. I was gone. No forwarding address; no forwarding phone number; nothing.

I got to San Francisco, got a P.O. Box, and became a police officer up there. Then I began a campaign to educate the LA community about what was going on. I pulled all my retirement money out and spent every penny of it. I'd fly down to LA, and for a while I had to have a bodyguard 'cause I got real nasty threats from LAPD. I spoke to sixty gay and lesbian organizations in the greater LA area about what was going on and what they could do.

I got an attorney who promised me that we could change the system. We would make it possible for gays and lesbians to become police officers in LA, so I hired him and filed the first lawsuit in the country by a police officer for discrimination based on sexual orientation. Since then, officers throughout the U.S. have come forward. I got over a hundred phone calls a week from gays and lesbians who are police officers, in the academy, or wanted to be police officers. I've been on "60 Minutes," "Phil Donahue," and "Geraldo Rivera." I've gotten calls and letters from kids from all over the world who said, "Thank you for a ray of hope. I always thought I was the only one. It is so great to see a positive role model."

The City Council voted to settle my lawsuit three times, and each time Chief Gates washed it. Finally they set up a meeting with myself and Chief Gates; at first he hated my guts—he wouldn't shake my hand, and he told me what he thought of me. When I explained to him that I couldn't have come into LAPD to become an activist like he believed because I had only told my mom and dad that I was gay two weeks before my lawsuit was filed, he changed his tune. He started listening to what I was saying, but he said, "As long as I am chief of police, we will never have a liaison in the gay community, and we will never recruit gays and lesbians." They brought in a new police chief, I had two meetings with him, and we were able to reach an agreement. The lawsuit settlement included recruitment, hiring, and promotions of gays and lesbians in LAPD. My attorney got the City Council to agree that every single department in the city of Los Angeles would recruit, hire, and promote qualified gays and lesbians. I got the police chief to agree that if a gay or lesbian officer is harassed, the supervisors will be held accountable if they fail to take action, and if the supervisors don't take action, the managers will be held accountable. So not only is the supervisor disciplined but the managers will be held accountable for not taking action to stop the harassment.

The City Council agreed to the settlement on February 10, 1993. I came back July 19. In August, I went back out in the field, and then in September I started recruiting gays and lesbians to become police officers. I'm not doing it for the department; it's my own time and expense. I'm not the liaison in the gay and lesbian community, except the gay and lesbian community sees me that way. The officers treat me better now, but management doesn't treat me any better. There's no blatant stuff like there used to be. For most gay and lesbian officers, it's not perfect but it's a thousand times better under the current administration. The lawsuit changed that.

When I first came on, you had to make a choice: you could be gay or a Los Angeles police officer. You could not be both. If you walked into a room of police officers and they knew you were gay, they'd clear out. If you walked into a gay party and people knew you were a cop, they'd clear out. You were a part of both worlds and a member of neither. You were alone; you were isolated. There are still people who hate you because of the historical relationship. For years, our job was to enforce laws against homosexuals; throughout the 1950s it was against the law to serve alcohol to a known homosexual in California. LAPD was raiding gay and lesbian bars all the way up through 1992.

My lawsuit and those who worked on it have changed things to a large extent. Now it isn't taken for granted that all police officers are heterosexuals. We have to make a change. It's up to us to get in there and change these perceptions. They're not going to change themselves. The best proponents of gays and lesbians in law enforcement are heterosexual law enforcement officers in San Francisco because they've worked with openly gay and lesbian partners. In virtually every case, gay and lesbian officers are outstanding in their field. Unfortunately, gays and lesbians must make a choice whether they're going to go to an agency where they're going to be forced to stay in the closet, or whether they're going to go to an agency where they can be open about their lifestyle. If you choose LAPD, you can be open but there're going to be problems, and you have to be willing to confront them.

I've achieved my lifetime goals. I've done everything that I'm going to do. I've had the greatest impact that I'm going to have in this world. I've always believed that if you save one life, you've justified your existence. From what people have told me, I've saved hundreds of lives.

Sue Herold

Department: Los Angeles (CA) Police Department
Age: 31
Rank: Police Officer
Job: Patrol
Years in Law Enforcement: 9

Sue works patrol on the evening shift near West Hollywood. On break at a coffee shop on Santa Monica Boulevard, she talked about the incidents leading up to her joining Mitch Grobeson's law suit against the Los Angeles Police Department for its treatment of lesbian and gay officers.

Growing up I'd play "cowboys and Indians" and "cops and robbers," and I was always the robber or the Indian. I was the little rebel, I always liked guns, I was a tomboy, and maybe that drove me into a more masculine profession.

I knew I wanted to be a cop about a week before I started processing to go into the department. I realized I was looking at fifteen years of college to get my Ph.D. in psychology, and that was going to be an extended period of time to live at home with mommy and daddy and not be able to be myself. In other words, it was a long time not to be able to date women, go out to gay bars, and things of that sort. So, I thought, "Okay, I'll be a cop." One of the sergeants from this department had been recruiting me for a long time. Finally, I realized that being a cop was pretty much an "out" where I could be a psychologist and carry a gun and a badge and do nice things for nice people. It's kind of a helping profession…an alternative helping profession.

When I looked at the hiring policies of the city of Los Angeles, I noticed that it said, "We do not discriminate on the basis of age, race, ethnicity, religion, and sexual orientation." I thought, "Whew. I can go and be myself." I thought that until I got into the academy—that's when I realized I couldn't be myself and that little line was a bunch of crap.

I was almost twenty-two when I entered the academy. It was an ugly experience for me. I would come into the locker room, change, and people would separate from me. They would change where I couldn't see them, or where they couldn't see me. When I would take my shower after physical training, some of the girls would leave the shower.

The first time that anything really got thrown in my face was when we had a speaker come in who was obviously gay. Before he walked into the room, we were prepared like we hadn't been prepared for any other speaker. "There's a gentleman who's going to come talk to you, and he's homosexual. We don't want any fag jokes or any sissy jokes. Just listen to what he has to say, and if you don't like it, keep your mouth shut." It was terrifying to hear, "Hey, somebody go up there and shut that fag up," while sitting in the classroom with my fellow recruit officers. There were some really ugly comments about body parts, where they didn't belong, and bombs being placed into certain body orifices. I was terrified, and this was relatively early in the academy.

I don't know how it got out, but there was a rumor that I was kissing some female in the academy parking lot. That never happened and it would never happen—I'm not that stupid. I think the rumors came from the fact that I didn't have a boyfriend that I could produce. He didn't have a name, he didn't pick me up, and he didn't drop me off. And, I'm not the most effeminate thing that ever walked the face of the earth.

One time during the academy the gal that I was living with, a classmate of mine, had a party at her house. I had gone into my room to be alone for a while because the party was getting out of control, and I had had way too much to drink. Four of my classmates came by one at a time to proposition me. It's almost as if they were out in the hallway rehearsing.

I had invited someone I was dating to this party, and she brought her ex-boyfriend as her cover. We found ourselves talking in my bathroom. The door was open, and she was crying. I innocently gave her a hug—there was no kiss, no rubby, no feely, and no touchy. The next day my classmates were saying I was French kissing her and feeling on her breasts. One of the guys who propositioned me came up and said, "People are talking about you and everybody's saying you're into girls." I thought to myself, "It's very true. Now, is it any of your business?" All these things barrage your mind, "If I tell them the truth, what are the ramifications?" In a split second, you have to make up your mind if you're going to out yourself or not. I chose not to. I said, "Hell no, I'm not." He said, "The more you deny it, the more we're going to know it's true." I thought, "I'm damned if I do and damned if I don't." That's when I started having problems at work.

I was outed in the academy. This classmate that I'd rented a room from was really homophobic, and she set me up. One morning I woke up, and the phone was ringing. It was my roommate's phone, so I didn't answer it. I ran downstairs to see if her car was still in the garage, and it was not. I went ahead and answered the phone, and it was my girlfriend. By the time I answered, the answering machine had picked up, so the entire conversation was recorded. I didn't have a whole lot of clothing on, my housemate's son also lived with us, and I thought, "If they come home, this is going to be a very large point of embarrassment, so I'm going to dash in my room, throw some clothes on, come back out, and erase the tape." By the time I came back, there was nothing on the tape. I thought that was kind of strange. My classmate knew that my girlfriend was going to call me at nine o'clock in the morning 'cause she had told her the night before that I'd be awake around then. So she parked her car around the corner, waited for the phone call to come, came back, took the tape out, and replaced it. She took the tape to the academy and played it for my classmates. From there on, it got ugly.

I would come in late to work so I wouldn't have to shower with the girls and make them feel uncomfortable. When I was in the locker room, they wouldn't talk to me. I'd ask somebody a question, and they wouldn't respond. People were totally ostracizing me. I couldn't understand. In a nutshell, I didn't have classmates in the academy. I had people that went through the academy with me, but nobody broke their back to help me. I was almost failing, I tried to get into study groups, and my classmates said, "Study group is closed." So, I went through on my own. If we're all in the academy, if we're all classmates, what does it matter who I sleep with?

Somehow I managed to make it through. When I got out, my training officer, who was a really neat guy, tried to let me know he knew I had somebody at home. He was saying, "I know what's going on, and I'm teaching you the other side of being a cop, which is taking care of home first." He also explained to me how I got outed by the "drop a dime" mentality. A lieutenant at the academy called my lieutenant to say, "You've got a lesbian down there, be careful." That call came before I ever showed up and is what pervaded my career ever since.

One time, my twenty-year veteran partner and I rolled up to a code-30 audible, which means that the alarm company can actually hear things going on inside of the business or residence that's being burglarized. My partner and I sat in the car as I saw the suspect coming out of the window. I told him, "I'm going to get out and try to prone this guy out [get him on the ground]." He agreed, and the suspect agreed to some degree—he put his hands up, he turned all the way around to show me that he didn't have any weapons, and then he was "ass and elbows"—that's all I saw. I went on a foot pursuit of him, and after fifteen minutes of requesting a backup, I got the suspect in custody and the cavalry was there. It's like they were waiting for me to either take him into custody or get my butt kicked. When the station is only eight minutes away, there was no way that backup could have been fifteen minutes away. In my career, it's never taken me fifteen minutes to get to a backup call, especially when it's a foot pursuit. If it did, it would be time for me to retire, 'cause I'm either driving or walking too slow.

Another incident happened where my partner and I were in an area that's infested with gang members, narcotics, guns, and parolees. Ironically, I had just been talking to my partner about all the troubles I had been having with the department, and he was basically telling me that I was full of it. We put out a man-with-a-gun backup call: "We have a man; he has a gun. We also have an additional suspect, and we don't know if he's armed or not." So we prone these two suspects out [got them on the ground], and there's two of us and two of them. We asked for a backup; nobody came. A black-and-white [police cruiser] passed right behind us and didn't stop. About ten minutes after that a backup showed. We got the suspects in custody, put them in the back of the car, and my partner said, "I'm sorry. I will never, ever doubt you again. You're right. This is fucked up." He was the first person who actually understood what I was talking about.

When I was over at Pacific Division, I worked for a guy named Mitch Grobeson. When he says he was not given backup, he's not lying. On several occasions, I was the only officer that responded to his backup calls. I had heard that he was gay, and I knew he wasn't going to get backup. They said in roll call, "Let's not back him up. Let's get the fag before he gets us." I can remember them saying, "Fuck him, he's a faggot."

I got paper-fucked. When I was five minutes late, they would ask me for documentation explaining why I was late and how I wasn't going to be late again. They requested a deduct—took time out of my pay or my compensatory time—for when I was more than ten minutes late. And to the guy that walked in twenty minutes later than me everyday, they said absolutely nothing. I'm one of the few Los Angeles police officers who's ever had a personnel complaint for being late to work. For a total of maybe two and a half hours of being late to work, I lost a full day's pay.

In October of 1989, I joined in Mitch Grobeson's suit. What brought it on was all the things I've just explained and then some. The "then some" could be summed up in one word: frustration. I started realizing that I was having some physical ramifications from the stuff that I was dealing with at work and that basically my career was over. There had to be a sacrificial lamb; there had to be somebody who was going to open their mouth. I chose to be that sacrificial lamb and say, "Here I am. Do what you're going to do to me. Just make sure that when you start to do it to somebody else, you'll think twice."

There are gay and lesbian Los Angeles police officers who would like everybody to believe that things have changed. Those officers are only looking out for themselves and not for the community and not for prospective gay and lesbian Los Angeles police officers. Change in an organization as old as this is going to take a long time. It's certainly not going to change overnight. If it did, I would be concerned that it wasn't a real change—it was simply a facade. I think some of those gay and lesbian individuals in this department are only interested in the facade. They're not interested in the real workings and how things are going out here.

I didn't get any support from other gay cops because if you hang out with Sue, it's guilt-by-association. I really can't blame them. I'm still a problem child, a trouble maker, and a rebel. I'm sure I will be seen as that for the rest of my career.

I don't recommend law enforcement as a career. I don't want to sound like a whiner, but I have an ulcer, I have shingles, I have high blood pressure, and according to several psychiatrists, I'm 9 percent nuts. It's a neat job, but the decision needs to be given a lot of thought by a young gay or lesbian, because this is a profession that for years to come is going to be dominated by macho, chauvinistic, egotistical, and sometimes racist men. They'd be crazy unless they gave it a lot of serious thought and had no other way to earn a living. I keep doing it basically because I like my job, and right now this is the most money I can make. The only thing I know how to do is be a cop. This is all I'm trained to do.

I kind of wish I wasn't gay. It's a hard life to live. I hope my son isn't gay because if he is, he'll have to put up with all the same crap I've had to put up with. When you walk into a restaurant and you want to have a nice, relaxing, romantic dinner with your significant other, everybody looks at you. Why can't we just live and let live? There's always going to be that homophobe, or that racist, or that White supremacist who is going to raise children to be the same way. Why would you want to grow up and live in a world of hate? I certainly didn't want to. If I had had a choice, I would have been straight. But I didn't have that choice; it wasn't offered to me. Why would I want to raise my son to have to deal with all this crap?

Marc Goodman

Department: Los Angeles (CA) Police Department
Age: 28
Rank: Sergeant
Job: Supervisor
Years in Law Enforcement: 6

The first openly gay officer to be promoted in the LAPD, Marc lives in gay-popular West Hollywood. A founding member of the Los Angeles-area gay and lesbian law enforcement organization, Pride Behind the Badge, Marc works out of the Seventy-seventh Street Station in South Central LA, ground zero for the Rodney King riots.

Ever since I was a kid, I knew I wanted to be a cop. It seemed very natural when I was growing up. I loved all the police stories, the different television shows, whether it be *Hill Street Blues*, or *Cagney and Lacey*. I used to play cops and robbers with all my friends. There was not a lot of family encouragement for me to enter law enforcement. As a Jewish person, I had three career choices. I could be a doctor; if I was not so smart, I could be a lawyer; and if I was really stupid, I could be an accountant. None of those appealed to me, although my mom pushed me really hard to be a doctor. I attended medical school for almost a year, but it's not what I wanted to do. I called my mom from med school and said, "Ma, guess what? This dream I've been pursuing is your dream."

When I was applying to LAPD, I was acutely aware of the questions I thought were there to weed me out. I had been warned that they didn't hire gay people, but I knew I wanted to be a cop, and it didn't seem to me as if my sexual orientation should matter one way or another. I was still really coming out to myself, so during my background investigation, when they asked me about my girlfriend, I gave them information about a female friend of mine, 'cause she was a girl, and she was my friend. I don't know if that was exactly what they meant.

In the academy I played the game. My friends would ask me, "Are you married? No? Tell us about your girlfriend." I'd make up stories that would cover my tracks so nobody would know I was gay. Not being out sucked because for the most part, gay people are invisible, especially gay cops. Since the 1970s, police departments have had really strong anti-discrimination policies that include Blacks, Hispanics, Asians, women, race, and religion, but the advent of policies including sexual orientation is relatively new. Even in the departments that have them, they're not well enforced. Cops joke about everything and everybody, but they know they can get in trouble for saying certain things. With gay cops, they have no idea we're there, so you get to hear every sick joke and the horrible, dreadful, hurtful things they say about gay and lesbian people, 'cause we're invisible. We're always undercover; we're perfect for undercover assignments, because many of us live our lives that way, constantly censoring ourselves and watching what we say.

When I went through my police academy class, I was playing "Joe Straight Boy." Come to find out there were six or seven gay and lesbian people in my class of seventy-seven recruits. I was doing well; people kept telling me, "Marc, you're going to be the next chief. You can go as high as you want." It didn't seem to me that the best thing I could do to enhance my career was to declare my homosexuality. I wanted to keep it real quiet.

The first gay cop I heard about was when I was just about to graduate from the academy. There was a cop by the name of Grobeson who had some trouble with the department—he alleged he had received some harassment at the hands of the department. He ended up quitting in lieu of being fired. A fundraiser was being held for him. I went and talked to him, and he ended up introducing me to other gay and lesbian officers. That changed my life.

If there's one thing that's more rare than a gay cop, it's a Jewish cop. I'm Jewish, and I was also a member of the Jewish police officer's association, the Shomrim Society. In May of 1991, there was a Jewish festival in Los Angeles that attracted about thirty-five thousand people. The Shomrim Society got together a bunch of off-duty cops in uniform, the department gave us a black-and-white, and we went out there, kissed babies, and shook hands. It was a real community relations and public relations effort. The community loved it, and the department liked it. It made us look good because we were bridging the cultural-religious gap between the community at large and the department.

In June of 1991, the gay pride festival was coming up. One commander had given us permission to recruit at the gay festival, "If you can get some gay cops to come out and participate, you can recruit." He didn't think it would ever happen, and neither did I. There were no openly gay cops on a force of eight thousand, which should give a good indication of the climate at the time. Somehow Chief Gates found out that the commander had given us permission, and he went ballistic. The rumor was you could hear him screaming at the commander all over the police headquarters building. He revoked the decision. By then it was being picked up by the news media not just in Los Angeles, but internationally. What galvanized me into action was in Chief Gates' denial and revocation of the commander's permission, he gave the explanation that never in the history of the Los Angeles Police Department had we had off-duty, uniformed officers recruit at any community event, and we were certainly not going to do it with these people. I figured, "The chief is a man of good will. Obviously he doesn't know that one month prior, I was in the Jewish community, off-duty, in uniform, and recruiting." Through the chain of command, I let it be known that actually we *had* done it before, and there was a long-standing practice of reaching out to all communities. And the word came back down, "No, I hadn't." I'm like, "Yes, I did." "No, you didn't." Well, he's the chief of police, about thirteen civil-service ranks above me, and you can see who won that argument: "No, we didn't." But we did, and that's what really frustrated me. I said to myself, "What do you call it when one group of people have certain rights and privileges and another group of people cannot do the same thing? That's discrimination." For the first time, it hit me really hard that I was being discriminated against, and I did not like the feeling. It went totally counter to my upbringing. The very first day of the police academy when they swear you in, I swore all these things about being a cop, about having integrity, about doing the right thing, and about treating all people with dignity and respect regardless of their background, and this chief was setting an example that ran completely counter to that. I said, "This is wrong, and I've got to stand up to it." That's changed my life permanently.

Eventually, the police commissioner overruled Chief Gates, and we went to the event. There were six of us: three men and three women. There were peo-

ple from the media, the press, and television from all over 'cause this was history. I was scared, really scared. I had been shot at, my police car had been shot,
I had been in some really knock-down, drag-out fights, vehicle pursuits, foot
pursuits, arrested all types of stone cold, hard core, gang member, murdering,
drug dealing people, but I was never as scared as I was thinking about partici-
pating in this event. I had heard all the rumors—gay cops don't get backup, gay
cops get things put in their lockers, they get nasty notes left on their lockers,
nobody'll want to work with me, nobody'll want to change next to me, and I'll
never get promoted again. All those things made it very scary. I remember
walking from my car in my uniform through the gay festival, and I felt like I
was going to the gas chamber. It was the longest walk of my life; it was like slow
motion. I was watching all these people in t-shirts and jeans having a good
time, and there I was in my long-sleeve, dark-blue wool uniform, walking the
last hundred feet to my death. I knew it had to be done, but it was so scary,
because I didn't know how we were going to be received. I didn't know what
the department was going to do. I didn't know what my partners were going
to do. But I made it.

I hooked up with all the other gay cops that were there, and they informed
me that all day long, people had been extremely supportive, and people were
very friendly. It was probably one of the most moving experiences of my life. I
had people coming up and thanking me for being there. It was really moving,
and given the dismal public relations the department was having so shortly
after the Rodney King incident, they couldn't have paid a million dollars and
gotten a P.R. firm to give them what they were getting out there. The gay and
lesbian festival in LA attracts between 350,000 and 400,000 people every year, and
I swear I shook hands with every one of them. They loved us, and we were on
all the television stations. On Monday morning it was time to go back to
Rampart Division, and I was afraid my career would be over, nobody would
talk to me at the station, and nobody would have anything to do with me. I was
wrong. It took three weeks for that to happen. It didn't happen right away.

At the same time the gay pride festival was going on, there was a lot of
post–Rodney King dissention amongst the officers. It was so bad that federal
mediators were brought in to talk to minority representatives from all the
officer groups. I attended this meeting representing the Jewish police officer
association. There were probably 100 or 200 people in the room with the federal
mediators. We had a couple of high ranking chiefs in our department, representatives from the Black cops, the Asian cops, the Hispanic cops, women
police officers, Jewish police officers, Irish police officers, members of our police

union, and all the high ranking officials from our police union. We went over a lot of hard issues and talked turkey about racial conflict among officers; it was a very powerful session. Before we started it off, because many people in the room didn't know each other, the federal mediators came in and said, "I'd like to go around the room. On a light note so we get to know one another, I'd like for you to think of something most people don't know about you that's different or unique or might be funny." I wasn't going to do it, but right before this went down, I asked one of the coordinators of the event, "I see you've got Black cops, Jewish cops, Asian cops, and Hispanic cops here. Wasn't there something that happened in West Hollywood a couple of weeks ago with gay cops? Were those cops invited?" She goes, "Oh no, they're not really an organized group, and they really don't have anything to add here." That bugged me a lot. So after maybe the seventy-fifth person, it was my turn, and I said, "I'm Marc Goodman, from Rampart Division. I'm here today representing the Shomrim Society and something most of you probably don't know about me is I was one of the cops that participated in the recruitment event last weekend at the gay and lesbian pride festival." People were spitting out their drinks, they were dropping their food, the chiefs next to me were keeling over, having heart attacks and stuff, and the room became dead silent. That was my real coming out, because I was saying it in front of deputy chiefs, commanders, captains, lieutenants, sergeants—people I work with. That was powerful. I felt that was really important, that I had the courage to stand up in front of these people and say, "Hey, I was there."

After I came out at this event, my commanding officer was immediately notified, "You've got one there, and you've got to do something about it." There's an old saying in police work, "Telephone, telegram, tell a cop." It's all the same thing—once you tell one, it's all over. So I got back to Rampart, and I started having partners coming up to me and saying, "Hey Marc, come here. Let's talk." They'd take me out to the most quiet, desolate part of the parking lot and say something like, "We've been partners for a long time, and I need to let you know something. There's a rumor going around the division that you're a homo. I know it can't be true 'cause we worked together, we kicked down doors together, we jumped over fences and caught bad guys, and you don't wear a dress, so I know you can't be that way. But Smith over there is spreading the rumor, and if I were you I'd go ahead and kick his ass." And I'd say, "Actually, I am gay." They'd look at me and go, "Yeah, right. Sure you are." "No, really, I am." "No, you're not." I was like, "Believe me, I have good intelligence on this. I would know." My partners would then look at me quizzically and say, "Oh, that's cool. Well, we got along pretty good before, we were part-ners, and if you need anyone to work with, screw all those other assholes. I'll work with you." Ten minutes later, another guy would do the same thing. That happened to me seven times in one week. At least they had the courage, the balls, and the dignity to talk to me about it which made me respect those par-ticular people even more. The fact that they couldn't believe it showed me how effective I was at playing the game. That was eye-opening to me, 'cause I, like most other gay cops, lived in constant fear of being discovered. Most gay cops live in constant fear they're going to say something wrong—somebody'll ask them, "What'd you do this weekend?" and they'll put out the wrong pronoun.

Among the cops I work with, the response was really good. I was very lucky in that I enjoyed a fairly good reputation. I wasn't supercop or anything, but most people liked working with me, I had a good time, and I was pretty capa-ble of doing the job; that helped me enormously. I couldn't have asked for a nicer, more professional group of people. It was nice to finally have the free-dom to be me. It was an incredible burden off my shoulders. Of the gay cops I've seen on the job who have had really hard times, most people didn't like them to begin with, and once they found out they were gay, it added fuel to the fire, "I knew I didn't like him for some reason. He's a homo."

I had a couple negative experiences. After I had come out to several officers at the station, it got back to this captain who called me into the station. Being called into the captain's office is something that's not good—normally the cap-tains are so far above us we never have any contact with them. He sat me down, made me feel like a suspect and said, "There's a rumor going around the station that you're a homosexual." It was real apparent both through his body lan-guage and the words that he used that he was no big fan of gay people. He said, "You don't have to tell me, but as your commanding officer I think I should know." I was like, "As your employee should I know what you're doing in your bed?" Of course I didn't say that. I thought, "I've got nothing to hide. I told everybody else. If he wants to know, he can know." So I said, "Yeah, actually I *am* gay." He said, "Oh, I see. Well, you've created quite a unique personnel prob-lem for me because there are all these other cops and what are they going to say? In order to deal with this situation, I'm going to go into every roll call and let all the cops know you're a homosexual. This way they can watch what they say around you." I said, "Well, sir, I'd prefer you didn't." He said, "No, no. I feel that the best way to manage this personnel crisis is to deal with it head on." That really infuriated me. I didn't want to be insubordinate but I came back with, "Well, sir. Rather than telling every cop in the division what my sexual orientation is, how about if you have your police officers comply with federal, state, local law, and department policy regarding nondiscrimination of everybody, and this won't be an issue." He thought about it for a second and said, "I see what you're saying." That captain, however, went on to tell every sergeant and lieutenant in the division.

Two sergeants from the "old school" were the "keeper of the faith." It was their job to see that no women made it through probation. Needless to say, they were not enamored with a gay cop. They made my life miserable for a couple of months. One was making such wild allegations that I went to the senior captain, and he told the sergeant, "You better stop it." The guy was starting to build a paper trail against me with the purpose of giving me a personnel complaint. It got so bad that basically the captain issued a restraining order against this sergeant: "You don't have anything to do with Goodman. If you need to tell him something, have it sent through somebody else."

There are some male pigs in the department who every time a woman walks by, "Check out the tits on her. Oh, baby." They'd talk to you about their dates, what they did, and go into graphic detail. One of the nice things that happened when I came out was when my partners would go off with, "Check out that girl over there," I'd say, "Yeah, her boyfriend's not bad either." It was a freedom that was really nice.

On the other side, I've had some very positive experiences. One time, I was up at the desk, and we had a new cop who had just transferred in. A rather effeminate man came to the front desk and made some type of report. As soon as the guy went out, this officer was like, "Man, what a fucking faggot. Why do those people have to be like that?" He was saying it right in front of me. All these other cops' eyes were getting huge 'cause they were watching this guy hang himself. The nice thing was, I didn't have to say a damn thing. All my fellow officers were saying, "Why you gotta to be like that? Why you gotta make fun of gay people? What do you care what he does in his bedroom?" They got all over him. Of course, the minute I left, they said, "Don't you know? Goodman's one of them. Watch what the fuck you say." But that's okay; I don't have a problem with that. My negative experiences decreased enormously because number one, I was no longer privy to all the hateful, anti-gay, so-called jokes that were being passed around, and number two, other people were correcting people on their homophobia, and I didn't have to.

My big fear was with the locker room: "Okay, these guys will work with me but they certainly don't want to change next to me." Shortly after I came out, one day I went in, and there was nobody in the locker room. It was five minutes before we were supposed to change, there was not a single person in there, and I said, "Finally it happened. This is the day I'm waiting for. Nobody wants to change next to me. God damn, these people, why can't they see I'm not like that? It's not about a sexual thing, I just want to change my clothes." I was sitting there wallowing in self-pity and feeling terrible. I got changed, and I was just about to leave the locker room when a cop came up and said, "Hey Marc, what's up? What are you doing here so early?" It was daylight savings time, and I showed up at work an hour early. That's why there was nobody there.

The great thing about coming out was that I could finally integrate my life completely. I didn't have to act one way with one group of people and another with another group. I could be me. I felt as if ten thousand pounds of weight had been lifted off my shoulders, and it was wonderful. If anything, it has increased my promotability. I've got high name recognition throughout the department, and it's only effected me in positive ways that I'm aware of. I wish more people would come out. I know literally hundreds of gay and lesbian police officers that don't come out; if they did, things would get better.

Post—the Rodney King beating, I and another woman became the first two openly gay people to go to the academy and lecture the recruits. When I come in in my uniform and speak the same language, they hear the message more clearly. I go over our holidays, I talk about gay pride celebrations, Stonewall, the appropriate terminology, some of our symbols like the lambda and the pink triangle, and give them some insight into gay and lesbian relationships. Now, from day one when baby policemen show up at the police academy, they're indoctrinated, "There are gay cops in this department."

I tell students right off the bat, "I'm not here to change your mind. I'm not here to make you think the way I do. I'm just here to share information." We make the analogy that the same way that gay and lesbian people are oppressed minorities, so are police officers. Very few kids in the class acknowledge knowing any gay people, even though obviously all of them do. We ask, "Where do you get your impressions from?" We talk about Billy Crystal on *Soap*, we talk about the two or three snippets that they show of the pride parade every year, and then we talk about, "Okay, you see a six foot-two drag queen dressed like Liza Minnelli, and you think that's what gay people are all about." I say, "Let's take another piece of media," and I talk about Rodney King, "If I just landed here from Venus, and all I saw was Rodney King and the beatings, then I would think that's what police are all about. But you know that's not the case." The latest addition to our class is a sergeant with twenty-five years on the job who came out as having a gay son. He'll say, "I've got twenty-five years in this department, I'm straight, I'm Catholic, and I did everything right. I've got a twenty-one-year-old son, and I just found out he is gay. If you were to stop him in a traffic stop, he deserves all the best treatment in the world—you owe it to me, and you owe it to the department." It's a really powerful message.

Closeted gay officers have a lot more stress from the constant fear of being discovered than out gay officers. As a former closet case, it's kind of like living as a Jew in Germany in 1942. "When are they going to get me? When are they going to find out? When am I going to be discovered?" It's incredibly stressful. Closeted gay cops go through enormous amounts of personal grief trying to hide themselves. A lot of gay cops compensate for it either by being married, by talking about women like dogs and being extremely misogynistic, or by harassing gay and lesbian people on the streets to show they're not one of us.

Being an openly gay officer has its own stress in that you're always wondering, "What are they thinking? Are they thinking, 'There's that gay cop.' What's the first thing on their minds? How do people perceive me? When it comes time to strip search somebody, are people wondering what I'm doing?" By comparison, on a scale from one to ten, the stress of being a gay cop in the closet is about a nine and a half and the stress of being an openly gay cop is maybe a two or three. For me, this is the way to go. I don't know that the numbers would be the same if I was working for a rural sheriff's department in Kentucky because I don't think they'd be that tolerant. But in my department, and for me, this is much less stressful.

Heretofore the history of our people—gay "copdom"—has been to lie and deny, "No, I'm not. You know I've got a girlfriend." So the rumor mills go. When you've got the courage to stand up to these people and say, "So what? What are you going to do about it?" It takes away all the fun for them; it takes all the power and all the wind out of their sails. It really disarms them. I've found that to be really a powerful tool.

Law enforcement is a great career; I recommend it to anybody. I try to encourage gay people to consider it as a career, because many young gay and lesbian people don't think they can do it, "I can't be gay and be a cop." I try to go out there, act as a role model, and let gay and lesbian youths know they can do anything they want. I stress the fact that they can become police officers, firefighters, doctors, and lawyers. Too many gay kids grow up without role models and therefore see their options as extremely limited—the boys can become hairdressers and the girls can become gym teachers. I want them to know they can do anything they want.

Dorothy Knudson

Department: Chicago (IL) Police Department
Age: 31
Rank: Patrol Officer
Job: Patrol
Years in Law Enforcement: 4

Dorothy's picture sits next to that of her grandfather, a "big, Irish cop" from Minneapolis on her mother's dresser. She once appeared on the Phil Donahue Show with a group identified as the Gay and Lesbian Alliance from the University of Chicago. In her newly renovated city house that she shares with her partner and her dogs, she talked about life with the Chicago Police Department.

I excelled academically my whole life, and I told my family I was going to be a doctor. But once after watching *Hill Street Blues*, I turned to my brother and said, "I'd like to be a cop." He got really mad that I would want to be a police officer, because I was going to be a doctor. Why would I want to be a cop? That was the only time I really toyed with the idea. It was kind of thrown on the back burner.

Law enforcement always intrigued me, partly because women are victimized so much in our society. I saw it as an opportunity to work with women in a crisis situation, whether they've just been beaten by a partner, raped, or in any way victimized. A lot of it was just really practical. In Chicago, there are a lot of very good benefits, the income is very good, and there is tuition reimbursement. I don't like working inside, and it seemed very intriguing and exciting. In 1990, I was hired by the Chicago Police Department.

I'm assuming the department knew I was a lesbian when they hired me. The only two ways they could know during the application process was they still use the MMPI [Minnesota Muliphasic Personality Inventory] that has sexual orientation questions, and I answered those honestly. And, they do a background investigation where a detective comes to your home and interviews you. At the time, I lived in a one-bedroom apartment with a woman who was in the military. I had gay and lesbian books and periodicals laying all around the house, and unless he was really stupid, I don't know how he could not have known.

I was out in the academy, and I did very well. Overall, the instructors were pretty good. People probably said a lot more behind my back than they said to my face. I ended up being our class commander; I graduated number one academically. I worked very hard, I earned some respect, I never gave up, and I didn't give in.

I challenged homophobic remarks as much as possible. A lot of the coursework is actually boring and was written in the '60s and '70s. One time, the instructors were dealing with victimless crimes, and said, "things like gambling, prostitution, and homosexuality." I said, "Excuse me, but homosexuality is not a crime. There's a human-rights ordinance protecting gays, lesbians, and bisexuals. Don't say homosexuality is a crime. Don't tell these people who are going to have badges, guns, and handcuffs that it's a crime." There were also other things to confront, like plain, old misogyny, which is another one of my pet peeves. A lot of homophobia is just misogyny in a different form.

I had an advantage being a lesbian. Straight men are very threatened by gay men, and it would have been trouble if I was a guy. A lot of guys are intrigued, a lot are amused, and a lot of them just don't like queers, but I was okay. I had comments from guys who were particularly homophobic who said they respected and admired me for being out, but that didn't mean they liked the fact that I was gay. As one guy put it, I had "balls." I cringed and said, "No. Ovaries; big ovaries."

After the academy I spent six months at the Twenty-third District at Addison and Halstead, which is in the heart of the gay community in Chicago. I had chosen my training district—that's one of the perks they give to the class commander. I knew the streets fairly well, and I thought, "These are officers who deal with gays and lesbians all the time, so they shouldn't have problems dealing with me." Actually they did, but everyone was always very nice to my face, and I never had anyone give me a hard time. I think a lot of people assumed that because I was so out I was what's called "heavy"—well connected—and therefore no one wanted to mess with me. The officers acted and responded very professionally, at least around me. I never noticed any officers being verbally abusive, flippant, or unprofessional around anyone who was obviously gay or lesbian. But I found I didn't like working in the gay and lesbian community 'cause that's where I go to have fun. My idea of fun is not coming home, changing clothes, showering, going to a nice restaurant, looking over at the table next to me, and seeing a person I wrote a couple of traffic tickets to earlier in the day. It's not relaxing. I wanted to be able to go there and not be at work still.

From there I was transferred to the Eleventh District, which is on the city's west side and is a very impoverished community. It's a very high-crime, very busy district, and I love it. The officers are great. They're mostly newer officers and very hard-working. I like the fast pace, and I like working very hard. I also really like what I've learned, how I've been able to grow, and the amount of anger I've been able to experience towards our society. I'm in the poor Black community on a daily basis, and the oppression and racism of our society is overwhelming. I hear a constant rage. I always understood it academically but until you see the nihilism, the pain, and the suffering on a daily basis, you don't understand how overwhelming it is. Whatever I can give to the citizens there, I give. When I encounter a human being, my philosophy is, "What can I do for this person? What can I give?" I take that with me everywhere, but especially to work. I love being there.

Most of my fellow officers are pretty amused by my being out and by the way I deal with it. For example, the guys were being vulgar men one day. They were sticking their tongues out, motioning up and down with their tongues, and joking around with each other. I walked by and said, "Amateurs. You're all amateurs." They liked that, and they thought that was funny.

If my fellow coworkers are teasing and calling each other "faggot," I explain to them why that's offensive. I hear faggot a lot. How do you degrade a man? You turn him into a woman—it's the biggest insult. I explain, "Not only is it homophobic, it's very insulting to women, 'cause what you're saying is, 'Only a woman would want to suck a dick.'" I think a lot of them understand.

The biggest thing has been to establish myself as a woman, not as a lesbian. The guys are always talking about how women would rather work inside and how they don't get out of the car, and I haven't seen anything to back that up.

My partner and I have a reputation for being in the thick of it all the time; establishing ourselves as good, hard-working police officers in spite of the fact that we're women was the toughest thing to do.

I had a couple of negative experiences but they turned into positive experiences. I found a ring in the hallway, and I put up posters by the locker room and the radio room that read, "Found: One woman's ring in the basement hallway." Someone doctored it up to say, "Found: One woman in the basement, see Dorothy Knudson." Finally after it'd been up for about a month, someone wrote the word "dyke" by my name. I was amused it took a month for someone to do this, but a lot of the guys who work with me were very angry. They were angrier than I was. I was very touched.

I'm very out, and I'm very comfortable with my sexual orientation. Police officers are like sharks—blood's drawn, and they have a feeding frenzy. With me there's nothing for them to feed off of: I'm comfortable, I'm out, there's nothing I'm trying to hide, and there's nothing I'm ashamed of. If you're out, it's just not fun. If I'm not bothered by it, it's just not fun.

In 1991, I was appointed to an advisory committee on gay and lesbian issues for the Chicago Police Department, and the *Windy City Times*, the Chicago gay newspaper, did an interview and put my picture on the cover. As a result, officers who were closeted started avoiding me like the plague. In fact, there were a few I wasn't sure about, and after that, I knew. I think it's starting to wear off. I'm not seen as so dangerous 'cause I haven't been outing people for the last four years.

In the Twenty-third District, there were officers who wouldn't help officers they didn't like. In the Eleventh District, it's different. My partner and I had an experience one morning at 5 A.M. where we were fighting with a guy in an alley. We were fighting with him, and we couldn't get him cuffed. I'd get him down on the ground, and he'd get up. We're tussling and trying to get his arms pinned so we could get him cuffed. We were in a really bad, heavy gang, and drug area. I called for help, and there were officers who were on the other end of our district just sitting down for their breakfast. One officer in particular was very homophobic and very misogynistic. He jumped up from his breakfast table, ran outside, got hit by a car, got back up, got into the squad car, and still came. That's the type of district I work in. It doesn't matter who's calling for help, it's, "Go." That's how we all are and how we have to be. We know that things can get very bad, very quickly, and we're in a lot of danger if we're not there for each other.

I had a really interesting conversation with a woman in Toronto who is a Black, lesbian, feminist radio-show host on one of the smaller stations. She was questioning how I could claim that I'm a lesbian feminist and a cop because it seemed so hypocritical to her. I explained, "Minorities play an extremely important part in law enforcement. The idea of an all-straight, White, male, police force scares me. Minorities have to be a part of law enforcement. It's what you do and what you take with you to the job that defines the job. The job doesn't have to define the cop, the cop can define the job." Our society is what's oppressive. The police are just the most obvious arm of that oppression. I use that a lot on the job. I go to work realizing I'm probably the only contact someone who's disempowered is going to have with the power establishment. I recognize that, and I don't let people insult me or offend me—whatever they want to say is fine because it might be the only chance to vent. Just as long as no one tries to hurt me. I draw the line at physical injury. I explained this to this woman. I don't know if she agreed, but I think she understood a little more why I was doing what I was doing.

There's a lot of stress on the job anyway, but it would be even more stressful for me if I were closeted. Whether it's in seriousness or joking, a lot of verbal gay-bashing takes place 'cause straight men tend to do that. They tend to limit what they say around me. It would be hard to be closeted and have to hear that all the time. Another stress has to do with not having partner benefits. If I were married, and I got shot and killed tonight at work, my husband would get a ton of money. If I get shot and killed tonight, my partner is not recognized; she's not going to get the quarter of a million dollars. If we live to ripe old ages and I happen to be the one who dies first, my pension should continue to her as if I had been married. It's not fair.

I think law enforcement is an important place for gays and lesbians to be. As more gays and lesbians come out in general, they're going to have more involvement with the police department because they'll be victimized more as out gays and lesbians. We need to be there; we need to be visible in every aspect of life.

Lynn "Rosie" Rosenberg

Department: Metropolitan Police Department, District of
Columbia
Age: 35
Rank: Police Officer
Job: Patrol
Years in Law Enforcement: 3 1/2

*Wearing a silver badge on her left hip, a gun on her right, and a Washington Redskins
sweatshirt, Lynn spent the afternoon before heading for a vacation in the Bahamas talking
about being a D.C. cop.*

I never thought I'd want to be a police officer; it never appealed to me. I
started out as a photographer, and when I couldn't find a photographic job,
my father said, "Why don't you try the Navy. You can get in as a photographer." So I went into the service as a photographer, and I loved it.

I was twenty-one when I discovered I was gay. When I went to boot camp, I
was still straight, but after that, I realized I might be gay. I was closeted for so
many years in the military thinking, "If I fuck up and the wrong person knows,
I'm going to go to jail." I signed re-enlistment papers with questions saying,
"Are you a homosexual? Are you gay? Are you lesbian?" It wasn't one question
you could slip by and say, "Maybe I just didn't read it right." I lied on official

government documents, and it really pissed me off that they made me lie, because otherwise I couldn't re-enlist.

I was close to the witch hunts, but not part of them. My lover and I got stationed in Puerto Rico together, and she had a record of being brought up on charges of homosexuality in the military. We lived together, we were lovers, and people around us were falling. Usually when people around you fall, NIS will pressure them and get a list of everyone who is gay. It was real close a couple times. It was scary, and it was awful to watch. My lover had been the victim of a witch hunt before we met, and she said NIS followed her everywhere she went. They never really hung her on anything. They brought her up on charges, but she never got fried. Now she's almost going to retire.

In the military, I spent ten years in the closet. I had a very nice career, moved up the ladder quickly, and my last tour was here at the Pentagon. That was the most closeted tour. You get real good at changing your pronouns, like most gays and lesbians do. But after my ten year career, it was time to get out. I was tired of being closeted and tired of changing my pronouns all the time.

I got out of the Navy and bought a dry cleaner franchise. I always wanted to own a business, and I fell into this trap. I spent about a year doing that, going down the tubes, losing everything I ever had, and it was time to get out. So there I was desperately trying to find a job, and I hit the streets of Washington. In bad economies, photography is one of the first things to go; if you have one photographic job that's semi-decent, you have ten thousand photographers going for it. Then Dad stepped in again; he said, "I read in the *Washington Post* that the police department is looking for photographers." So I went down and talked to this guy who said, "Become a regular officer and work with crime scene search teams. You go out and photograph a crime scene, take fingerprints, and those kind of things." I said, "That sounds good; plus I like being in uniform—I don't have to buy clothes."

So at thirty years old, I became a cop and went to cop boot camp. Once I actually hit the streets, I thought, "This is kind of fun. I like this." That's when I thought I would stick with doing patrol versus doing crime scenes where you get there after everything's all taken care of. Now I get to be the first unit on the scene and jump into the fun. That's how I became a police officer, and I love it. It's pretty diverse. I get to do something different every day. The basic is the same: I drive around in a scout car, I have a partner usually, and we do a lot of domestic violence calls.

I was out in cop boot camp. There were about eight women and probably twenty-five or thirty guys that made up my class. We did everything together;

we ran together, we ate together, we studied together, and we played together. At some point in the very beginning, I came out. It was totally accepted as far as I know. There's so much stress on becoming a cop it's like who the hell has time to deal with anything else. It really wasn't too much of an issue at all. Nobody cared who did what, as long as we got through cop boot camp.

The guys were kind of macho when you got them together; when you got them apart they were normal people. Together they have this macho crap going on. I'd hear them talk once in awhile, and I'd hear derogatory comments like, "Faggot." They'd be telling a story and they'd say, "these three faggots came up…" In the academy, I would let a lot of stuff go 'cause I was still trying to feel my way through. But then came time for multicultural sensitivity awareness week and everybody was bitching. I'd been hearing these derogatory comments off and on for weeks. When the gay community came in, there were two men standing in front of us giving a lecture on homosexuality. The first thing they said was, "How many of you have a friend, relative, brother, or sister that is gay?" I looked around the room and every one of those little sons of bitches raised their hands. I couldn't believe it. I looked at all these people, and I thought, "You bunch of hypocrites."

After boot camp, I got to my district. I'm totally out there. Everybody who wants to know, knows. After being so closeted, I feel like I'm free. I came out to my training officer right away. He was like, "Great, that way we can look for women together." That's how it started. We didn't talk a lot about it with the other guys, but it slowly started coming out. One on one they asked me about the lesbian life. One time it was a bright, sunny morning, and I remember talking to another officer. He was having relationship problems, and right then I was having relationship problems, too. We were agreeing, "Yeah, relationships suck," and he looked at me and said, "I never thought I'd be standing here talking to a woman about a woman in a relationship." We started laughing, and I told him, "Relationships are basically the same. You have the same kind of things going on; you have two people interacting, and you have trust, loyalty, love, and infidelities. Mine happens to be with a woman, and yours happens to be with a woman. The difference is you're a guy, and I'm a woman. That's it." He's from the world of gay-bashing and rednecks. It dawned on me at that moment that a lot of the guys have accepted me as a person; I happen to be a lesbian also. I don't run around with a big lambda on my forehead screaming, "I'm gay, I'm gay." But if somebody asks, I tell them. The police community is so small that if you tell one person, everybody knows. They'll come up and ask me questions, and I'll tell them the truth. Maybe they won't have so many prejudices if I can help educate them a little. I'm not on any crusade, but if they ask me, I tell them about my lifestyle and my life. The biggest thing I don't know how to overcome is, they think that homosexuality is about sex. I try and tell them that it's not really sex, even though sex is a big part of anyone's life. It's a culture. It's a lifestyle. It's my life. It's not really sex, and it's hard to get them to understand that.

I was in traffic court one time, and we were sitting around waiting to testify. There might have been fifteen or twenty cops in the room, and I didn't know any of them well. I knew this one guy from the academy, and he was a real ass-hole. Everybody in the room was Black and male, except for me and maybe one or two other people. He was telling a story, and he said, "...that fucking fag-got," and it struck me wrong. I don't even remember what the story was about, but he kept saying, "Faggot," and my heart started racing real fast. These were a group of people that I'd just had a little interaction with; I didn't even know their names. I stood up and said, "That's really rude. If you want to tell your story, tell your story, but that'd be like me telling a story and saying the word 'nigger.' Faggot to me is like nigger." I thought we were going to have to fight right there. One guy in the crowd said, "She just called you a nigger." I got a new respect for this guy 'cause he looked at me and said, "No, she did not. She was trying to make a point, and she made her point. And I'm sorry." That real-ly impressed me.

Another time, in roll call this guy said, "...and that god damn faggot." He turned right around to me and said, "No offense, Rosie." I said, "Offense is taken. If he's a gay man or homosexual, say 'That man there,' or 'That homo-sexual man,' if you want to identify him. Don't say it like that. He's not a 'fuck-ing faggot.' He's not a 'god damn faggot,' he's a person, so identify him a different way." You can't harp on them all the time, but once in awhile I'll stand up and say something.

I think the real issue for me was being a woman. The guys make up the most of our department. It's a man's world; it's always going to be a man's world. You might be the only backup for the guys on the street. They wait and watch each woman who comes up there. They want to know if she's going to get into it, they want to know what she's going to do. They want to know, "Can we trust her? Will she back me up? Will she get in and fight? Will she shoot somebody if they've got a knife at my throat?" They look at every new female that comes up; it's almost like a little test. I tried to tell them that just because you have a gender difference doesn't mean you're not going to get in there and try. It's tough being a woman in a man's world; it's a cliche, but it's true.

Being a cop is a macho, tough kind of world. I'm not really dykey; I'm not macho. I have long finger nails, and I'm like, "God damn, I broke my nail again" after we fight or something. It's a man's world, and we've got to try and fit in as females, and that's hard. We've got to do everything they have to do, and if we can't, we have to make up for it in other areas. Where I lack in the physical, I make up in the mental. I have to out smart them, and a lot of times I have to talk people into handcuffs if I don't have any backup. You have to use your head more. If we have a real big guy sometimes we use reverse psychology, and my partner sits back, and I go to arrest them. Sometimes they don't want to beat up on a woman, and sometimes we just have to fight.

I came down for one of the marches recently and marched around just like everybody else. God, it was packed—crowds everywhere. I've never been arrested—that'd be kind of embarrassing. But if I saw a group of police officers attempting to arrest somebody at a gay demonstration, I would be on the side of the police officers. I would jump in and assist my fellow officer, there is no doubt in my mind. Usually people act like idiots. We don't just run in and arbitrarily grab people and arrest them. We take a lot of abuse before we arrest in a crowded situation. You've got fifty zillion chances, and if you choose to be arrested, if you want to be martyrs, then you will be arrested. If I had to choose between standing with my gay sisters and brothers and jumping to the police, I'd jump over on the police side and assist.

I really love what I'm doing. We have a lot of fun on the job. We laugh a lot, and we cry a little bit sometimes, too. I love it 'cause they have faith in me; they have confidence in me. I work real hard, I care, and I do all the bull shit stuff they ask me to do. They like how I work, I make a lot of lock-ups, and I'm not afraid to fight. I know I'm going to get my ass kicked, but I still fight, and they know that. This whole job is reputation. I don't know how, but I have a real good one. I just hope it stays there.

Most of my experience is positive. A lot of shit happens, and you try and not drag all that negative shit with you. You got to let it go, 'cause sometimes it just gets to you. Some of this stuff you take home, but you try not to. It's the little pleasures that make you feel good and make you feel like you have an impact on people's lives. Sometimes you're so overwhelmed that you feel like you have no god damn impact whatsoever—you're just squashing these little fires all over the place and we're never going to get control of it. But then once in awhile you help people out, and it feels good.

B.

Department: A Metropolitan Police Department
Age: 42
Rank: Police Officer II
Job: Patrol
Years in Law Enforcement: 7

*Having been an officer with both a university and a metropolitan police department, B. has had
the "pleasure" of experiencing two police academy classes and two departments. A solidly built
man with greying hair and a thick Boston accent, B. wore an "Army" t-shirt with a pink triangle
embedded in the top of the "Y".*

W hen I was five or six years old, we lived in Boston, and my brother was
two years older than me. One time we were with a bunch of kids, and
we ran up the block. We went around one corner and as we ran, my little legs
couldn't carry me as fast as theirs, so they were separating from me more and
more. By the time I got down to the end of the block they were no where in
sight. I had no idea where I was, and I started crying. Finally, a police officer
came over and picked me up in his arms, got me to calm down, asked me
where I lived, and took me home. I always remembered that police officer as
being someone I could depend on, someone I could trust. Being a cop was a
very respectable thing in my mind.

I always had the desire to be a cop, but when you're gay there're only certain options open. Police always seemed so para-military, and the military has this macho image. When you think of gays, you think of feminine guys or you think of females as complete bull dykes. I figured that there was no room for someone like me to be a cop. I didn't think there would be any gay cops, and so I didn't pursue law enforcement for a long time.

I moved out of my parent's home when I was seventeen and worked as a musician for a long time. I got my own apartment, and I started going to some gay liberation meetings. I was smart enough to know that there was really nothing wrong with being gay, but I couldn't *feel* it. At one point, I remember riding on a subway train in Somerville, Massachusetts, and the guy sitting across from me kept staring at me. I found him kind of attractive, and I kept staring back. He got off at a stop and I followed him. It was the beginning of having sex with other guys in a kind of sleazy way. That went on for years— quick sex, movie houses, places where I could go where nobody would see me, where I could be anonymous. It felt very exciting in a way.

Shortly after my father died I met my first lover. Even after we split up after twelve years we were best friends until he died last year. He really loved me for who I was. About seven years into our relationship, he was sucker punched by the kid who lived across the street. My lover went into a coma for a week, lost hearing in his left ear permanently, and had brain damage. It was really awful. This was my first experience with hatred. I always knew that there was hatred but I didn't understand how much people really wanted to hurt gays. It took him six years before he really started to get his personality back.

I met a guy in San Francisco who'd been a cop there for fourteen years, and we became friends. He became an inspiration to me, and I figured, "If he can be a gay cop, why can't I?" So at the age of thirty-two, I decided I was going to go for it. I checked into Boston Police, and they had an age limit of thirty-two. I just missed their exam, so I tried for a job with a university police department. Eventually I got the job and was with them for four years.

The university police was an eye opener. Going through the academy was like going through boot camp. That first academy was tough. This was typical in the academy—the drill instructor would run up to somebody and get three inches away from the recruit's face and start screaming, "Are you looking at me, boy? Do you like me? Are you a faggot?" If the recruit said, "No, sir. I don't like you," the instructor would say, "What's wrong with me?" Then the recruit would say, "Sir, I do like you." Then, "You must be a fag." They used it like it's the worst thing you could possibly be. They turned it into a little fucking game. Hearing that kind of stuff used to make me really uncomfortable.

Knowing that I was gay, I had to make up that I had a girlfriend. I'd say, "I'm dating this nurse back at work." I dated a nurse for awhile, mostly for cover. I didn't want to admit it at the time, but there was still a part of me that figured I could go straight. If I was a more dishonest person, I could be living somewhere in the suburbs with kids and occasionally having sex with men.

There were a couple of guys at the university that were starting to figure it out before I left. I had a good friend who you knew was gay when you met him. I introduced him to one of the guys I was working with, and he probably put two and two together. He would say things that indicated that he knew I was gay, and he would make comments about fags. I remember getting a phone call at home one day, and I think it was from one of the guys I worked with. He said something like, "I need a blow job." I just hung up on him. It scared the piss out of me.

Once one of the guys I worked with said, "So, B., how do gay guys feel about that?" I said, "How the hell would I know?" I still don't understand why I couldn't come out to him, but these were the same people I'd heard making negative comments about gays, so I couldn't trust them. Even if they made it look like I should trust them, it would look like a trap to me. Back then I could get fired. Even though there were gays that worked at the university, I knew the people that ran the police department would have found a way to fire me if they wanted to. I didn't like keeping it hidden. They'd all be talking about their girlfriends or the wives, and I'd have to either make something up or just not say anything. You get sick and tired of lying about who you are.

There were these bathrooms at the university where there are what they call "glory holes"—guys put holes between the partitions and have oral sex. I remember once having to arrest a guy who turned out to be married. I felt awful for him. This was something he did occasionally. It's not something he made a life out of, yet it was going to haunt him for a long time. I had to do it. It was part of my job. He actually fought me and tried to run. I don't blame him. As much as the system oppresses somebody like that, it oppressed me even more. If I ever got caught doing something like that, I'd lose my job; I'd lose everything. There's no self-esteem in that kind of stuff, either.

I came out to southern California on a vacation and just loved it. I decided to apply for a job in the sunshine. Plus, I wanted to work for a city department. I flew out here several times to take the test and got hired the first week after I moved out here.

When I started at the police department, I was definitely not out. I went to the academy again for six months. This one was even worse. There were instructors that would make comments about fags, and I would sit there and think, "This is disgusting. I don't want to have to listen to this crap." I remember one instructor saying, "Did you hear they're actually letting fags on this department now? Isn't that disgusting? That's really sick."

I read in one of the gay rags that SOLO (Society of Law Officers) was being formed. I remember calling and saying, "I can't give you my name. All I can tell you is that I've been hired by a police department. I don't want to let you know who I am." I still didn't believe it wasn't a set up. After a couple of years, I finally got to talk to another out officer. We worked at the same division, but I had never seen him. It was a relief to talk to him, and I stopped pretending right around that time. I didn't make up the fact that I had a date when the boys would say, "Let's go out drinking." I would go once in a while, but I didn't feel like I had to go to prove I was one of the boys.

Then my first lover died from AIDS in August of '92. A week later, I was sitting in the lineup room and the Sergeant was explaining what a hate crime is. He said, "Suppose someone is walking down the street in a neighborhood known for its gay population, gets beat up, and called a fag. That's a hate crime." Somebody in the back of the room says, "That's a matter of opinion." Another person quips in, "Oh, yeah. Cruelty to animals." I was fuming. I almost stood up and started screaming at the whole bunch of them. At the end of lineup I said, "Sergeant, I've got to talk to you right now." We got in the office, and I started yelling, "My friend just died from AIDS, and he was a better person than anybody in this lineup room. And you people have the nerve to say things about gays and fags?" He says "What? I didn't hear anything." I said to him, "I am not going to put up with a comment from anybody about AIDS or gays ever again. If anybody says anything I'm going to take them to task. I will sue their asses off them." That day I became the talk of my division.

I think because of the way I came out of the closet, people are a little afraid to say things to me. I like that, because I don't have to listen to their bullshit. I don't like it, because they don't feel as free around me; I can tell a lot of guys are uptight. I spent a couple of years being one of the good ol' boys, so even though people look at me a little askance, they all know me, and they all say hello to me. Plus, I'm not the kind of guy that's going to let them get away with not talking to me. I'll go over, look right in their eyes, and just because I know that they'd rather not even deal with it, say, "How you doing? How's it going?"

I have never had any trouble with not getting backup. I have to say that when it comes right down to it on the street, guys do back you up, and it's us against them on the street.

I think the community needs gay and lesbian officers out there. I'd love to see a whole lot more gay people going through the academy. The more people we have in law enforcement the better.

Judy Nosworthy

Department: Metropolitan Toronto (Ontario, Canada) Police
Force
Age: 30
Rank: Constable
Job: Community Patrol
Years in Law Enforcement: 6 1/2

*A community patrol constable, Judy covers her beat on a mountain bike. A tall woman, she was
dressed in her blue constable uniform and biking shorts. At the time of the interview, her partner
was pregnant with their soon-to-be-born son.*

I grew up in a suburb of Toronto. My parents still live in the same house, and
it wasn't a very "happening" place. When I grew up it was a nice, quiet,
clean, waspy suburb, and I was a nice, quiet, clean, waspy kid. I went to the
University of Toronto and did a four-year honors degree in English Literature
and political theory. Nobody was banging down my door in 1985 saying, "Judy
Nosworthy, we want you." I needed a job. The two summers prior to graduating
I worked for the police force in their intelligence services doing clerical work,
and I found it very interesting. When I graduated, the people that I'd worked
for said, "Why don't you become a police officer?" At that time, I wanted to be
a musician. But two years later, I still wasn't a musician, and I thought,

"Perhaps I should look at being a police officer." So I applied, and I've been a police officer now for six years.

I had my first relationship with a woman after I got out of college. I always knew I was attracted to women; my family didn't always know, my friends didn't always know, but I always knew. For the first few years on the job, I was kind of vague about it, I didn't really say anything. But police work is such that you spend a great deal of time with the people you work with. We work ten hour shifts for seven days in a row, and then we get a pile of days off. You work seventy hours with these people, and you practically know their bodily functions. When you're doing general patrol, a lot of time is spent sitting in a car ten inches away from somebody. What do people talk about? Sports, their family, their house, whatever.

When I met the woman I'm with now, we very quickly decided we had the same goals, hopes, and aspirations. Life was wonderful, except her ex-girlfriend outed me at work by way of a very explicit public complaint. I was a well-respected officer and on the way up the ladder as a female in a male-dominated world. She basically said I was seeing her ex-girlfriend, and she was very explicit as to a variety of sexual acts we engaged in.

I spoke to a few senior officers who were gay or lesbian, and they said, "Keep your mouth shut, let the dust settle, transfer out, go somewhere else, and start again. This is a mark on your career." I wasn't too happy with that, not because I wanted to be a shit-disturber, but because I realized that this is a significant part of my life, of who I am, and how I relate to the world. My home life is very important to me. I couldn't brush it all under the table.

That was a very difficult time. After a few weeks of serious panic, I realized that knowledge is power. Coming out to my parents was a big deal; coming out to people you work with, but really don't know, is not.

I'm sure everyone I worked with suspected I was a lesbian. You can do a lot with a rumor, but you can't do much with the truth. Prior to being out, there was a lot of talking behind my back, but once they knew, there was a lot of support. We've gotten a lot of support from straight police officers—my partner at work has been incredibly supportive. One of the things that was really amazing to me was how people congratulated me when they found out we were having a baby. People have been really great—offering advice and helpful tips, how to survive these months, what baby things to get, and what things not to get. It's been a real educational process in terms of people who may not knowingly know someone who's gay or lesbian now seeing someone who doesn't have a repulsive lifestyle and someone who has the same concerns they do. They see the sameness as opposed to the difference.

I haven't experienced very much abuse. It's so bloody boring. I feel my being outed has shown the people I work with and my supervisors I'm not a wimp. It's been a career advantage, in the sense that it's shown more of what I'm like as an individual, and how I can handle very stressful situations. It's been really freeing. I don't walk around saying, "I'm Judy Nosworthy, the lesbian police officer. How are you?" It has very seldom come up except as, "How's your girl-friend?" "You got a good doctor?" "What hospital are you going to?" Things like that. It's become very normalized.

One guy was looking to intimidate the shit out of me. He said, "I hear you got your girlfriend knocked up." I said, "Yes, I did." He said, "How did you do that?" I said, "Great skill." Then I explained exactly how it was done using all the correct terms, the drugs used, the prices, and everything. He kind of stood there with his mouth open and said, "Wow, that's really cool." Since then he's been great.

The gay and lesbian officers backed off completely. I've gotten very little, if any, support from them, because they are not out. They're still part of the rumor mill, and they're afraid that by association, they will be linked. But everyone knows about them anyway.

If someone steps out of line, I'll take them aside and say, "Listen, that was not called for." I can take the regular locker room skirmish back and forth, and there's enough formal structure to keep people from getting too out of line. Police work is this macho thing, and it gets a little bit rude. I think it's the way guys talk to each other, and if you want to be a part of the group, you have to give up some of your individuality.

My partner faces the same stressors as other, for lack of a better term, police wives—the alienation and the evening shifts. She hates them. For seven evenings from five P.M. to three A.M., I'm gone. The support just isn't there for her. I've fallen off my bike and been beaten up a couple of times. I don't come to work everyday thinking this might be my last day on earth—one assumes one is going home. Prior to claiming my outness, if I were to get killed at work, they would have had a big funeral and said what a wonderful person I was. There would be five thousand police officers from all over North America, and they'd be sending all of this stuff to my parents saying what a great person I was. Meanwhile, my partner would have sat somewhere in the back row or proba-bly outside. That put things in perspective for me. It was very important for me that they know. Getting hurt is a part of police work. I know that if something happens to me, they won't phone her as the next of kin saying, "Your friend's in the hospital," leaving a message on the machine; they'll treat her as a partner. My fears are probably very much like everyone else's. Most of the people I work with, their big fear is if something happens, you hope it's not some asshole who goes, gets your wife, and brings her to the hospital. That's my hope, too.

In metropolitan Toronto, same-sex spouses are recognized if they've been common law for three years or if they have a child in common. Once my partner got pregnant, I phoned up our legal department saying, "I was there every step of the way, for every testing, and every ultrasound; I signed every check, and I've taken complete responsibility for this individual. The child that comes of this is ours." I've done everything a male would have done if he were unable to impregnate his wife, so I applied for same-sex spousal benefits, and they said, "Yeah." Once the baby's born, it's considered "in common," and from that point on, we are spouses. This has never been done by a police officer.

Being a police officer makes going to parties very difficult. The gay and lesbian community is fraught with recreational drugs, and I have a real problem with that. If I go to a function where someone is partaking of recreational drugs, I have to leave. You don't like to arrest your acquaintances, so basically it means you go to parties at eight o'clock, and you leave at eleven. In the gay and lesbian world, parties start at ten-thirty and go 'til four. That's been problematic.

A lot of times I don't want to come downtown to the bars because I work here. I've just spent ten hours in this eight-block area, and I know every inch of this pavement. I don't want to go home, get cleaned up, and come back; it's like a factory worker partying at the factory. People find it very difficult when "Judy the cop" would be in the bar saying to the bartender, "Don't serve drunks," and telling the people who are drunk to leave, versus "Judy the person" coming into the bar ordering beer. The expectation is that if you're a police officer, you're always a police officer. Well, when I go home, I go home; that's it. I don't feel compelled to pull speeding cars over, and unless there's something life-shattering, I very seldom get involved in things.

A lot of people have never had to deal with gays or lesbians. Sometimes you run across people who are just plain ignorant, and there's no point; they're not going to get it. You just have to walk away. There's no point forcing a confrontation. If somebody says, "The Bible says it's wrong," well that's your interpretation of the Bible; mine's different, and that's okay.

A lot of how you get treated as an individual, whether you're gay or straight, male or female, Black or White, is the way you treat yourself and the way you present yourself to other people. If you present yourself as angry, people treat you in an angry fashion. If you treat yourself like a piece of shit, if you don't look after yourself, or if you don't have any respect for yourself, how can other people respect you? So many people in the gay and lesbian community don't treat themselves well, so they get treated poorly by the world around them. But if you treat yourself with dignity and respect, other people treat you that way, too.

I never set out to change anything. I didn't say, "Let's join the police force which is really homophobic and rock the foundations." What I'm finding is I'm changing a lot of things just by virtue of being here. I have made people think, and that's been really amazing.

Ferenc

Department: County Law Enforcement Agency, Seattle, WA
Area
Age: 33
Rank: Police Officer
Job: Patrol
Years in Law Enforcement: 9

Ferenc emigrated from his native country of Hungary when he was seventeen years old. He first dreamed of being an American police officer after listening to the radio program The Voice of America in Budapest. Nine years later, he accomplished his dream in the Seattle, WA area.

I was sixteen years old and living in Budapest, Hungary, and I used to listen to my shortwave radio that my mom and dad bought me for Christmas. I ran into a radio station called *The Voice of America*. This was back in '77 at which time women were entering law enforcement in the United States. I was very much interested in the United States, and they had an interview with a lady deputy sheriff in Texas. She was talking about her job, of speeding tickets that she was handing out, and of how surprised people were down in Texas to see that it was a woman walking up to the car when they were stopped. When she described her job, I got hooked. From that moment on, I started to think, "Wouldn't it be neat if I could be a police officer." I tried to put my hands on the very little information available on American law enforcement, and typically that ended up to be *Kojak* on tv. I made up my mind that within a year I was going to be a police officer.

Hungary was a communist country, and the police over there were used to oppressing people for political reasons. If you said the wrong thing, that would be a crime, and you went to jail. I didn't want to be a police officer in Hungary, so I waited to immigrate when I had the chance. I don't know if my parents really knew. I was an only kid and I was never very talkative about my inner feelings. I was one who walked along the streets of Budapest for entertainment, went to movies by myself, and didn't really talk about my dreams and aspirations in life. At the time, I was attending a Merchant Marine vocational high school. As far as they knew, I wanted to be a sailor—they did not know I wanted to be a police officer.

I did not want to tell my mom because I was afraid she might give me up to the authorities, but she figured it out. Mothers have this sixth sense. I was planning a trip through school, and she told me one day, "You're not going to come back, are you?" And I said, "No." She told me that she could make me stay in Hungary, but she was not going to do that, because if my life didn't succeed in Hungary I could blame her. If I emigrated and my life didn't succeed, then it was my fault. She didn't want the responsibility over my life choice, and she allowed me to go. It was very painful. I left shortly after my seventeenth birthday. I'd never been away from home other than for short, supervised trips.

My motives for leaving Hungary were purely political. I was a very idealistic young man. I knew full well what democracy, freedoms, and civil liberties were. I understood very well that the Hungarian government was oppressing me. I was not allowed to talk, I was afraid to criticize my government, and I could have been arrested. I did not want to serve what I considered a Nazi regime for the rest of my life.

When I came to the U.S., I moved in with my sponsor and his wife in the Seattle area. I started to attend college in September of '79, and I majored in law enforcement. I was about twenty credits shy of graduating when I went for a summer job collecting coins from parking meters. In December, they offered me a temporary job for a month, and January 1, they gave me a pay raise and asked me to stay permanently. For the next four and a half years, that's what I did until I became a U.S. citizen in 1985. I immediately filled out an application for the police department and became a police officer in May of '85.

I had been a police officer for three or four years when I quit dating women. Then one beautiful day out on patrol, I stopped to eat on my beat. I walked into a restaurant next to a gas station, and there was a boy that was pumping gas who came in to eat, too. My breath went away when I saw him. He was about nineteen, had a hard gymnast's body, had big, beautiful, baby eyes and a very happy personality, and was just as cute as can be. He said, "Hi, officer." I looked at him and said, "Would you like to come over to my table and have lunch with me?" He did, and we started to talk. I still did not realize that the attraction was sexual. I just had a crush, period. We started to hang around, and I was very quickly becoming attached to him and was basically falling in love with him. He started to make so many sexual jokes that I started to realized, "I could actually have sex with him." While it lasted it was the most beautiful romantic relationship in my life.

At the time, the police department was not part of my private life. I did not talk very much. I had my usual escape routes about why I wasn't married. Since I don't socialize very much with other officers, it never came up in conversation. Now since I have come out, I have been coming out to friends, family, and some people I work with on the department. I have gotten to the point that if someone would put the question to me, I would say, "Yes. I am." Hardly anybody's that moronic.

This year in June, I participated in the gay pride parade as a police officer. It came about in a roundabout way. I joined an organization for gay police officers, and one of the deputy prosecutors said, "We're going to have a police car, and there's also a straight motorcycle officer who's going to be there who's very supportive of us." He asked me if I'd like to be in the parade. I was planning to watch it from a distance, but I said, "Yeah." So I sat in the patrol car and waved at the crowd; I recognized about two dozen people who also recognized me. I figured I'd see my face on the cover of the local newspaper or on the news, but nobody had a clue. I went to work the day after wondering, "Are people going to look at me funny?" But nobody brought it up. It wouldn't bother me if people knew. I already know what I am, and I call myself a faggot but not in a demeaning way. Our department has procedures and policies to follow, and our department manual specifically forbids harassment. If anybody was antagonizing me and I made an internal affairs complaint, they would get days off without pay—disciplinary action. I'm sure I'm going to run into discrimination, but it's not going to be open because the department doesn't tolerate it. Nobody wants to lose stripes, lose rank, or have days off because of it, and I would call them on it in a heartbeat. There's no support system for anti-gay sentiment, at least at my precinct.

I'm sure that there are people who I work with who don't really know, but it should be obvious to them. I work out at the local gym where at least five or six other officers also work out, and I wear a triangle with the rainbow colors in it. It's obvious to me that that's a gay sign, but a lot of people look at it without a clue. I don't play the macho stuff very much, so I'm almost certain that they've got to know that I don't date women. It's basically an open secret.

It's not hard being closeted because doing police work is a job that I do, and it's the way I make a living. Being gay is a sexual lifestyle issue that is not in conflict; we're talking apples and oranges. I'm not asking what a heterosexual is doing in the bedroom because it's not an issue. I'm out in my private life, and if someone called me at work I would be out there, too. The issue doesn't come up much.

I'm a police officer and that's my job. I'm also gay with my personality, my wit, my charm, my looks, and my body. If you like that, let's be friends. If you don't, then walk away.

Donna Loring

Department: Bowdoin College (ME) Campus Security
Age: 44
Rank: Chief
Job: Chief of Campus Security
Years in Law Enforcement: 10

Donna's Chief of Campus Security office sits in the basement of a building on the edge of campus. At work on a summer morning, she was dressed in a white blouse and blue cotton slacks. Behind her desk was a poster reading, "Oh Great Spirit, grant that I may not criticize my neighbor until I have walked a mile in his moccasins." She and her partner have been together fifteen years.

My grandfather was the first police officer on Indian Island, and he was like a role model to me. I always wanted to grow up and get into law enforcement like my grandfather. I was afraid that if I had to take a lie detector test and they found out I was gay, I would never be allowed in. Luckily, I never had to. After I got out of the military, there was a government apprenticeship program where you could study to be law enforcement, and they'd pay for your salary while you were learning. I went in to the Penobscot County Sheriff's Department as a detective because they didn't want to put me on the road without academy training.

My favorite area of law enforcement was investigating—the detective work. I always enjoyed a good investigation, the chase, figuring out how something happened, and then bringing someone around to admitting it. What I liked the least was putting people into the penal system and the way the court system worked. Whether people want to admit it or not the system is geared to the wealthy. If you have a lot of money, you can get a good attorney who can get you off of anything. It's not a fair system.

I went to the police academy, and after I got out, I went on the road. I didn't like it, so I left to go to college full-time. Then there was a reserve officer position that opened up with the Penobscot Nation. I applied for it and got it fairly easily. I started there as a reserve officer, and within a year, I was the chief of the department.

I look back on a lot of stuff, and at the time I didn't see any problems, but I think they were there. It was very subtle. When I was with the sheriff's department, there was a deputy sheriff I was paired up with who was a sergeant, and he would not leave me alone. For example, my patrol area covered Penobscot and Piscataquis Counties, and most of it was in the woods. He'd take all these side and back roads and say to me, "Do you know where you are?" During my first week I'd say, "No, I don't." And he'd say, "You're not very observant. You're not going to make a good police officer." Eventually I quit. I decided I wasn't going to take that bullshit.

As a deputy sheriff with the county, there were a lot of comments and very subtle things about the "Indian deputy sheriff." I was with my own people at the Penobscot Nation, so there was nothing there about being Native American. However, they didn't like it that I was a woman. When I first became Chief of Penobscot Nation, the guys said to me, "We heard rumors that you were coming aboard, and you're going to have to prove your leather." I just sloughed it off, but on a lot of calls, they would take their time on backup or they wouldn't come to back me up at all. I'd have to handle the call myself.

I'm not very out—I don't talk about my private life. It's nobody's business. The president of the college doesn't talk about his sex life, nor does the dean or anybody else. Why should I? My life is just as private as anybody else's. I do a damn good job, and that's all that's expected of me. When I'm at work, being gay doesn't even enter my thoughts. I just do my job. I don't look at myself as a gay or lesbian doing police work. I look at myself as an individual, as a person doing this work on a professional level. The emphasis should be on how well I do my job, not what I do at home on my own time.

The people I work with probably know because my partner calls me just about every day. Whenever we have a department party or something, she is always with me. I've never come out and told anyone—we just talk about

things. They'll talk about their husbands or wives, and I'll talk about my partner. It's something that's understood. Do they have to come out and say, "I'm
heterosexual?" No, they just talk about their family life. So why the hell should
I be any different. I'm accepted, and she's accepted. I don't make a big deal about
it.

Walter

Department: A North Carolina Sheriff's Department
Age: 32
Rank: Deputy Sheriff
Job: Patrol
Years in Law Enforcement: 9

A self-described "Durham [NC] boy," Walter is a slight man with a thick southern accent. In a favorite dessert spot on Durham's Ninth Street, he talked about what it's like to be a gay deputy sheriff in North Carolina.

One of my dad's uncles was a cop, and he used to come over to my grandmother's house where I spent a lot of time. He was an authority figure, and I liked the uniform, the patrol car, and the respect that he got in the county. Instead of college I chose law enforcement; it was my second choice.

I went into the National Guard right after high school and stayed for eight years. I was twenty-four when I started my career with the sheriff's department. Every deputy sheriff does jail time where you work in the jail before you go out on the street as a patrol officer. I spent nine months in the jail, and then I went out on a patrol squad. I never had a hard day in the jail. I treat people like I want to be treated; some of the other deputy sheriffs in the jails were hateful to the inmates. A lot of the deputy sheriffs got into fights with the inmates, but I never did. I played cards with them through the bars. The whole time I was in the jail I never thought about being gay. When I had to dress somebody out to go, I had to take all his clothes from him, put them in a bag, give him his toothbrush, deodorant, soap, and all that, and then I would give him his orange jumpsuit. I'd tell everybody I was turning him into a carrot and putting him in the carrot patch upstairs. Some of the guys were cute; the cute ones I looked at, and the other ones I didn't pay attention to.

After nine months, I went out on patrol where I don't play any favorites. If I stop somebody for something they've done wrong and they're drop-dead gorgeous, they get the same ticket as an ugly customer. Some of my friends say, "If you stopped me, would you give me a ticket?" I say, "If you do anything wrong, I'll give you a ticket." The sheriff's department is really not a traffic organization; we are more of a property checking agency. I would rather check your house while you're at work than be out writing citations for minor traffic offenses while your house is getting broken into. On patrol we ride around and check out a few public areas where people want to have car sex. I've driven up on girls and guys, girls and girls, and guys and guys. I check ID, make sure they're legal age, give them back their ID, and say, "Y'all need to find a better place to do this." Some people might not be as easy going as I am. One of the funny questions I ask is, "What are y'all doing out here?" And they say, "We're just talking." "Do you always talk with your clothes off?"

As long as there're gay people in the world, you're going to have to have gay cops. Gay people in the community need gay cops 'cause we know how they feel. I've seen some straight cops laugh at somebody, or I've heard two of my cop friends say, "We're going to go sit on the gay bar tonight so we can pull drunk drivers out of there." I said, "Do y'all want me to go sit on the straight bar and pull y'all's friends?" One time I had a bar owner call the highway patrol commander, the sheriff, and the city police chief to have them call the dogs off. One was a deputy sheriff and supposed to be patrolling out in the county, so he got demoted for being out of his area.

I'm not worried about being fired for being gay 'cause if I'm not a deputy sheriff, I'll be something else. I got a knack for making money; I can do a lot of things. I climb trees, I got a tree company, I spin compact discs at parties, I have done a little bit of modelling, I've done construction, and I've been a termite inspector. I've done it all, and I'm not going to be worried about starving. I'm very well-liked at work, and I don't believe any of them would turn against me. I have a reputation for being one of the better officers. We have some lazy people, we have some really good officers, and I'm one of the good ones, so I don't think they would change how they felt about me at all because of me being gay. I don't look gay, especially in uniform. This sheriff doesn't know, but the last one did. He wouldn't have fired me. But the election's in three days, and we don't have to worry about this one anymore, 'cause he will not be re-elected.

When I told my mom, she said, "You don't look like a gay person." I said, "What's a gay person look like?" You can't pick them out going down the street unless they act a little nellie. I've never been called a homosexual, or gay, or faggot in public. I guess that's why the other deputy sheriffs either don't believe I'm gay, or they don't care because I don't act nellie. I'm out just by the way I act at work; I don't act any different other than watching a guy walk by which I do but nobody notices. I don't act like the normal gay person you'd see walk-ing down the road with a little pocket book or walking a little funny. Talk prob-ably goes on behind my back, but I don't know about it.

Some of the guys at work know, some of them think they know, and then some of them are just dumb as dirt. Most of the guys I work with don't know or don't believe it. They may have a suspicion. Some people have seen me going into one of the local bars, and then they go back and say, "I saw Walter going into that fag bar." I love to go dance; I drink one or two drinks right when I get there, and then I dance. I think dancing and being around other gay people is a real turn on.

The guys that know would rather see me come to a call to help them if they're in trouble than some of the other guys, 'cause if it comes down to a fight, they know I'll go. I'm not a violent person—I can get a lot farther by talk-ing to somebody than I can by beating them up. They like to see me come because we'll solve the problem, get back out, and go home safe. Most of the guys would rather see me come to a call, and they come just as fast to help me.

Some of the guys joke with me now. Last April 1, me and two of my buddies were down at the gas pumps, and I said, "I got married over the weekend." And one of the guys said, "What's his name?" I said, "I'll never tell." I hear plenty of gay jokes at work, and I tell some! Most of the guys that tell a gay joke around me know I'm gay, and they're telling it to see if I laugh. Most of the jokes are funny, and it doesn't bother me at all. You can tell a joke about somebody because you're prejudiced or you can tell a joke about somebody to be funny. When they tell a joke around me about somebody being gay, they're clowning around with me. They can tell some awfully racial jokes, and I don't play any part of that. If they start talking about hateful or racial stuff I leave, and they know that.

I think being gay may have slowed my process of being given rank, but if I don't ever get promoted, that's fine 'cause I like my schedule, I like patrol, and I like the way the guys treat me. If they think they're spiting me by not giving me a promotion, that's fine 'cause I'm comfortable right where I'm at. Maybe one day I'll be sheriff; that's the only other step I want. I don't want anything in between.

Being gay's a lot of fun. I dated a boy in Thomasville, North Carolina, and we went out with one of his friends. We were sitting in a restaurant, and his friend was acting a little nellie in public. Three rednecks were sitting in the corner. The one that acted a little nellie went out to the bathroom, and when he walked past the rednecks, one of the rednecks said, "Faggot." He said, "Jealous," and walked into the bathroom. So he walked back out and sat down, we finished eating, and we started to leave. One of the three guys walked out and confronted him. I pushed him to the side and said, "You need to leave or I'll have you arrested." He said, "You can't have me arrested; my dad's the chief of police." I said, "I don't care who your dad is." So the guy's brother came out, and I had to put him down. If he had never opened his mouth, everything would have been all right. I used to keep my mouth shut because I thought I'd get beat up, but now I'm not going to get hurt 'cause I'm gay. I might get beat up because of something else, but not because I'm gay. No way!

I don't have any problem being gay in the law enforcement community or out in the regular community, and I don't worry about being a cop in the gay community. I'm going to keep doing this unless the sheriff gets rid of me, and then I'll go to another agency and get another job. I got a saying: "Where there's love, there is no wrong."

Greg

Department: City Police, North Dakota
Age: 33
Rank: Police Officer
Job: Patrol
Years in Law Enforcement: 9

In his current job for eight years, Greg has worked exclusively in rural, municipal police departments. Sitting on his living room couch and surrounded by antiques, he spoke of the trials and tribulations of being a gay cop in a rural setting.

When I was little I always wanted to be a police officer or a firefighter. When we were running around the neighborhood on our bikes, I was always the one making the siren noise. I went to school for political science, didn't see it going anywhere, so I switched over to law enforcement to help people and make a difference in people's lives.

The only police officer I knew growing up was the father of a classmate. I saw him often 'cause I worked with his son in a restaurant, and he used to come in all the time. In fact, when I went to school for law enforcement, he encouraged me not to become a police officer. He said, "It's a very thankless job, and it's very frustrating." He said he wished I would have gotten a hold of him before I went to school, because he would've said, "Don't do it." But I was halfway through school, I didn't know what else to do so, and then I still was excited about doing it.

I went to tech school to study law enforcement. The tech school was similar to the military in that it was very regimented, and we wore uniforms, had inspection, and stayed with the same people through the two years. I started to realize from the attitudes of people I was in class with as well as the teachers, it was going to be very difficult for me. Basically, if you weren't a White, straight, male, it would be difficult.

I had gotten my ear pierced when I was seventeen years old, and I knew I couldn't wear my earring at school because I was told, "Men don't wear earrings." So I didn't wear it at school, but I had a job out at the mall and wore it there. A lot of people from school came in to the store, and someone told one of the law enforcement teachers. He called me into his office one day, and asked me why I wore an earring. I said, "No particular reason." He said, "You can't wear it here, and we'd prefer you didn't wear it anywhere because someone will think you're a queer." It made me really angry; I wanted to tell him, "They'd be right," but I didn't. I continued to wear it when I was at work because I thought, "When I'm on my own time, I'll do what I want." And I never heard another word about it.

Initially, there were a lot of faggot jokes and things like that. As time went on, it started to go away. Two people were really bad and continued to make comments the whole two years. I'm sure that's just the way they were and they weren't going to change. But a lot of people did. I'm not saying they changed their thoughts about it, but I think they changed in knowing they shouldn't say things in front of certain people. As time went on and I got more comfortable, if people were telling jokes about Blacks I would call them on it. If it was a fag joke, I probably wouldn't say anything 'cause I didn't want them to think anything, but that probably made them think something 'cause I was speaking up for all the others. It was a lonely and hard time being closeted because it added so much pressure.

My first job was in a town of roughly twelve-thousand people and fifteen officers. Overall, it was a pretty pleasant experience. I don't think I could've stayed there real long, because I don't know what the reaction would have been to my being gay. There were fag jokes from a few people, and I thought if they found out I would be ostracized and out on my own.

From there I went to another small town. That job was a disaster, and I hated it. In the department and in town, if you weren't born there, you were an outsider and they didn't want you there. If they had known I was gay, they would've drummed me out of town. It was bad with them not knowing; I just think it would have been a disaster had they known. I was glad to get out of there.

Then I came here, and there's one friend in the police department that I'm out to. We became really good friends two or three years ago. I helped him and his wife move, and we became really good friends. One time I was talking to his wife, and I told her. She said she didn't think it would make any difference because his sister is a lesbian, and he's dealt with the issue. I finally told him, and he said, "I don't care." It hasn't changed things at all. It felt great to know he felt that way. He's been a big help at work because if somebody says something, he sticks up for me. It's kind of like we're brothers. He's told me of two officers that have come up and asked him if I was gay. He just says, "You need to ask him." They haven't said a word to me, but from what he tells me, there are several people who have some suspicion.

There're 110 people in the department—sixty some are officers. I think if I came out to the department there would be a small group, maybe fifteen, who wouldn't care because I've worked with them for eight years. They know how I work, they know I'm a good officer, and they can count on me for backup. There would be a group who would not say much of anything. They have very limited contact with me, and may make jokes behind my back. Then I think there'd be another small group that would be very vocal. They'd probably put magazines in my mailbox and not back me up. So it would be a mixed reaction from the department, but I think for me, it would be better than keeping it all inside.

A couple years ago, a detective and my lieutenant were talking about an incident that happened in front of the adult bookstore where somebody had got ten hit with a blow dart. Someone made reference to, "Oh, a pee-pee pumper." It's really frustrating to hear that kind of stuff; it makes me very angry. I don't know where to go with it because they're in positions of power, and where do you go above them? It's very frustrating to hear supervisors make reference to queers, faggots, or other minorities. It's tough to work in an environment like that.

It makes it very hard to go to work and to listen to people talk the way they do. It makes me angry at myself for hearing those things and not saying anything, or seeing so many people harassed by officers. A guy came in to the police station a couple years ago who had been beaten up; his face was bleeding, he was effeminate and was with a couple other guys who were acting effeminate. They told the officer what happened and the officer told him, "You shouldn't be down there," and didn't take the report. I see things like that, and it makes me furious. In a way, I hope it's caused by fear and ignorance so if I did come out, it might make it a little easier. Maybe if these people realized that they've been working with me for eight years, and they've been able to get along with me, then they can get along with gays in the community.

It is terrible not being out because there're Christmas parties, softball teams, cookouts and barbecues, and everybody brings their spouses. I think I'd be a lot more at ease, because I'm always on edge, wondering, "What are they thinking? What do they know?" I guess it would be better if I just said, "I don't care what they think or what they know."

One officer made a comment about me a couple weeks ago, and there's no doubt in my mind that if something happened to me, he wouldn't come around the block to help me. Maybe if I come out and affirm what they're thinking, it will only get worse. These older officers have a lot of power, and it would be tough for me to work on their shift.

What keeps me from coming out is fear of the unknown. I don't know how to do it; I don't know how you actually go about coming out. Do you announce it to everybody? I used to deny things, or when someone would say, "Look at that woman," I would agree, but I don't do that any more and haven't for quite a few years. I guess nobody's asked me point blank. I think there're people who know, 'cause when I say I'm going somewhere, they don't ask me, "With who?" I've made it pretty clear through the years that I don't ask people about their private lives, and they know not to ask me. So for me to come out, I would have to somehow initiate it, and I don't know how to do that.

It's something I want to do and something I feel the need to do. At this point in time, though, I'm running for the state legislature in North Dakota, and I couldn't come out before the election because the election would be over. I know I want to do something, but I can't do it before November. When I was making the decision to run, I never thought it would come up. I guess I was very naive.

If you're closeted, it causes more stress and pressure. There's one guy I've arrested several times; he's always in trouble. One of the last times he got arrested, he told a friend of mine that he was going to go to court, plead not guilty, and tell them I was gay. I hate to say it, but since that time, I've seen this guy driving without a driver's license and I haven't done anything about it. I'm afraid of what he's going to say or do. I'm in fear that someone's going to out me.

Being a cop has put a strain on my relationship more than once. When we run into someone I work with, I change and distance myself. If we're walking down the mall, I'll move away so they don't think it's anything other than two friends. Everywhere we go, I'm looking over my shoulder and hoping, "I hope we don't run into so-and-so." I think if I was out at work it would help me loosen up a little bit and not be so afraid of who's going to see me. 'cause we'll go to the store, a movie, or the mall, and I run into people from work, and I'm sure they wonder, "Who's that?" He feels bad and says afterwards, "You didn't introduce me," and I feel like crap for not doing it, so it just takes a toll on the relationship.

I'm starting to become cynical. Being in law enforcement has changed my personality negatively and made me into a kind of person I don't want to be. I said when I started in this job that once I became cynical and hated everybody, I was going to quit. That's easier said than done after you've done it for eight years and you don't know what else you're going to do. I try not to bring it home, but it's become a part of my personality. It's a hard job, it's a thankless job, and I wish I could do something else. I can't see myself doing this for twenty more years. The good thing about law enforcement is you're your own boss and you have job security. But it's time to get out unless I can switch to something else in law enforcement. I need a change. I've been in patrol eight years, and I know that's where I'm going to be 'til I'm done. It's just too negative. If you take yourself and your job seriously and you're conscientious about what you do, it just eats at you; it's too hard.

Sara Raines

Department: Duke University (NC) Public Safety
Age: 32
Rank: Detective Sergeant
Job: General Investigator
Years in Law Enforcement: 6

On a Sunday afternoon in October, Sara talked about her experiences at Duke University. Wearing a t-shirt reading, "It's OK to be gay," she sat in her living room filled with books and cats.

I went to undergraduate school at Duke in the late '70s and majored in religion and history. When I came to Duke I was not out. I had a girlfriend, and we became roommates later on, but we were very closeted. I was not out to any of my professors, because I didn't think they'd understand. It was a very conservative atmosphere.

After graduation, I applied to the Coast Guard Academy. Unfortunately, I didn't know that they did background checks. I had gone to the trouble to marry a friend of mine as a cover because I had lived in the paranoid times of very conservative Orange County when I was growing up. What I didn't find out until years later was that the guy I married told the background investigator that I had some questionable things in my background. He said, "She's gay; you don't want her." I wanted to do my patriotic duty and serve my community but was turned down because of my background. Eventually I decided I could do law enforcement; the sort of skills that I used in the Coast Guard were similar to the skills in law enforcement.

I applied to a local municipal department, and the woman who did my background investigation was "family"—gay. I got lucky—they hired me and sent me to the police academy where I got a really good education. I worked there as a reserve officer which meant no pay. I couldn't make a living as a reserve officer, so I started looking around for full-time law enforcement. Duke had been recommended, and I thought, "This is good because I went to school there, and I already know something about Duke."

I called Mr. Dumas, the director of the department, and he hired me as a security guard. As soon as he had an opening, he promoted me. I got lucky again, because the guy who did our firearms program liked me a lot 'cause I turned out to be a great shooter. I didn't believe in guns and had never shot one before going into the police academy. I just did what the instructors told me, and I turned out to be a really good shot. So the first thing they did once I became a public safety officer was send me to general instructor's school, which meant that I could teach any academic subject in the police academy. After that they sent me to firearms instructor's school. Whenever a new school came up I said, "I'll go." I later became the shotgun armorer, which means I'm the only person in the department who's authorized to take shotguns apart and fix them. I made it to the rank of corporal, which means you're a training officer, and I taught in the police academy.

We investigate whatever comes our way. The population of Duke University is about twenty thousand employees and ten thousand students; it's like a small town. Anything that's in a city, we've got at Duke. I work in the medical center mostly and investigate medical center crimes which range from homicide to white-collar crime.

My first year or two working at Duke I was still relatively closeted. I was paranoid about people finding out, what they were going to think, and what they were going to do to me. I worried about it a lot. I was still married, and I mentioned "my husband" a lot so people knew I had one. I was also really worried about proving myself as a woman. It's harder for women to break into law enforcement, let alone gay women. So I was really concerned not only about being forced out of the closet professionally, but also worried about proving myself as a woman who could do the job. There was a lot of misogyny among some of the more redneck types about whether or not women could do the job. And unfortunately I got a training officer who didn't like women.

He was very aggressive, short, and had little-man syndrome. He would tell me to do something, and then take over. After thirty days he gave the shift commander an evaluation which said I didn't know anything based upon the fact that I did not take notes. He also said I was too timid and not capable of doing the job. I was so mad. I said to the shift commander, "I don't take notes because I know this stuff; ask me anything." He did, I told him all the answers, and he was like, "You do know this stuff." I said, "As far as not being able to do the work, I do this work already, and I don't have a problem. The reason I don't do more out on shift is because my training officer does it for me. He will not give me a chance, he will not leave me alone, and he's always butting in." After the shift commander had a talk with my training officer, I spent thirty more days in training, and then they promoted me. I think that was a female thing as opposed to a gay thing.

I'm fortunate that my life partner used to be a very good cop at Duke. Even the rednecks thought that she was a good cop. We sort of favor each other, and people used to compare me to her. She definitely paved the way, and the way had been paved for her by yet another lesbian cop who worked there. We've had several lesbian cops come on board since then, and since I'm actually part of the hiring process now, I do my part.

Being closeted was hard. There were a few rednecks in our department who were very vocal, "Rush Limbaugh all the way" rednecks. It's taboo in our department to say any kind of racial slur. Mr. Dumas used to guard Martin Luther King, Jr., and he believes in civil rights, so the rednecks had to take it out on the gays. Some of the guys used to make jokes like, "I'm happier than a faggot with two assholes." Pretty crude stuff. That would bother me as much as if they said something about a lesbian. It was very hard for me to keep my mouth shut but I was still thinking of going into the FBI and stayed closeted to make it. But, I was also afraid for my job. I loved it and didn't want to lose it. Finally, I was concerned about my safety. There are a lot of ways cops can get other cops hurt by doing nothing.

I came out so subtly and slowly that people didn't even really notice. People liked me when I was closeted, and they still liked me afterwards. Coming out was a very slow process, but I think it worked out okay because I never shocked anybody. I didn't put them on the spot. I injected little stuff into conversations until they got the big picture. People were not shocked, but I have never been a sign-carrying, in-your-face kind of radical lesbian-type anyway.

At some point I discovered that Duke had an anti-discrimination policy including sexual orientation. I would ask discrete questions about how the policy worked and then saw it demonstrated. People who discriminated against gay folks got disciplinary actions. I was like, "This is great! They really can't do anything to me, and I won't lose my job just for being gay." Then I was like, "Okay; it's safe."

Somewhere around the third year, Mr. Dumas scheduled himself to come in to the training periods to prepare everybody for his retirement. He said, "I'm not going to be here forever, and you guys have to be ready for the new age of police work. When I became a police officer you had to be over six feet tall, male, uneducated, and straight. Now you can be short, female, gay, and educated. We have some of those people in the department, and they're some of my best officers." I was like, "He knows about me." I don't think he was actually speaking to me, he was just trying to make a point. That was the crowning moment that it's really okay. He's been most supportive.

About that same time, I went to firearms school with a bunch of redneck guys. I was the only woman in the class, and I was gay. There were two hotels we could stay in; one was a real nice hotel, and the other one was a Days Inn. I had checked into the Days Inn. The guys were talking about the motels saying, "You guys don't want to stay in the Days Inn; that's right around the corner from the gay bar." I was like, "There's a gay bar right around they corner?" I thought, "This is cool; I can have something to do at night." Then some of the local officers were saying they would go to the gay bar, lie in wait outside for people, and beat them up. Then I thought, "Maybe it's not such a good idea to go." These men talked about how it was okay that Black people and "Orientals" had civil rights, but not gay people. They started telling stories about how much fun it was to beat up gay people, how gay people didn't have civil rights, and how gay people were "against the Bible." They went on and on for over an hour, and it scared the piss out of me. I realized that the fraternity of police does not extend to gay people everywhere.

More recently I had a problem with training a cadet who was closeted because she wanted to get on with a federal agency. I didn't know she was gay when she first came to my squad. When I started training her I said, "There are two personal things you need to know about me as your training officer. One is that I smoke which you may find offensive, and we can work around that. The other is that I'm gay. If you have a personal problem with that you can request another training officer." She was pretty cool. However, towards the end of her training period, someone started making jokes to her like, "Have you learned to be a good lesbian yet?" She went ballistic because she thought she had everybody fooled. They were making the jokes 'cause of me, but she was so paranoid she started bringing in straight pornography books and stopped talking to me. I was hurt 'cause I did not know what was going on. Then a buddy of mine pointed out that she did not want to be associated with another lesbian, so I let her have her distance, and after a while she got over it. However, during the time she stopped talking to me I was still theoretically her training officer, and the assistant director asked, "What is going on with you and this cadet? I have been hearing you guys have been fighting." I said, "I'm not fighting with her. She's just had an attack of homophobia, and she'll get over it." The first thing out of his mouth was, "Is she going to back you up if you have a call?" I was really impressed because his first concern was for my safety.

Now that I'm out, not only do I want to be a good example for other lesbian cops, but I want to show people that justice works for everybody. Come to Duke because we're going to treat you fair.

Karla Buchting

Department: Barnard College (NY) Security
Age: 34
Rank: Supervisor
Job: Security Supervisor
Years in Law Enforcement: 7 1/2

Karla, a tall woman with dark brown hair and brown eyes, played center for her Gay Games flag football team. After a successful, semi-final game that put her team in the gold medal round, Karla nursed a beer and her bruises in a Manhattan pub and talked about her experiences in campus security.

I was born in Nicaragua. After my parents divorced when I was four or five, I grew up in Massachusetts. All the way back in third grade, I couldn't wait to play house, play daddy, and put the kids to bed, so I could give mother a good night kiss. At fifteen, I met a lover who was twenty, and we stayed together for nine years. I told my family I was gay when I was fifteen during Thanksgiving dinner. My timing was priceless. At that time, my mother went from one side to the other. One minute she was telling my grandmother, "Keep an eye on Karla 'cause she's a good looking woman, and the boys will be after her." The next was, "Keep an eye on Karla because she has a lot of male tendencies, and I only see her hanging out with women."

I was out in high school. If there were people that didn't like it, they didn't voice it to me. I took a woman to my prom. That was a blast. I went in a tux, and she went in a dress. When we walked in, the guys came over, and were like, "You look great." They were high-fiving me. I think there were some people that wanted to have prejudices but couldn't because they knew me. I was very popular; I got voted the most popular female my senior year.

After I graduated high school, we moved to San Francisco for four years. Then we moved back to New York, and I've been here ever since. I was doing guard security at the Natural History Museum, and my supervisor was "family". She respected the work I did, and she knew that my aspirations were far beyond being a security guard. She wound up getting a good position at Barnard, and she recruited me.

I started out as a guard with mostly foot patrols of the dormitories. When I applied for supervisor a year and a half later, my co-workers were not too positive because Barnard had never recruited from within, and I was an out woman. Most people stereotype supervisory roles as being filled by men. I didn't let that bother me—when I sent my application I told them, "This is a woman's college. It would be good to have a woman at this level." I sold myself on that. I think my being there's been positive for not only the lesbian students, but especially for women of color. It sends up a flag that there's not discrimination even though at times it seems like there is. It's a predominantly White woman's college, and only for the last four or five years has it become more intermingled in terms of ethnicity.

I've never really had fear about my job because of being gay. Even when I thought they didn't know, I didn't have a fear of them finding out. I've been out all my life, and if you don't like me because of that, I'll go on. It's not been something I've laid awake worrying about, and I don't think being a lesbian has hurt me on the job. I wouldn't have been there as long as I have if it was a problem—there's always a way to get rid of you. I have respect from the deans and from people in high levels of the administration. It's how you project yourself. I do my job dignified, and my sexual orientation has nothing to do with my performance. I've had a good seven years there and have gotten commendations, so I think I'm safe.

The security field has always been ruled by the good old boy type of staffing. Being a woman in this field, you are a minority right away. When I go to conferences, if there're thirty men, there're three women. In this field, they haven't focused on orientation; they've looked at color or gender first. I thought law enforcement would be an area of great acceptance, and it wasn't until I started knowing people in it that I realized it's not as accepting as I had viewed it. There's a lot of pressure to keep in the closet, but I haven't had any first-hand horror stories.

I think all the guard force that works for me knows. I'm not a lipstick lesbian—I think my appearance is sort of labelling. Most people think I'm gay whether I admit it or not. It's something that any rookie that comes in finds out as part of their training, "By the way, the supervisor's a lesbian." In a way, it bothers me that it even has to be a topic, but I guess it's human nature to gossip.

I've had comments made to me, but they've always been by perpetrators, people we're arresting. The most recent was when we were making an arrest of a guy that was harassing his girlfriend. When we went to remove him from one of the dormitories, things got heated, and eventually he came out with "dyke." In those situations, even the men who are uncomfortable with the idea of homosexuality come to my defense. They're the first ones to step in, be protective, and tell whoever it is to shut up. When the gay issue comes up—especially when it's in a slanderous way—they get offended.

I'm proud to be a dyke, but I don't think I appear like one of those "I hate men" dykes. I think the guys at work realize that the stereotypes they have been brought up with are being contradicted by the people they know, and it's made them more comfortable. Sure you may still have some people that don't respect me, or who think that it's unnatural, but they accept me as Karla. If you've opened a mind even a little bit, it makes a difference. Guys have said to me, "Before, I may have whistled at lesbians and said, 'Hey, baby, this is what you need.' I don't do that now because I realize that's messed up." So you change people in little, tiny ways, and hopefully you change the world.

When people are scared of something, they're scared 'cause they don't know about it. When they're able to sit down and talk to somebody that's real, sometimes they see your point and sometimes they don't. For the most part, I'm very up front with people. To the ones that have thought about conversion being an answer, I tell them, "If we go by your solution, then I could get a gay man to convert you." That's when they see the light that conversion is not a possibility.

I've never let any of my occupations hinder my private life because to me, my private life comes first. I can always get a job—if times are rough and I've got to be a messenger, I'll do it. Better that than lose my dignity. The same people that I might choose to put above my private life would not be there when the chips fall, so they're not worth it in the end. I wish more people thought that way, but everybody's got to do their own thing to survive. You answer to yourself in the end. I'm always proud of who I am. I can't sell out for ignorant people.

In the community, you get the old, stupid stuff about, "You could handcuff me tonight," and, "How do you use your night stick?" I don't look at it as a big compliment. I kind of get turned off by it because I think they're just going for the image, they're not going for the person. If me being in law enforcement gets them all hot and bothered, then I haven't gotten them hot and bothered, just what I do has. That makes me uncomfortable, because I think, "What if tomorrow I tell them I'm a street cleaner, then they wouldn't want me." So that turns me off right away.

When I get my degree in criminal justice, I would like to move back to California. If I stay in security, I would like to go for an associate directorship or directorship. Right now, I just want that piece of paper, and I want to be out of the East Coast. As much as everybody says New York is a melting pot, and anything goes in New York, I think it's untrue. I think there's a lot of prejudice in the city, and there's a lot of conflict and anger between races. I want to get out of that. I was raised in the country and want to get back to being in a natural environment. So when I get the degree, I'm out of here. From there, I don't know what I'm going to do.

It's good that you show yourself in numbers. Gays and lesbians need to affect the good old boy system. You need gays and lesbians in law enforcement because you have a lot of people that are very prejudiced. Even though you're trained and indoctrinated to do the job, you walk in with your own prejudices. I don't think you leave them in your locker when you put the uniform on. Gay and lesbian officers need to be detectives, they need to be lieutenants, they need to be borough commanders. They need to show that their orientation does not affect job performance. And in the gay world we need heros. We need people that we can look up to and aspire to be. It'll show little girls they can be whatever they want to be.

Jim Blankenship

Department: Pineville (WV) City Police Department
Age: 33
Rank: Patrolman (Former)
Job: Patrol
Years in Law Enforcement: 1 1/2

Jim worked for the Pineville City Police Department until he was fired for being gay. Although he won his grievance against the city, he never worked as a police officer again. Now a manager in the auto sales business, he and his partner live and work in Morgantown, WV. On the night of their fifth wedding anniversary, he reminisced about his earlier career.

I was always fascinated by police cars. As a kid I always played with them, and in cops and robbers, I was the cop. Any time a sheriff's deputy pulled up in our community, I was out there to look at the car.

I grew up in Mullens, West Virginia where there were probably three thousand people. Pineville, about the same size, was the county seat eleven miles away. I come from a large and popular family, I was president of my high school student body, and I'd worked as a disc jockey at a local radio station in Pineville, so people knew me. Being from southern West Virginia my parents taught me what gay people were—nellie queens who dress up like women. The only gay person I ever knew of was a man that was raised in my Dad's community, and the community got together and beat the shit out of him.

I really didn't think going into law enforcement was possible, because I didn't see myself as that masculine. After graduating high school, I was on a student work-study program as the dispatcher for the city of Mullens. I was put in a cute little uniform and given the badge, but not the gun. About midway through the summer they put me in one of the cruisers to ride along with another officer. After I got that initial excitement of law enforcement I decided I'd go into the academy and into law enforcement. It was like a childhood dream.

When I was dispatcher, a man used to make jokes and little gay slams at me in hopes of bringing me out. He finally came up to me and said, "Have you ever been to a gay bar?" I said, "Of course not; why would I go to a gay bar?" He said, "I'm picking you up at eight o'clock tonight. We're going." Why I didn't say no, I don't know. We went to this bar, we got in the parking lot, and he said, "Are you ready to go in?" I said, "Yeah," and he kissed me. I went, "Oh, my God. I'm going to be queer now because I've been kissed by a man." He brought me out of the closet screaming.

That was scary because I wanted to be a cop, but everybody knows you can't be gay and a police officer. It was a bit of a dilemma, but I felt I could hide it. I went into the hyper-masculine mode and started working out. I was real self-conscious of making sure that my every hand gesture was of the masculine side. I used to be real self-conscious about my pinky. I was afraid that if my pinky went in the air, something was wrong. When I was real young, my Dad made a comment about my pinky and my hair. He said, "The next thing I know you're going to squat to pee." That always stuck with me.

When I went through the academy, it was not required for police officers in West Virginia to go through the academy. City police officers didn't have formal training. They gave you a gun and the badge, and said, "Have at it." At that time, I was the only trained police officer in the city of Pineville, so straight out of the academy, even though I still considered myself to be a greenhorn, all the other officers came to me when they needed something.

I remember the fear during my training—I remember my instructor making gay comments. He would say things that were borderline positive, like, "Don't assume that gays are wimps. If you ever work in Charleston don't go into the gay section by yourself." But, any time the subject would come up, there were always faggot comments. One question I asked got a big response. We were in drug identification asking questions about different drugs and what was legal and what was not. Poppers were common in the gay bars, so I asked, "Is poppers, or what is known as amyl nitrate, legal or illegal?" The instructor turned and said, "Considering faggots are the only people that use it, we don't give a shit." The entire class turned around and wanted to know how I knew about poppers.

We were instructed on what we could and could not get away with with gay and lesbian people. Pretty much anything you wanted to do to a gay person, you could have the support of the rest of the police department. I remember a gay wedding one officer found out about and called in for backups to go in and arrest the people for public intoxication. In another case, one officer liked to harass one well known gay person in the community. He would pull him over for "no tail lights," and if his tail lights were burning he'd bust the tail light and write the ticket. I knew to protect my identity.

For example, I remember pulling over a guy one night going through town twenty miles over the speed limit. I pulled him over, walked up to the car, got his driver's license and registration, and asked him to come back to the cruiser and have a seat. He came back, sat down, and he said, "The next time I see you in the Palace (a gay bar in Charleston, West Virginia) I'm going to read your fucking beads." I said, "Okay, have a nice day." That was one queen that got off for speeding twenty miles over the limit 'cause I knew he was going to call the mayor and go, "You know what that nellie queen did? He wrote me a ticket."

I remember my chief of police saying, "You've got to have a drink with us while you're on duty," 'cause they drink on duty. They were out screwing around on their wives, and they couldn't figure out why I wasn't going. At one point, they really pushed me to go out with this one girl. They would take me to her trailer, she would make very forward sexual advances, and I didn't respond. I think there was a certain amount of suspicion beginning to arise.

Towards the end, when the suspicion was rising, they would send me out on calls unprotected. The pressure was becoming more and more intense. They sent me out on every shit call they could. There were nights that I was the only officer doing any work out there. They called me to go pick up one of the town drunks, and I got into a wrestling match with him. I got back to the cruiser, called for backup, and no one ever showed up. I should have seen the handwriting on the wall, but I kept thinking that if I laid low enough things would be fine. Once they sent me out to a garage to check a prowler. I was walking among the cars and instructing the other officer to go down the back alley. When we met at the end, he had his weapon drawn and aimed towards me. I still have nightmares about that one because I think he probably was going to kill me but didn't have the nerve to do it. He swore he thought I was the prowler.

I was outed—that was the end of my career. One of the deputies that I was real good friends with told me I needed to ride with this guy and show him around. He rode with me a lot. He started telling me personal things about himself, and we got to be close friends. He was sitting in the cruiser one night and started crying that he had some things he wanted to talk to me about. He started telling me that he goes to "The Park," a gay bar in Roanoke. Immediately I thought, "I've been there." I started consoling him and saying, "It's okay. I've been to The Park, it's all right." I totally spilled my guts to this guy, showed him pictures of my lover, and told him everything. It turns out he was a plant by the city and the county to find out if I was gay.

A couple of days went by, and I got a call to meet him behind the jail. I stepped out of the car, and he hit me across my face with a night stick. I broke my glasses, I cut my eye, and I wrestled him and cuffed him. I put him in the cruiser, placed him under arrest, gave him his rights, and took him to the magistrate's court. The whole way to court I kept asking him, "Why are you doing this to me?" He kept saying, "You're a faggot." I said, "You told me you were gay, too." "I'm not gay. I just needed to know if you were a faggot or not."

When I got there, they took him out of the cuffs, sent him home, and that was the end of it. I showed up for work the next night, and the police commissioner met me at the time clock. He told me that the city had determined that I should be on immediate suspension, and he asked for my resignation. He wouldn't come out and give me a reason why. He kept saying, "You know why." I didn't resign. That was probably my first real standing up to anyone. He went back into the chambers where the entire City Council was meeting. He came back and said, "Okay. You're fired."

I left work totally devastated. They made me leave my uniform there—I went home in a t-shirt and pair of pants. I didn't know which way to turn. I filed a grievance against the city which I eventually won. I had been hired by the state of West Virginia under the CETA program, and I tried to get on in a couple other departments. The CETA program moved me to a rescue squad and trained me as an EMT—emergency medical technician. I tried to get on other departments but there was no way in God's green earth that they would have me. The frustrating part was I knew I was a good cop. When I was a cop, if other officers needed backup, I was there to take the punches. I spent many a night in the emergency room, but I was never afraid of going out there and getting in the middle of it. I wasn't big-headed—I was fair with people. I may have been a little blue light happy—I pulled people over for thirty-two in a twenty-five—but that was just immaturity. I was a good cop, and I couldn't understand why all these people were at the hearing. The ironic thing was there were a couple of deputies who were gay and who I had slept with. Why I didn't expose them, I don't know.

Everyone in my community knew what had happened. I couldn't go anywhere without getting faggot calls. I started getting harassed by the city police in the town I lived in. I would get pulled over for going twenty-seven miles per hour in a twenty-five. The state police came and arrested me saying I had purgered myself in court—it turned out to be a case that I had never even testified in. They accused me of accepting bribes from a big drug family in Pineville. They didn't have the balls to come to my house; they called me up on the phone and said, "Are you busy? Meet me over by the high school." I went to the high school, I stepped out of the car, he placed me under arrest, he put me in the back seat of the cruiser, and off we went for a drive. I didn't know if they were taking me to jail or out to kill me. I answered all their questions the best I could, and they turned me loose, saying, "Find your own way home, faggot."

I decided I really needed to get away from that. I moved to Morgantown and went back to the university. I look back now and it's probably the greatest thing that ever happened to me. I really miss law enforcement—I had a passion for it—but my life really has changed. After I was fired, I became a radical queen—an in-your-face type person. I got very involved in the gay community, and it definitely changed me.

I have a great deal of respect for police officers who are out there doing a good job. Some of the guys that I worked with can burn in hell as far as I'm concerned, but in Morgantown I think the police officers are well trained and are sympathetic to gay and lesbian problems.

The gay and lesbian community was not real kind to us as gay cops. Not only would you have the straight community down your back if they knew about you, the gay and lesbian community was not kind. I felt that I was viewed as the other side.

Most gay people that I knew in law enforcement were very successful. I think they work harder because they have to. You've automatically got one strike against you, and if you're going to make anything out of your life, you'd better be busting your butt to get it better. I busted my butt on every opportunity, and I still feel that I had to do more than a straight person. I have to bust my butt to make sure that I'm successful.

The most important thing to me was that I was trying to be the best I could be. I never understood why people didn't accept that and just let me be. I still feel the pain and humiliation from being dismissed. It will never be clear to me why people had to do that. I really believed I was a good police officer.

Cheri Maples

Department: Madison (WI) Police Department
Age: 41
Rank: Sergeant
Job: Street Supervisor
Years in Law Enforcement: 10

Cheri was one semester away from finishing her coursework for her Ph.D. in social policy when she decided to become a police officer in 1984. For the past three years, she's worked the night shift supervising patrol officers. Over coffee on her back porch on her day off, she talked about her experiences on the MPD.

I grew up in a working class, poor family, with two alcoholic parents. I was pretty much on my own. When I was a kid, there weren't any role models. I can remember thoughts of, "I'd sure like to be a police officer," but I can remember thoughts of, "I'd like to be a lawyer," and, "I want to play little league baseball." I didn't consider it a viable avenue to me at the time, so I didn't think about it seriously.

I made the decision to drop out of school and come on the Madison Police Department. When you're growing up, the idea of being a police officer appeals to the cowboy sense in some of us. I also saw it as a logical next step. I was helping to support a family, and I knew that by going into a nontraditional arena for women I was going to make what I was worth. Some of it was just an economic decision. Cops here make good money, especially cops with degrees.

The decision was difficult because I didn't have many supporters in my immediate community. I had pretty leftist politics, and there was a very big question mark for lots of people about why I would do this. It was a pretty radical shift. But as police officers, 80 percent of the work we do is crisis intervention. Most people see us as crime fighters, but we really are peace keepers. That is very much in keeping with what I was doing before.

The academy was difficult because I had been making decisions in organizations that operated by consensus decision-making. It was really interesting to be in an organization where, "You'll do it because you've been told to do it." When we got out into our field training experiences, there was a button campaign going on directed against lesbians. The buttons being worn said, "Straight as an arrow," and "Happily hetero." It wasn't exactly a wonderful culture. At the time, I didn't feel comfortable telling any of my male field training officers that I was a lesbian. Once I got on the streets, things got better.

I've had people who have had trouble with my being lesbian, but working side by side with these people they start to understand that you're not a heck of a lot different from them. You have a family that you go home to, you have things that you do when you get off of work, and you have the same concerns that they have. I think that's had a huge impact. But, there are some people who have never been willing to say hello to me since I walked in the door at the Madison Police Department. There's one guy who won't even grunt at me if I say hello. I don't get comments to my face because they know I won't tolerate it—I would have written people up for that. But behind my back, definitely. I don't want to imply that Madison is this great place where there is absolutely no price to be paid for being out. It's been harder in this arena than any other one I've been a part of. A lot of times I feel more exposed than I want to feel. I always feel like, "Why do I have to be making these choices to be out and visible, and why can't some other people help a little bit more?"

My ex-partner and I were together for ten years, and I helped to raise three kids she had from a marriage. My oldest son was a year and a half old when I started the academy, and I got pregnant with my second son, my biological son, during my third or fourth year on the department which really sent up a hullabaloo. People were wondering if they'd made a mistake about me. Here I am this out lesbian and it's announced at a training session that I was pregnant. The room got so quiet you could hear a pin drop. Finally, somebody said, "Congratulations." It spread like wildfire, and I think people were really confused. They could not figure how in the world this had happened. My other family wasn't recognized, but when you have a child that's your biological child you have this base in common with other people who have gone through a similar experience. It was fascinating. Again though, it was more exposure than I was comfortable with.

Ten years ago there were still a lot of difficult attitudes toward women on the department. People with those attitudes still exist, but they've had to go underground. Now we've got a culture that's 25 percent women. Downtown, you're going to find mostly female officers on any given night. I think it's been a harder road for the minorities in the organization. The race thing is more paramount than the gender thing although we certainly have minority females that understand that their battle has got to be waged on both fronts and for some of them, on three fronts.

Madison is a wonderful place because we've had the support in terms of numbers to make a difference and the camaraderie of each other. We have the highest percentage of women in the country. Once you have the numbers, people can be themselves and not feel an incredible pressure to blend in with the majority culture. Our department is such a unique place because I feel comfortable talking about my partner the same way as somebody who's married. There are enough of us that it's just not an issue.

The numbers have brought two things. One is more exposure to people working side by side with more of us. A lot of the lesbian officers in this organization are extremely good police officers. It's impossible to work side by side with these people and not see that. It's impossible to do this job on a cold winter night and not coffee up with somebody eventually and start to learn things about people. It's impossible for attitudes not to start changing as a result of those kinds of numbers and those kinds of conversations. And when you have enough numbers where you can have those conversations among eight or nine of you, you don't necessarily care if you're overheard. All of a sudden it becomes different. Both of those factors have been important.

Most of us here have the luxury of coming out and doing it comfortably. I've heard horror stories all over the country of people who don't trust backups to be there, where their life is literally going to be on the line. They are possibly going to be killed because they're going to look behind them and not see somebody there. Whenever you have to go in the closet to do your job or to be part of your family, you lose a piece of yourself. That invisibility is a major stressor. Whenever you're having to keep secrets on any level, it's stressful, and when your safety may be an issue, it's extremely stressful.

Everybody's going to get needled in this job. If you're an African-American, Hispanic, or Asian officer, you're going to hear racial slurs all the time. If you're a man, everybody you arrest is going to call you a faggot. And if you're a woman, everybody you arrest is going to call you a lesbian; that's the first thing out of their mouth. That's the most insulting thing they can think of to call you. That's why I've been convinced that homophobia is about gender roles, it's not about men loving men and women loving women. It's about stepping outside of what's perceived to be socially acceptable gender roles. When somebody calls you a lesbian they're not saying it's a terrible thing that you love a woman. You are stepping outside of who you are supposed to be.

All of us have to ask ourselves a question every day, "Is this the most effective arena for me at this point in my life?" I'm having a hard time dealing with the victims of poverty and racism every single night, and the cynicism that's a part of that. I've always said that when I can't feel things in my heart, when I feel shut down, it's time to start looking. And lately I've had more of those experiences than I'm comfortable with. But yet I have been a part of changing some things in a real positive way in this profession.

The only hope that I go to work with each night, other than staying alive, is to do the next right thing in front of me. I've had some tremendous opportunities to do that, and I've made a difference here and there. Every now and then I get a call where a small miracle happens, where you have one of those experiences that is so powerful it makes up for all the shit you've taken, for all the crap that people are throwing in your face, and for all the times you've been in situations where people might have a gun in your face.

The world is a-changin' and I think gays and lesbians need to be on all fronts and in all places. In this job, having a strong sense of who you are is more important than your sexual orientation. The people that do worst in this job are people who are real worried about what other people think of them. Being a minority officer of any kind—whether it's female, African-American, Hispanic, Asian—you need to have a stronger sense of yourself. We need people fighting for us at all places. When you take the risks and you're willing to be who you are, it's not just for you, it makes a difference for other people, too.

Pete Zecchini

Department: Miami Beach (FL) Police Department
Age: 34
Rank: Police Officer
Job: Patrol
Years in Law Enforcement: 13

Pete works the night shift on Miami Beach. He lives in a neighborhood of art deco homes and well-groomed lawns along the intracoastal waterway. After working all night, he sat on one of two white sofas in his living room, wearing a white t-shirt with a rainbow on the back and blue MBPD shorts.

I knew I wanted to be a policeman when I was in elementary school. My dad had some friends that were policemen, and he was good friends with a judge. There was a cross guard out in front of my school, and her husband was a policeman. Every day after school, he would come and sit there on his motorcycle and talk to his wife. I always used to go and talk to him. To this day, they still send Christmas cards.

When I was eighteen or nineteen years old, I moved out of the house. I met a lot of people, started going to clubs, and was having a lot of sex. I was working at a gay bar back then, life was going nowhere, and I started going down the tubes. I got caught up real quick in the gay lifestyle.

I was in a hole, and I don't know how I was able to pull out of it. I moved out of Los Angeles and up to the mountains of California. I hibernated for six months. I came down one day and joined the Coast Guard. That was the way to change my life around. That was my way to snap out of it.

I spent four years in the Coast Guard, and I was in law enforcement for three years of that time. After the Coast Guard, I joined the South Miami Police Department and was down there for about five years. I was a patrol officer and a detective. I was out there—everybody knew I was gay.

My last year in South Miami was pretty difficult. My supervisor screwed me every way. If I was late, if I didn't look right that day, if I wasn't handling my cases quick enough for him, he would screw with me. He would change my days off, he would make me work different hours, and he would take cases away from me and assign them to other people. He was the only supervisor I've ever really gotten into it with. I confronted this guy, and we had shouting matches, "You're doing this because I'm gay." He outright told me one that it was and that I couldn't do anything about it. The day he said that, we went to the chief's office, and I said, "Repeat what you told me in your office." He said, "I don't remember talking to you. I don't remember having any conversations with you." Stupid me. I was naive to think this guy was going to say anything.

In South Miami, I was hurt by one of the gay business owners. Me and a lesbian officer were working undercover one night in plainclothes and happened to walk by the manager of a club. He was smoking a joint and got arrested. The owner of the club called up my chief of police the next day and said, "Pete and this other officer are gay." The chief called me in the office and had me listen to the tape of the call. He wasn't letting any cat out of the bag, but he thought he was. I still feel pissed off. I still feel in a gray zone being a policeman and being gay: not accepted at all by the people you work with and treated as a very suspicious character by the gay community, too.

Being a cop in Miami Beach is miserable. I had told somebody that my lover was sick, and it got spread around the department. That hurt me very much. I went to a training class and part of the training was a physical training course. They were doing physical take downs, putting us in choke holds, and that kind of thing. The instructor came up to me to demonstrate a choke hold, he pushed on my throat, and I spit. Not a lot—it was like a cough—but a spray did come out, so he says. I didn't think anything of it. I didn't even know I had done it to him, but I took his word for it. I came in to work the next day, and everybody was coming up to me and saying, "I hear you vomited on the instructor." I walked in the building, and the instructor walked up to me and said, "Hey, I know your lifestyle, man, but don't worry, I've talked to somebody, and I'm not that afraid of catching anything." Then I found out that this guy went in and had them do an injury report because I spit on him. His reasons were because I'm gay I might have AIDS. Then the jokes started up again, that I had vomited on him and that he was going to get AIDS because I'm a faggot.

A couple days before that, we were at the shooting range. When I got there I sat down off to the side drinking a cup of coffee. Not a lot of people knew I was there. They were saying, "faggot this," "faggot that," and, "Miami Beach is turning into a bunch of faggots." I couldn't believe it. There were a couple of people that knew that I was there, and I was kind of shocked to not hear them say, "Hey, shut up, Zecchini's around the corner."

I haven't met a gay-positive straight person. I see a lot of people that are friendly and nice, and if you pass them in the hallway you can say hello. But are they going to sit in the same car with you? Are they going to invite you over to their house to meet their wife? Or are they going to ask you to go to their parties? I've never had anybody do that. I think I was tolerated by the majority of people. I've never had anybody come up to me and call me "faggot" in my face, but I don't think being tolerated is enough. I can play the game just like anybody else, but I don't. Everybody always says, "You've got to go the extra mile to try to get along with these people because of who you are." I don't know why—it's not my problem; it's their problem. Like I said, a lot of people say hello, and a lot of people will be pleasant, but nobody wants to sit in the seat next to me.

I don't feel effective as a policeman anymore. You can't do your job effectively if you've got all these things to worry about. I'm scared that I might not be backed up. That has happened, several times. The most dangerous time for me was one night when I got dispatched to a burglar alarm call at a business. I got there, and there were two kids inside the store. I advised them on the radio that I had two subjects inside the store and that I needed a backup. The dispatcher got on and asked for a backup. Nobody came on the radio for what seemed like several minutes. Finally, a guy who was at the other end of the city got on the air and said he'd back me up. On my way up to the call I saw five policemen sitting inside a restaurant five blocks away, and none of them got up to come and help. You don't do that. If a cop calls off something like that, you go. Doesn't matter if you're eating, doesn't matter if you're pissing, you get up and you go. Normally in a call like that, five or six or the whole shift will show up. Only one guy showed up, and it took him ten minutes to get there. I ended up going in and arresting the two kids myself.

I was working off-duty at a gay bar one night a few weeks ago, and I got into a fight. I got on the radio and asked for a backup. Nobody got on the radio, so I just walked away. I decided not to arrest the guy. I retreated, 'cause nobody would come. I've done traffic stops before, pulled over people, and asked for a backup and nobody would come on the air. So I'd just get back in my car and drive off.

There's other little subtle things. If a straight cop makes a traffic stop, a lot of other cops will drive by and make sure he's okay. That doesn't happen with me; they won't come by and check on me. There's one or two guys that might, but if they're on a call, forget it. So I have to be even more consciously aware of who's in service. I think about it all the time. If I'm going on a call, I've got to think about things other guys probably don't even concern themselves with. Will they back me up? Will they help me if I get hurt? I can't count on their being there.

I feel like the loner out there. I think, "If I get hurt, am I going to have the same treatment?" When cops get hurt, all the cops come to their side. They'll put their parents up in a hotel, and they'll make sure they get out to breakfast in the morning and out to lunch. They'll drive them around. Will they do this if something happens to me? How are they going to react? What are they going to do? That goes through my mind all the time. I'm scared to death. If something happens to me, what's going to happen?

The majority of the guys I work with think they're God's gift to saving the world. I'd probably do a lot better if I got on to day shift where there're some more mature thinking people, but I've got this stuck-up thing in my head right now that they want me to quit. They can't call people faggots in front of me, they're having a hard time arresting gay people in the park, and they're real upset about it. I don't want to give in to them. I sit there and pretend like noth ing bothers me at all. The smarter ones probably know it's not true. We've got one guy that's working off-duty at a gay bar, and the guy walks around the police station with a bumper sticker on his suitcase that says, "AIDS is a cure for faggots." He can take our faggot money; it doesn't bother him one little bit.

When I was on day shift, I was close to one officer. We were friends, and I knew there was no barriers because she was gay, too. I never got the feeling that she understood a lot of things that I was going through. She gets along better with people at work than I do. I can get along with anybody, but I have this need not to play the game to get along. I want to have true friendships, I want to be truly honest with people, and I want to be able to sit down next to straight guys in restaurants and talk to them. But I know I can't do that. She can do that, and it doesn't seem to bother her. I don't think she cares about what other people think about her. And, it's not the same for a lesbian. These guys aren't threatened by them; it doesn't bother them. They talk like they would like to be the third person in any sexual relationship with a lesbian.

I'm a policeman just like them. Why can't they treat me like they treat each other? I don't understand that. If they treat me like shit, if fellow officers don't respect me, how are they going to treat these people on the street? Because of that, I've given gays a break when I've stopped them. Somebody's got to cut them a break sometime. The job requires a lot of human skills, and what's wrong one time can be completely different the next time. I've heard so many stories about policemen mistreating gay people, I just felt that if there was something minor, it could be overlooked.

Last year I felt I was being discriminated against. I didn't get a pay raise because I had some personal problems at home that required me to use some sick time. You're allowed to use twelve days of sick time, and I used thirteen, so they denied me a pay raise. I was the only person in the history of the Miami Beach Police Department that has ever been denied a pay raise because I used too much sick time.

I can't do anything if I'm discriminated against, or if I'm mistreated. I can't go to my supervisors and tell them that these guys won't back me up and I'm getting the shit knocked out of me because it's taking them ten or fifteen minutes to get to a call I'm on. I can't tell a supervisor when somebody calls me a faggot. I can't tell a supervisor when somebody beats the shit out of somebody that's gay. Miami Beach has an anti-discrimination ordinance—that's fine for average, everyday, gay people that think they've been discriminated against in a job, or if they're fired. But I can't file complaints like that. If I'm discriminated against, I can't sue anybody. Do you know the repercussions of a policeman suing or accusing fellow officers? I would be an outcast far more than I am now. You don't hand up other cops. I might end up dead, not just not getting any backup. They could set me up, they could do all kinds of things. I don't think there's anything beyond their capabilities to get back at me. They've done it before; I've seen them do things to others.

I'm happy when I'm at home. I can't wait to get out of work. I go in there every night, answer my calls, and just can't wait to get home. That's not a very healthy work environment. I have no idea where I'll be in five or ten years. I don't even know where I'm going to be next week. I'm scared to death. If I can't do the job, if I can't work with these people, I don't know what choice I have. It's been a hard few years and I'm not sure if it's worth it any more. As a matter of fact, I've been thinking about getting out of it.

Gwendolyn Gunter

Department: Minneapolis (MN) Police Department
Age: 29
Rank: Police Officer
Job: Patrol
Years in Law Enforcement: 2

Over lunch on a sunny, June day in a cafe overlooking Minneapolis' Loring Park, Gwen took a break from her job as a Housing Enforcement Team investigator for the Minneapolis Police Department. A powerfully-built woman in a crisp, blue uniform, she also plays rugby and has a bachelor's degree in psychology.

My mom died when I was seven. I have six older brothers, and they pretty much raised me. My dad was working all the time, so I was in the streets a lot. I was in trouble a lot at school—always in the principal's office. I worried about what I was going to do when I grew up 'cause being a housewife didn't appeal to me. I knew I was gay in the back of my mind, and I didn't want to be a gym teacher which is pretty much what is expected of the jock and the lesbian. Even though when I was growing up the most important people in my life were my coach and a gym teacher, I didn't want to do what people expected.

I grew up in Evanston, Illinois, but when I got older and went away to school, I moved to Chicago. I used to get harassed by the cops a lot. In a matter of a year,

I had been harassed by the police six times and gone to jail twice. Each time I had been mistaken as a Black male. One of these times, the police snatched me up in a matter of seconds, and I was off to jail. They tried to hit me up for information about what was going on in the street. First they took me up to their office where they sat me down and handcuffed me to a huge chain they had mounted on the wall. The chain was one that is used on ships to pull in the anchor. Then I was put in a cell with a male prisoner. The watch commander ordered that I be moved. From there, they put me in the closet and handcuffed me to a chair. It was absolutely humiliating and terrifying. I remember sitting there thinking, "This is bullshit."

I had another incident where I was riding my bike about one o'clock in the morning, and I stopped to write a note to leave on my friend's car. There was a state trooper across the street talking to somebody, and before I could finish writing the note, he was in my face, "What are you doing?" By this time, I've got major attitude towards cops, and I said, "What does it look like I'm doing? I'm writing a note." He goes on and on, and I said, "If you would leave me the fuck alone, I'd be done by now and be gone." He's like, "I just want to know what you're doing. You don't belong here." Then I lost it, "Why don't I belong? Last I looked this wasn't South Africa." He goes, "I can take you to jail." I said, "Fucking take me to jail. I'm leaving a note on my friend's car—is that against the law?" It got to the point where he was like, "Okay, come on, let's go. I'm taking you to jail. If you hadn't gotten smart with me and just told me what you were doing...." I said, "I did tell you what I was doing. Why did you come over here? What was your probable cause? If I was a White man, you would not have thought anything about it." He goes, "There's been a lot of car break-ins in this neighborhood in the last couple of weeks." I said, "Why didn't you just stand over there and wait and see if I was going to break into the damn car? I saw you standing over there. I would have to be a really stupid criminal to try to steal a car with a state trooper right across the street." I said, "It's not the *fact* that you approached me, it's the *way* you approached me. If I was a White person, you would have come over and said, 'How're you doing, Ma'am. Is there a problem? Can I help you with something? I just want you to know there have been a lot of car break-ins and somebody could call the cops because they could think that you're getting ready to break into this car.' I wouldn't have a problem with that." It turned out we had a really good conversation. This was one of very few positive interactions.

With all of this, I used to sit around with my friends and bash cops. Just two days before, I had taken the test for the police department in Chicago. I had been sitting around with my friends trashing cops, and I thought to myself, "If only assholes *become* cops, then only assholes will *be* cops." I wanted to bring my experiences of being harassed by cops to the police department.

When I took the test to become a police officer in Chicago, a quarter of a million other people took the test, too. I ranked "very well qualified" but since there were so many people, it took six months before they sent out letters calling for interviews. During that time I decided I wanted to move to Minneapolis 'cause I wanted to train for and play rugby. I figured if they wanted me, they would call me. Two months after I moved here, a friend of mine said, "They're hiring for the police department," so I took the test. A month later, I got a letter saying they wanted me to come in for an interview, and two months after that, I was hired. I had already started the training here before I heard that Chicago wanted me to come in for an interview.

Because we had so many minorities in our recruit class, it gave me a lot of strength. The guys I came on with are like my family. Without a doubt, I trust them with my life. Even if they don't agree with some things I believe and say, they'll be the first to back me up. There's two different types of backup. Say there's a person with a gun and I get dispatched to the call. I hope another squad will volunteer to come and be in the area in case something goes wrong. Those are the types of situations that are scary because they're not obligated to come. The other type is when an officer needs help, and that tone goes out on the radio. You get backup then. It's those situations where there's a person with a gun or there's a domestic, and people know you're there—will people put themselves in an area where they can get there to help you if you get in trouble? Also, when you're out on a traffic stop, it's customary for cars to roll by you and to be in the area. At night it's not even unusual for a car to not only roll by but just sit there while you're doing your traffic stop. My partner feels she does not always get the backup she may need. After riding with her, I know she doesn't. There have been times where shots have been fired, my partner and I have pulled over a car fitting the description of a vehicle that's supposed to have a gun in it, and no one has rolled by. Some women will not ask for backup for fear that they will be judged as "pussys" by some of the male cops.

Everyone in my unit knows I'm gay. They know my partner—whenever I'm invited to a function they invite her. I'm very straight forward with them, and they're very straight forward with me. When I decided to become a cop, I made up my mind that I wasn't going to be in the closet. I tell people, "When you become a cop, you're going to give up a lot things, but never give up your self-respect." I felt like I had so much going against me anyway, what difference does it matter that I'm gay? Let's face it. The most underrepresented people on most police departments are Black females. There are a ton of gay women, there're a ton of gay men, but there aren't too many Black females. They just don't want us. I was more concerned about being a Black female, 'cause historically they have treated us like shit. The first Black female to ever join the police department retired after the minimum amount of years. I can only imagine what she had to go through. Being lesbian is the least of my worries.

The most common thing that I run into is people using the word "fag." Within the first month my partner said, "Fucking fag." I said, "Time out—that's offensive to me." He's like, "Why? What am I supposed to call them?" I said, "You're supposed to say, 'gay men'. That's no different than if someone said, 'That nigger.'" I know he still uses the word, but I planted a seed, and he doesn't use it around me. He's more cautious of who he says things around which is really all you can ask for. You've got to chip away at it. When I walk into a room, I'd much rather see them stop talking and change their way of thinking and living than for me to do it. You don't come out of the closet to make things easier for yourself. You come out of the closet to make things easier for the people after you. When you come out, you know it's going to be hard. Your only gratification is that it won't be as hard for the next person.

If I were a gay man, I don't know if I'd be out. It's the last of the ole boys' network. I think that a lot of the men on the department assume that if you're not married or you're not fucking someone on the department, "you're a lesbian." And let's face it—straight men think lesbians are erotic. I've had cops tell me that they think two women being together is very sexy; it's their fantasy. But every single person who's ever said that to me has also said without missing a beat, "Gay men make me sick. I can't stand the thought of it; it repulses me." It's a threat to their manhood. It's really hard for gay men. I can see where a gay man would really be in fear for his life every single day from his fellow officers.

Being a cop is a hard job, and the hard part isn't being on the street. Dealing with the people that you work with is the hardest part about this job 'cause you never know—they'll smile in your face, and they'll stab you in the back. It's a lot easier to tell who the criminals are on the street than it is in the police department. There are a few people on this police department that I feel like if I was in a dark alley and they had the opportunity to take me out, they would. I know there are some guys in this department that would do the same to a gay man 'cause he represents the scariest thing in the world to them—a man loving a man and not ashamed of it.

I seem to represent everything the old boys hate in this department—female, Black, and gay. The thing that makes it worst of all is I'm a good cop. When I first came to this shift, my sergeant was like, "When I saw your name on my list, I tried everything I could to get you the hell out of my precinct. I didn't want you here; I had heard all these bad things about you—you were a troublemaker, and you brought the morale down. I'm glad I got you because there's not one person on the shift that won't work with you. You're a damn good cop." That made it all worth it.

The main reason I joined the police department was because of the inequalities I faced as a Black woman being mistaken for a Black man. I wanted to do something about that. I wanted to be an ally to people; I wanted them to feel like they had someone on their side when they were stopped. Why I continue to do this job has nothing to do with that. I continue because of the kids. Every day in this country, a kid dies 'cause of some violent act either by a parent or another kid. The scariest thing to me about being out on our police department is that parents will not want me to be around their kids. My biggest joy as an officer is going into a classroom full of kids and one of them saying to me, "I want to be a cop like you."

When I was younger I had a gym teacher who paid seven dollars to send me to a basketball camp that changed my life. That's what I want to be to other kids—I want to be the influence that can change their lives. I kind of adopted a girl's basketball team, and I'm sending five of them to camp. I have this fear of a parent finding out that I'm a lesbian and not wanting their child to ride in the car with me. My biggest fear is that I won't be able to give to these kids what I know I can and what their parents don't. If I couldn't work with kids there wouldn't be any reason for me to do this job any more. I would be too bitter.

I came on the department looking for racism, mistreatment, and narrow-mindedness, and although all three have been present throughout my career, I've been pleasantly surprised. The majority of the officers have treated me more than fair, and I attribute this to the officers that came before me. Lieutenant Lubinski's coming out really opened the door for me and other gay cops. It also closed the door on intolerance. A Black sergeant who has been the target of mistreatment for the past five years has also paved the way. The people before me had it rough; so far, I've had it pretty good. Hopefully, those after me will wonder, "What's the big deal?"

Sandy J. Austin

Department: Metropolitan Police Department, District of
Columbia
Age: 38
Rank: Patrol Officer
Job: Narcotics and Special Investigations Division
Years in Law Enforcement: 20

*A compact and muscular woman, Sandy portrays the image of a woman who doesn't take much
from anyone. One of ten children, she carries in her wallet and proudly displays a picture of her
three-year-old granddaughter. On medical leave with job-related injuries, she talked about her
experiences as a D.C. cop over dinner at a steakhouse in the District.*

My mother died when I was eleven. The guy that we were living with
told me I wasn't his child, and he put me out. I ended up going to live
with my sister because she was the only one who would take me in. I really owe
her a lot, 'cause I'd probably be out on the street somewhere if I was still alive.
Life would be totally different. I was probably lucky compared to some of my
friends.

My brother-in-law was a reserve police officer who always wanted to be the
"police," but he was too short. When I was in eleventh grade, all I wanted to do
was write poetry and play drums but he thought I should get a real job. When
the police cadet test came up, he made me take it, and I passed. In the twelfth

grade about two months before I was ready to graduate, the police department called and asked if I still wanted the job. I said, "Yeah," 'cause I really didn't have anything else lined up. I took and passed the physical, and a week after I graduated from high school, I was a police cadet. Three years after that, I was a sworn officer. I still want to write poetry and play drums, but this pays a little better right now.

I like being the police. I like the excitement, and I like it that no two days are anything alike. I always used to say, "Why watch the news when you can make the news?" I like knowing what's happened first. I could give you all that B.S. about trying to help people, but I got over that a long time ago. Everybody has some of that naiveness about trying to help the world—you're going to solve all the world's problems—but once you get out there and realize people don't want your help and they don't like you, you give that theory up and go to something else like making money.

Before I came on the department, you had to be 5′7″; I'm 5′2½″. When we came on in '74 as cadets, we were the first group of short females. I went to one of the most dangerous districts in Washington, D.C., and I was 5′2″, female, and Black, so my early reception was not that great. I got the rookie treatment. For example, my first day in role call: you go to role call, you see an empty chair, you sit down, and then one of the veterans comes in and tells you, "That's my seat," so you get up. Then you sit in another seat, somebody else comes in and tells you you're sitting in their chair, and you get up. So what you have to do is wait 'til everybody is seated, then you see what chair is empty, and that's your chair. When they called my name and assigned me with somebody, I got the, "Aw, Sarge, I don't want to work with her" treatment. They only put me with people whose partners were off for the day. I rode with whoever was available. I'd get in the car, and they'd give me the, "Don't touch the radio. You're not my partner for life, and I don't want to talk to you" treatment. You've got to go through the rookie thing. I didn't drive a car for two months. I just sat on the passenger's seat.

As much as possible, I tried to leave the fact that I was gay separate from the police department because I had one lieutenant who figured it out, and he always told me that if the police department found out, they would fire me. So I kept that quiet for a while 'cause I wasn't quite sure if they could fire me or not. My first year I played the game going out with the guys, I went to no gay clubs, I didn't go out with anybody, and I was scared 'cause I didn't want to be fired. Once my first year was over, I said, "I'm not going to worry about this so much." I was in vice, I was twenty-one or twenty-two years old, and I must say, I was a dog. I'd do anybody. I didn't care if they were married, single, separated, living with somebody or not. I was just a dog and having a ball! I was fooling with this girl who used to be my neighbor, and her girlfriend found out. I was over at my sister's house one night, and she came over and broke my windshield and cut my tires. On top of that, she went to the nearest police precinct and told them the whole story about me being gay and messing with her girlfriend. When I got to work my lieutenant said, "Effective tomorrow, you're going back to uniform." I asked him, "Why?" He said, "Just because."

I said, "I ain't going for this," so I called our EEO office. The secretary asked, "What's your problem?" I said, "Sexual preference." She got real quiet and put me on hold. Then this female sergeant came on the phone; I went through the same thing with her, and she got real quiet. She said, "Can you come down now?" I said, "I'm on my way." So I went down there, and I got a Black female sergeant, a White male lieutenant, and a Black male inspector to talk to. I went through it, and the Inspector said, "I don't think there's anything we can do to help you." But the female sergeant said, "Oh, no, Inspector. She put a lot on the line. We have to do something." The lieutenant agreed with the sergeant, so the inspector said, "I have to listen to my staff. I don't know exactly what I *can* do, but I'm going to try to do something."

Nobody else knew I went to EEO except those three, but when I got back to my unit, a reporter called and said, "I heard you have a complaint. Are you willing to talk about it?" So it came out on the front page of the *Washington Post*. My ex-partner, who was working downtown at the time, called at seven o'clock in the morning and said, "You've got to go get the paper." I was shocked that it got all that ink; the headlines were so bold. It was on the radio, my telephone was ringing, and I was hearing from people I ain't heard from before. This was on a Friday, and the following Monday, I had to go to court. I got to court, and it was like that E.F. Hutton commercial—everybody stopped. My friends at work were always my friends, but I guess most of the high-ranking officials had been told to stay away from me. The only real problem I had was one of the females tried to get a petition to get me banned from the locker room but none of the other females would sign it, so that blew over. I guess what helped was I'm such a good police officer.

A lot of guys said they weren't surprised. People I work with on a daily basis were there for me, and those are the only people you really worry about. Those are the people who have to back you up, and those are the people who you have to backup. You don't worry about the people who work downtown and gossip all the time 'cause they're not out there with you on a daily basis. The people who were out there were cool.

People would never make comments to me. I learned that you had to make your reputation early on, 'cause if you don't, the police and the people out there on the street will eat you alive. I made my reputation quick. Nobody knows if I can fight or not, but they believe I can. Nobody would ever say stuff to my face, 'cause they don't know what I might do. I had a type of reputation where they think I'm crazy. I told people, "If you don't come back me up, I'm coming after your ass." I told people to their face, they believed me, and I wasn't playing.

I had a guy one day who was sitting in my seat in roll call. I told him to get up, and he wouldn't. I told him to get up again. He said, "I ain't." I told two or three of the fellas after roll call, and they took him in the bathroom and had a talk with him. He ain't never sat in my seat again. I don't have that kind of problems.

Don't get me wrong, I've been in trouble. My mouth gets me in trouble, because I don't take no bullcrap from anyone. I don't care what your rank is. A lot of times, especially when I was younger, I would speak before I thought. One time I had locked this guy up and parked his car right in front of our precinct. I was the only one handling the arrest, and this new sergeant came in and asked me about the car. He said, "I want you to move the damn car right now!" I said, "I'm going to move the car as soon as I get him in the cell. I'm the only one handling the arrest, so just give me a couple of minutes." He went on and on, so I cussed him out. It ended up costing me $250; my mouth gets me in trouble.

I've never been one who wants to go through the rank structure. I have a problem with the promotional process because if you could just take a test and get promoted, that's fine. However, once you take a test then you've got to go through a review board, and it's all favoritism. Recently we had a female who wrote the twenty-fifth best paper on the test for sergeant, and after going through the other phases they bumped her to 153. Too much favoritism. You see, if I studied for six months, wrote the twenty-fifth best paper, and got bumped to 153, I'd hurt somebody. I won't put myself through that. Before I got older and calmed down some, I stepped on a lot of toes. I just didn't care. But after I got in my thirties I realized that it wasn't quite beneficial to mouth off all the time, and it kept costing me too much money. So I calmed down, and I just mutter under my breath now.

I go just about anywhere I want to go, 'cause I have a gun. If something happens, it's going to happen anyway. One night we went to the gay club, and there had to be thirteen policewomen in there. These two women got in a fight, and we broke it up. About five of us decided we would leave, 'cause you could see where it was heading. But before we got out the door, one of the girls grabbed a bottle, broke it, and went at the other girl who was on the dance floor. She was getting ready to stab her in the back. I was the first one to get to her—and I ain't bragging, but I lift weights, so I think I'm pretty strong—but she must have been on something, 'cause I tried to get the bottle out of her hand, but she wouldn't let it go. So I was trying to break her arm because the bottle was coming toward me. A sergeant friend and four other policewomen jumped in, and the sergeant got cut and almost lost her thumb. We ended up having to lock the woman up, and we were up all night doing reports. It was hard 'cause up until that point, the females who were with me weren't out. I had to notify half the police department that we had a sergeant who was cut, an off-duty arrest, and three officers who needed to be put on the book to do the paperwork for the off-duty arrest. This report came from a gay club on women's night and went directly to the chief's office the next day. So everybody who wasn't out the day before, was definitely out then. We talked about it that night because one of them didn't want to make an arrest, and I told her, "There's too many people here that know we're the police for us not to make an arrest; if you don't make an arrest, it's going to be worse."

I would really like to see our high-ranking officials come out. I know it's not going to happen 'cause they still want to get promoted, and they believe being gay would stop them from getting higher. I keep fighting. The best thing I do is let people know I'm there, and they definitely know I'm there. Other gay officers come up to me and say they look up to me for being so open, but they wish they could be that open; they're afraid to come out. I think it's silly 'cause if you want to come out, you come out. I don't see what the big deal is. You come out, and you live your life. I think that's the best decision I've made because I feel freer than I ever could've been if I wasn't out.

Stacey Simmons

Department: Connecticut State Police
Age: 27
Rank: State Trooper
Job: State-wide Community Crime Control Task Force
Years in Law Enforcement: 6 1/2

The only openly gay state trooper in Connecticut and possibly the country, Stacey came out after a few years on the job. An activist at heart, she has ruffled a few feathers in her six-and-one-half years on the department. After attending the "Together in Pride" conference for lesbian and gay law enforcers in New York City, she relaxed over a beer in a deli in the shadows of NYPD headquarters at One Police Plaza.

My father is a state trooper in Connecticut where he's been with the department for thirty-one years. So I grew up with my extended family being my father's platoon. I grew up around the uniform, in a state police cruiser with a state police radio, and amongst police officers, so it was a very natural transition for me. My family has known that I was gay since I was seventeen, and let's just say it's been a rocky road. I was in college and ended up taking a police work class on a whim. I absolutely loved it, got an "A," and said, "Why go to college?" I applied, and luckily a year later, I was offered a position as a state trooper trainee.

When I was applying, I had to take a polygraph. They asked you whether you've ever had relations with a married woman or married man, with more than one person at a time, with dead bodies, or with animals. They asked you, "Have you ever had sexual relations with a member of the same sex?" (It is now illegal to ask your sexual orientation.) I knew that if I said, "Yes," I would not be hired. Then they asked you, "Under the category 'Sexual practices,' did you lie?" When they asked that and I said, "No," a picture of the face of the woman I was dating came in front of my closed eyes, and I panicked. I heard the polygraph machine go wild, and I was like, "I'm screwed." So at the end, we went over the test, and the trooper giving the test said, "I only have a problem with one aspect so far." I thought, "I'm gone. I'm dismissed." He said "Under the category about shoplifting…" And I was like, "What? I shoplifted a candy bar once when I was a kid. My mother caught me and made me return it and pay for it since it was half eaten. I was really embarrassed." He said, "Okay. We'll get back to you." I got the letter a few weeks later saying, "You have successfully passed the polygraph; here's your date for the next phase of the process."

Our academy was five months long; it's like Marine Corps boot camp. It was emotionally, physically, and psychologically challenging. It is the most difficult thing I've ever done in my life. We started with a class of seventy-four, three of which were women. One of the women dropped out the first week, and the other woman hurt her knee and had to drop out the third week. From the third week on I was the only woman. One of my mother's friends said to me, "That's great odds," to get a boyfriend. In reality though, the odds were nil. The majority of my classmates were ex-military. If you were a woman there was attitude from the department and from many of your peers as well. I had one instructor who would jog next to me during physical training and whisper, "You want to be a man? Is that why you're here?" Obviously I couldn't keep up with everything the men did physically; I got good-natured ribbing, though, because we learned to be a team. You start as individuals, they break you down to your lowest point, and then they slowly build you back up into what they want you to be—a state trooper, professional, aware, and educated. If you don't have the mental capacity to really handle that, you wash out. We graduated a class of forty-six of which there are thirty-eight left on the job.

The academy was very stressful, but it was great because I proved something to myself. I had gotten a lot of shit for being gay from my family and from the world, and this was something I had all for me. I did it all by myself; it was like a reaffirmation, "I'm okay. Look what I can do." It was the proudest day of my life when my father pinned my badge on me and I graduated. That was very emotional because my father's very important to me and now we had a common bond with the job. It was a bridge to mend our relationship that suffered due to my homosexuality.

I started out at Troop C in Stafford Springs, which is country. We had a little bit of highway but it's a country troop, and we do mostly criminal work. We had a situation arise at the barracks that I took offense to, challenged the commanding officer, and filed a grievance. I was young at the time. The commanding officer was not allowing women to work an overtime job. He stated, "No one under six foot and a fourth of a ton" could work it, and that was not kosher in my book. I challenged it, and eight troopers ended up getting paid for a job they never worked because this lieutenant had obviously participated in discriminatory practices. However, three days after I told them that I was going to file the grievance, I got notified I was being transferred to Troop H in Hartford, a highway troop. Even though I eventually won the battle, I lost the war. I spent about a year and a half in Hartford. Due to my challenge, among other things, the old lieutenant also eventually got transferred, so I put in my reassignment papers and went happily back to Troop C.

I'd gone through a year-long process of mulling over thoughts of coming out. There's such a need for gay cops, because gays are 10 percent, if not more, of the community that you police. You have Black officers, Hispanic officers, Asian officers, females, and White males. You have just about every category represented except for the gay community. So I said, "I'm not going to let that happen anymore." I'd seen gay victims of hate crimes who were afraid to come forward because of homophobic police officers, who were beaten and robbed, and who were frightened to go to the police because they thought the cop was going to be a second offender or that their names would be plastered in the papers. I was furious at that.

I felt guilty because I had been in a restaurant one night, and one of the waitresses was obviously gay and open about it. One of my troopers jokingly said, "That waitress likes you," and I said, "If she comes near me I'll smack her." We all laughed. I played up to that because I was so scared of what would happen if they found out I was a lesbian. A year later I came out on the job. I wanted to have a few years on the job, get my feet on the ground, gain respect, and have the troopers know me and like me before I did something like that. You can't just come in like gangbusters and say, "I'm a lesbian." That's too confrontational, and that won't wash in my work climate. I think my strategy was good.

I spoke with several politicians and attorneys looking at what my approach should be in order to protect myself. We had a gay rights bill going into effect in October of '91—I wasn't going to come out until that passed because I felt that would be crazy. I coordinated my coming out to the commissioner and the lieutenant colonel over a five month span. I worked through the woman who heads a training division in another local police department; she was my go-between because out of total fear I wanted to be anonymous until the day actually arrived. She would call the commissioner when I wanted to ask questions, and the commissioner would tell her the answer. I had set it up for October 11 of '91 which was National Coming Out Day.

About three weeks before the date, we had a major problem with lay-offs; the state laid off 111 troopers. I had missed getting laid off by thirty people, and more layoffs were possible. I was like, "What's going to happen? I'm going to get laid off; I'm going to be an out lesbian trying to find a job in another police department? No. I don't think so." So I had to cancel my meeting and my coming out. Six months passed and the layoff scare was over. Another meeting was set up for May 1 of '92. Unfortunately, it happened during the LA riots, so it was very quick. Needless to say, I was extremely nervous. I had the only openly gay Connecticut state representative with me and the woman who was my go-between. I felt confident that, "I have witnesses if anything happens." The commissioner and lieutenant colonel weren't surprised that it was me, so I guess the anonymity thing was useless. I was frightened to death and shaking in my boots imagining what a disaster this had the potential to become. The lieutenant colonel let me know that they knew when they hired me that I was a lesbian. I was surprised and said, "I hope I've proven myself to you," and he said, "You have." That was wonderful. However, look at those four years of stress I put upon myself feeling as if I had to hide my orientation, worrying about hiding my girlfriend's car in the garage, and scared to be seen going into a gay bar. As troopers, we have to be accountable twenty-four hours a day. If I was not going to be at my residence, I had to leave a phone number where I was staying overnight in the event of a major incident which might require a department mobilization. The sign-out book was accessible to all employees. I was so nervous that the troopers would find out that it was a woman's house I was staying at, so I would go in to the barracks the next day and white out and scribble over the phone number with as many pens as I could. I was concerned about protecting her identity as well as my privacy. Surprisingly, after I came out nothing ever happened to me. Sure there were troopers that gave me the cold shoulder—people wouldn't look at me, and they wouldn't say hello back—but I can handle that. I've been dealing with that all my life. I never once got a nasty note left in my box—never once got a comment made to my face. I think they knew that if I was brave enough to come out, then I would be brave enough to confront them or follow through on a complaint against them if I felt harassed.

I had told a couple of straight troopers that I was closest with that I was going to come out, and they were like, "Don't do it." They were frightened that I would get fired or black balled. Other gay troopers were also very frightened for me. Out of respect, I stayed away from them. I didn't want "guilt-by-association" to be a factor. I understood my wanting to be out of the closet, but I also understand them wanting to stay in the closet.

Telling my father about my plans to come out was the hardest, but I wanted him to know. He knew that I was a lesbian and ultimately I believe that he was more frightened for himself and his honor than for me. This was his department; this was his life; this was his livelihood. "Oh my God! He's got a dyke for a daughter!" When I told him I was coming out, he said, "I don't know if you can have your family behind you for this." I looked at him and said, "Are you threatening me with the family? How have you ever been behind me before?" I walked out on him. After I came out my parents didn't speak to me for six months. He came to me later and said that it wasn't as bad as he thought it was going to be. Nobody would dare say a word to him—my father's a very respected man; he's a legend in the department. I think he was afraid that people were going to say things to him or think less or him, but as far as I know, no one did.

My troopers came to me one by one because they were either supportive or just plain curious. We'd be working midnights, and one would radio me at three o'clock in the morning under some other pretense. And when we met up, they wanted to know, "What's going on? Why did I do this?" I would talk 'til my throat was dry because they wanted to know all about it, but they didn't want anybody else to see me talking with them. They respected me enough to ask questions directly. On the job, I never hid the fact that I was a lesbian, and I never made up boyfriends. I also had a crew-cut so if they were any type of trained investigator or if they even cared, they had a good idea. There had been whispers about me for years, so it wasn't a shock to them when I came out.

I didn't come out for anybody but myself. Sure, I had hopes and dreams of helping the community which ultimately have not really materialized, but I came out because I was tired of hiding. I was proud of myself, and I didn't want one more roll call with "That homo," and "That fag," comments to go unchallenged. These comments were so commonplace that I almost got used to them.

I had my spies who would come to me and say, "Watch out for this one; this one's saying that or this." They'd be saying things like, "Fucking dyke. What's she think she's doing? She's dishonoring the uniform, and she shouldn't be a trooper." But when I would see them in the hallway, they might not say hi to me, but they would never confront me.

Two years ago, I approached my department asking, "I want to wear my uniform at gay pride in Hartford." I'd seen uniforms in the New York City and Boston prides. The uniform speaks a thousand words in itself. I thought it would send a message to the people that the Connecticut State Police is compassionate, they have an openly lesbian trooper, and they care about serving the gay community. When they denied me the right to wear my uniform, I pitched a bitch because I knew plenty of troopers including myself who have given speeches or participated in various functions in uniform off-duty. When I was in the academy, we marched in a Jamaican/West Indies pride day parade because the department was trying to recruit people of color. So I brought all that up and also said, "I know for a fact that we have Connecticut state troopers who march in full-dress uniform in the Saint Patrick's Day parade in New Haven every year. Why are they allowed to march in that parade?" My superior said, "Because it's a tradition; it's honoring Irish police from back when." I said, "So you're telling me that these troopers can march in uniform honoring a saint that's been dead for a thousand years, but I can't march in a gay pride parade that's got to do with issues and realities that are very alive and well in the '90s?" I had him. The conversation ended very quickly with, "The answer is no. You can't wear it."

Well, I had bought a raid jacket normally worn by plain clothes detectives which I had worn on the job over my uniform one night, and a sergeant said, "You can't wear that. It's not authorized nor issued equipment for road troopers." I went in my drawer, pulled out that raid jacket with a huge "Connecticut State Police" printed on the back, and wore it during the parade. I said, "This is not issued equipment. Therefore, I can wear it marching." I heard through the grapevine that another sergeant tried to initiate an Internal Affairs investigation against me for disobeying orders which was very hush-hush. However, it never materialized. I still wonder who was in the crowd that saw me wearing it.

In 1993 I had an article in a local newspaper about what it's like to be an openly gay police officer. My sergeant wrote me up for it. Obviously, I wrote a rebuttal, but nevertheless, the negative observation report went in my official file. Silly me to think I had a First Amendment right. I called my union, and they backed me 100 percent. I ended up contacting an attorney and the Connecticut Civil Liberties Union, and the CCLU took up the case. Within a short period of time, the observation report got taken out of my file, I received a vague apology, and the administration and operations manual was changed to make the policy in regards to speaking to the press more black and white and not so grey as to be interpreted however one saw fit. Ultimately, two weeks later I was again transferred out of my country troop that I loved so much back to Hartford. Again, I won the battle, but I lost the war. But this is what you've got to do. You've got to keep fighting these battles, because some day you're going to win that damn war. And if *you* don't fight the battles, who's going to fight them? I think it's a safe bet to say that not many police departments are going to be receptive to gay rights issues for their officers unless we educate them. They're not going to hand these things over to you without you asking for it.

My next plans are to get sexual orientation included on the bottom of our application where it says, "We do not discriminate based upon..." I want medical benefits for my partner. When we're off duty we can't have people in our cruiser that aren't immediate family or spouses, and we get our cruisers twenty-four hours a day. It's unmarked except for when we're on duty; then we throw a light rack on it that says, "State Police." But I can't have my significant other in my cruiser, and every other trooper in that situation gets that benefit. So that's my next angle. I want the wording changed to include, "Significant other."

I haven't been doing too much in the last year and a half. The flack about the article and the subsequent transfer knocked the wind out of my sails. I have certainly had my peaks and valleys, with more to come, I'm sure. I come back like a ball of flame, but I usually falter because I don't have anybody else in my department who's out to gather strength from. My saving grace is the Gay Officers Action League, of which I have been a member since 1991.

I'm proud to be an activist. Anybody who marches in gay pride is a hero and an activist in their own way, no matter how loud or verbal they are. I'm just waiting for the day I get arrested at one of these civil disobediences. What's my department going to do about that? Maybe someday I'll feel strong enough to do something like that—not that I would be proud of being arrested, because I'd probably be very humiliated. But it's for a better cause, and I'll make a personal sacrifice for a better cause.

Why can't the world accept me for who I am? Why do you think we have activists? Because you don't give us what we should have based on the Constitution, and unfortunately we need to fight for it. That's why there's activism. If everybody was out and there were no heterosexuals hating homosexuals, there would be no need for gay pride parades and activism on the issue.

The parades, however, are important to remember how far we've come. Heterosexuals should be able to walk down the street holding hands, and so should I. I don't want to worry about getting jumped, being called a name, having objects thrown at me, or having my car vandalized because of it. When I hold hands with my lover in public, I have fear, but I do it. Some day I hope I can do this without a second thought.

I love being a trooper, and I love the road. I love being on patrol and am proud to be in this uniform and wearing that badge. I'm very apprehensive about the thought of being in print again, but know that some things need to be said. I hope someday the CSP realizes that I am a unique asset to their ranks and it allows me to proudly represent the department in an official manner as an open lesbian. I salute all other out law enforcement personnel and encourage those in the closet to follow suit. There is strength in numbers and there's a lot of work to be done.

Frank Buttino

Department: Federal Bureau of Investigation
Age: 49
Rank: Special Agent (Former)
Job: Investigator
Years in Law Enforcement: 20

Frank grew up wanting to change the world. Little did he know he would do just that. After a successful, twenty year career, the FBI fired him for being gay. His class action lawsuit paved the way for lesbian and gay agents to serve in the FBI without fear of dismissal. In his family room overlooking the Pacific Ocean on a rare, drizzly day in San Diego he talked about how one man changed an institution.

I always thought I wanted to be a teacher; I really never thought about law enforcement. In '67 after college, I went back to my home town and taught world history and African and Asian culture in the high school. During the second year I started feeling frustrated. A lot was going on in America at the time—the Democratic convention, the Viet Nam War was really starting to crank up, the assassinations of Martin Luther King and Robert Kennedy—and I felt I was teaching about history when all of this history was going on around me. I wanted to be a part of the history that was going on in America.

The idea of public service was really important to me; John Kennedy talked about doing for your country. I was very idealistic and was thinking in terms of how can I serve the country and have an interesting and exciting job. So in the second year of teaching, I started exploring other possibilities. I'd grown up in a small town, had gone to school twenty-five miles away, and had never really been away from my home town for any period of time. I thought about becoming a police officer or a detective in a major city. I was looking through brochures about law enforcement at the guidance office, and there was something on the FBI; I thought, "That sounds like it would be interesting," so I got the application, and the process began. The FBI had a wonderful reputation as the premiere law enforcement agency in the country. Ever since I was a kid you heard about the FBI, J. Edgar Hoover, and the clean cut, all American men—there were no female agents at the time. They were the elite of law enforcement.

It was a different America then, before Watergate, before the real Viet Nam War flap, and all that. It was a different way of looking at the world. People had more trust, faith, and confidence in the government than they have today, now that we know more about the way the government actually works. A lot of my peers were very idealistic. We went into the Peace Corps and did things that we really believed in. Then the disenchantment and reality set in. But prior to that period of time we had a wonderful optimism about changing the world. Looking back, it was certainly a naive way of looking at the world, but that was the America we grew up in.

I joined the FBI July 28, 1969. One of the fortunate parts of my career was that at different periods of time in our nation's history, different things were of priority to the government and to the FBI, so I was able to work with things that were really in the public eye. In the '70s it was the radical groups, and then after Hoover died there was a real emphasis on organized crime. Drugs became a real problem in this country in the early '80s, so I started working drug cases. Nineteen-eighty-five had been called the year of the spy with the Walker case, the Pollard case, and a number of other cases, so I decided I wanted to work foreign counter intelligence. At that point I had sixteen or so years in the Bureau, I had done a lot of arrests and kicking in doors, and I wanted to do something more challenging intellectually. The last case I worked was the bombing of a van that belonged to the wife of the captain of the USS Vincennes who had shot down the Iranian air bus. That case was never solved. Then I got suspended, and that was it for my career.

The bureau could be very draconian in the way it treats its employees. If you mess up or you do something wrong, even if it's an innocent mistake, they can be very harsh with their employees. That's a legacy of Hoover. Hoover was like a dictator and careers ended for very little reason. He created the bureau to look infallible, like it was always perfect, and like all the agents were perfect. You were always very much aware that your career could end very quickly and capriciously. The bureau was exempt from the Civil Service, and there were no hearing boards or anything like that. If they said you had done something wrong, then they could fire you with very little recourse.

As an FBI agent, they really frowned upon our getting involved in the community. They liked the agents to remain relatively anonymous, and as a result most people don't know FBI agents. Being an FBI agent is like being a closeted gay man in some respects. As agents we lead relatively anonymous, secret lives; you don't tell people that you're an FBI agent, you don't talk about your work, you keep secrets, and you are very discreet about your professional and personal conduct. It was pretty much the same for me as a closeted gay man. I was really living two secret lives, and sometimes three when I was working undercover. Someone once said that gay people are well suited for undercover work because we are chameleons; we blend in wherever we go.

I was very secretive and had a close circle of gay friends. Most of the people I was involved with were closeted also. They were in professions—some worked for the government, some worked as teachers—so they were in a similar situation. In fact, most of my friends were closeted. Some were so closeted that they were afraid to be involved with someone who was an FBI agent. On the other hand, others would be very trusting of me because they knew we all had a lot to lose, so we had this bond of trust that we wouldn't expose each other. Of course, I was never out in the gay community until I actually came out and filed the lawsuit.

As time went on, I developed a relationship with another man, and he was in the Navy. He would go overseas for extended periods of time, and it really bothered me. It was like a part of myself had gone, and I would feel bad about it, lonely, and lost. And you really can't share that with the people you work with; if you meet somebody and you really like him, or you break up with somebody, you can't share that personal side. You always have a mask. I found myself separating myself; I was very friendly and outgoing in the office, but I really kept a barrier between myself and my colleagues so they wouldn't get too close. I kept my relationships with people on a professional level.

Trouble started when my relationship was ending. I placed some ads in gay personals using a pseudonym and responded to a personal ad in a gay publication. I never met the person, I never told him I was an agent, but somehow he found out I was an FBI agent and where my parents lived. He sent my parents and later the FBI anonymous letters saying I was gay, and forwarded a copy of the letter that I'd sent to him. When the letter came to the bureau, they called me in, and I denied writing it knowing full well I'd be fired. About five weeks later, they called me back to Washington. Their first consideration was that I was a spy, and they wanted to know all the details of my homosexual life. This started a series of interviews, signed statements, and polygraphs about whether I'd been compromised. Of course I passed all of those polygraphs, and they realized I hadn't been compromised but they wanted to get into the details of my personal life. They asked point-blank questions about the kind of sex I engaged in. They literally wanted all the details of my homosexual life. They wanted the names of other gays and lesbians in the FBI and the names of my gay and lesbian friends, which, of course, I wouldn't give to them. Eventually they used that against me as a failure to cooperate. They felt I was hiding the identity of the letter writer, and I wasn't telling them all the details of my life. Those kinds of things are pretty personal. Looking back at it now I think they were trying to put enough pressure on me to resign. Later on when we got other FBI files we realized that everyone else at some step in this process resigned voluntarily or were told, "If you don't resign they're going to fire you." I did not resign, so they ended up revoking my top secret clearance and then firing me. They said they weren't firing me because I was gay but because I did not have a top secret clearance.

While this was going on I was still working in the office and being called back to Washington periodically for new polygraphs. I was put in charge of a major investigation, got my twenty year service award, and was promoted. It was very important for me that my work performance not suffer because I was afraid they would not fire me for being gay, but they would use the fact that I wasn't doing a good job as a reason to fire me. So during that period of time I got superior performance ratings and a promotion. I thought I would survive it and they would look the other way 'cause being gay had no impact on my job. But in September of '89 they proposed to revoke my top secret clearance, suspended me from the office with pay, and then did revoke my top secret clearance. I appealed that to the Department of Justice, and when my appeal was denied, I decided to file a lawsuit. Before I could see the judge to have a hearing date, the FBI fired me. From that point on, I was seeking reinstatement. Later on, we changed the lawsuit to a class action suit because other people came forward telling about their experiences.

The American people have a basic fairness about them, and a lot of people didn't think it was fair. Here is a guy who was a good agent, is a good person, did his job, and the FBI made an issue of it. He kept it secret, they found out that he's gay, and they got rid of him. I think people within the bureau and the general population would say that doesn't seem quite fair. I was probably the right person at the right time to fight this for a lot of reasons. If I had been only two or three years in the FBI I don't think I would have been successful. My record was the most important thing that I had going for me because it dispelled the notion that gay people couldn't do the job. We worked on the gay people as blackmail; we made the argument there had never been a case in American history of a gay or lesbian being blackmailed to betray the country. Most of the people that betray the country betray it for money, and often times it's married people with children who have some kind of financial problem. So actually heterosexuals are probably greater security risks than gay people. The thing that we tried to do in the case was make it into a simple job discrimination based on sexual orientation case. I always made the point, "Judge a person by their ability to do their job and not by something that didn't matter." For twenty years they trusted me thinking I was heterosexual. All of a sudden now that I'm gay I can't be trusted? This had no bearing on my performance as an FBI agent. Even after they found out I was gay, it had no affect on my job, and my colleagues didn't have a problem with it.

When we started, it was the Reagan administration, when I filed the suit it was the Bush administration, and we settled in the Clinton administration. They agreed to all of our demands relative to protection of the class, so I decided that I would not insist on reinstatement. That was the deal maker. The settlement was basically that homosexual conduct between consenting adults in private is not an issue for the FBI or the Department of Justice. They will treat homosexual conduct and heterosexual conduct the same. It doesn't automatically raise a security issue of blackmail, it's not a negative factor in hiring, they're not going to ask people, if it comes up, it's not going to be used against people, and they're going to hire an open lesbian in the next class. That's a big accomplishment in a greater sense. I am disappointed about not getting my job back. I really enjoyed being an FBI agent and miss the job, but the reason I didn't insist on reinstatement is that it would have prevented the class action suit from being settled. The government would have appealed it and probably would have delayed all of this for another four or five years.

It's not been an easy experience. In many respects it's been very painful, but I guess nothing that's really worthwhile in life comes without a price. It's going to take me a long time to really recover. I'm glad for the positive parts of what happened and feel very pleased with the accomplishments. But there was a price that I paid for all of this, and I have to live with it. One of the prices that's very painful was to have my personal life become public. I meet total strangers that feel like they know me. All of a sudden you're a public person that you never wanted to be. I can understand now why people don't file lawsuits and don't go public on things. My life will never be the same. In most respects it's better but in some respects I've lost a certain amount of privacy that I'll never reclaim.

The end result was good, though; I'm glad I did it. A lot of people have benefitted from it. I think I'm a better, stronger person for having been through this ordeal. It's made me more compassionate and empathetic toward others. It is causing me to reflect on my own life, put things together, and become more introspective. It's given me an opportunity to change other people's attitudes about gays and lesbians.

It was not pleasant getting fired from my job and all the attendant publicity, but it's much easier for me to live my life now. I can be open about things and not be so guarded with my family, friends, and neighbors. The closet can be an incredibly destructive place to be, although I understand why people don't come out. Often times there is a price to be paid for coming out. Everybody is the best judge of their own situation. I tell people that once they do come out, eventually their lives will never be better because they can be honest about who they are with other people and honest to themselves; they don't have to deny who they are. Being open and honest is a nice way to live your life.

I never found out who the person was who sent the letter; I don't know what his motivation was. The irony is if it was some anti-gay person who wanted to get rid of the gay person from the FBI, they were successful. But in a broader respect, it had the opposite effect because now the FBI is open to gay people. Push came to shove—I got pushed out but I shoved them into accepting gays and lesbians as a part of the bureau. From the point I filed a lawsuit, they have allowed four gay employees, including an agent, to continue working for the first time in the bureau's history. Although I didn't get my job back, a lot of other people have benefitted from it. Gay and lesbian agents and support people no longer have to fear losing their jobs.

It's never really been about me. It's about changing people's attitudes about gay people. There's no doubt in my mind that as the FBI and police departments change and have openly gay people, as all organizations have openly gay and lesbian people, the organization changes. It becomes more sensitive to gay and lesbian issues. As people come out in these organizations or as openly gay people go into these organizations we're going to change our society. We need gays and lesbians in these organizations for that kind of sensitivity. The FBI has changed, and it has a greater sensitivity. That's how we're going to change society—one on one and being a part of these organizations. The FBI will never be the same.

Part Two:
Detention and Incarceration

J ails and prisons are used to *detain* and *incarcerate* prisoners. Jails, managed by deputy sheriffs, house those awaiting adjudication and those convicted of misdemeanors, while prisons are managed by corrections workers and house those convicted of felonies. A wide variety of criminal justice professionals are part of the detention and/or incarceration process. Prisoners must be searched and given clothing, they must be fed and housed, they may need counseling or other rehabilitative services, they must be protected from themselves and others, and their court appearances and legal responsibilities must be managed. Inmates are rarely pleased to be in jail or prison and often take their resentments out on their keepers. While jail and prison atmospheres are more contained than the streets, as you will see, anything can happen, and concerns about officer safety and backup remain paramount.

J. D.

Department: A California Sheriff's Department
Age: 35
Rank: Deputy Sheriff 1 (Former)
Job: Jailer
Years in Law Enforcement: 3 1/2

J. D. came out after watching a Marcus Welby rerun about a lesbian doctor and her partner. Only the fourth African-American woman on the force, she looked forward to a long and successful career in law enforcement until a couple of homophobic incidents brought her career to a halt.

I didn't know what I wanted to be when I was a kid. I had the notion of getting into medicine or possibly being a firefighter; I never thought of law enforcement. I got into law enforcement as the result of having been laid off from a job. I needed a new job really fast so I went to work for Sears in their security department as a plainclothes officer. I was so good at catching shoplifters that sheriff's deputies were constantly encouraging me to get into law enforcement. One officer even pulled out his paycheck and said, "Do you make this much in two months?" I looked at it and went, "No. I don't even make that in six months." So, I applied and was accepted into the sheriff's academy. I was twenty-four or twenty-five.

I knew I was gay when I went into the sheriff's department, but it didn't influence my decision. I surely wasn't going to tell them that I was gay, though. In the academy I didn't have too much time to think about my sexuality. There was quite a large lesbian contingency in the sheriff's department. They were everywhere. I was shocked. They were very closeted, even among other deputies. There were certain phrases that they used that only a lesbian would use, one of which was "Sister." You don't hear straight women call each other sisters, unless they're with African-American people. Or, "Are you going to go to the Suite?" which was a women's bar. No other straight women would ever know that name. That was our way of communicating that, "We are a family." But we kept very much in the closet.

I didn't know any other way to be. I thought my job would be in jeopardy if I came out, although I didn't have any concrete proof of that. At the very least, I thought I would not be promoted, even though I knew one of my sergeants was a lesbian—I had seen her at the bar. She was quite supportive, but she was only one. The county in which we worked was very conservative and Republican. We didn't feel it was appropriate to come out, so we didn't.

The academy was hell in and of itself. Ninety-nine percent of the people going through the academy had taken law enforcement classes before or knew people in law enforcement, so they knew what to expect. I hadn't taken any classes, and I went in blindly. The intimidation factor was disconcerting to say the least. I've never felt so stressed out in all of my life. The first day was real typical. We had orientation and were able to bring significant others. I brought my partner although I let them know she was just my best friend. The tactical sergeants and officers were real nice, they smiled, and things were wonderful as long as family members were around. At one point the potential officers were asked to go to one room and family was asked to go to another. As we were walking into the room you could feel such tension that you wanted to leave. The expressions on the tactical officers changed from smiling to almost hatred. They began to yell at us, "Get in here. Sit down, and shut up. You are nobody. You will be nobody for quite a few weeks, so get used to it." This went on for an hour. We came out of the room and two people immediately dropped.

During our physical training we were ordered to do disciplinary push-ups. One time, we were down on asphalt doing push-ups, and the asphalt was hot. People were beginning to moan and groan. Finally one of the females stood up, tears in her eyes, and the sergeant started to berate her, "Why are you standing up, recruit? What the hell are you doing?" All she did was raise her hands. At least fifteen of us had suffered second- and third-degree burns, but instead of tending to us, they took us out to run the physical training obstacle course. As I started to sprint the last fifty yards, my hands began to throb. I couldn't figure out what the hell was going on. When I finished, I put my hands on my shorts, and when I took my hands off, there was blood on my shorts. Evidently I had blisters on both palms, and they had burst because of digging through the sand in the obstacle course. We ended up going to the hospital, and the majority of us had second- and third-degree burns on our palms. That was typical of what we went through. Eighty-seven started off the first week of academy training, and forty-nine graduated. My partner helped me get through it. I went home and cried every night. I didn't think I could make it. Every night she would tell me, "You can do this." She was very religious, and she prayed for me all the time. I felt like I had something to prove to myself, that I could do it, and then I'd have it made for the rest of my life. I just stuck it out.

After I graduated, I was assigned to the jail system, and I remained there 'til I left the department. I baby-sat female inmates—housed them, fed them, listened to them, and disciplined them. I left because of accusations that I had been carrying on an affair with an inmate. One inmate who I had to discipline quite often decided to create a horrible allegation.

I'd been working jail detail for about six months and was pretty much on my own. During my training period, my training officer continually stated, "In order to get to know the criminal out on the street, you need to get to know them while they're incarcerated. That way you'll be able to track them when you get out on the street." I was not only interested in doing that, I was also very interested in helping people. I made the "mistake" of getting involved with one particular inmate in the jail; she was having a lot of problems, she was really scared about going out onto the street, and she was afraid she was going to start taking drugs again. I was counseling her, and most of the time I counseled her in the hallway in front of a lot of people. Deputies and other inmates could see that all we were doing was talking, but it was misconstrued by her lover that I was trying to come on to this inmate, and she began to make a lot of waves. She began to complain to other deputies, other deputies began to watch me, and rumors started that I was having an affair with this inmate.

The captain called me down to his office, and I explained to him what I was doing. He said, "That's fine. You just need to be aware of these rumors and how it appears. Try to cut off all your contact with the inmate." One day an important tour was going to take place the next day, so we were supposed to take all of the workers and clean up the jail building, from head to toe. I was given a group of workers one of which happened to be the inmate I was to have no contact with. I told my senior officer, "We need to switch." He said, "No. It'll be okay; you're only going to be down there a couple of hours. You don't need to worry about this." So, I took this inmate and five or six others, and we went downstairs and cleaned up. The next day I was called into the captain's office and was told an investigation was being started because obviously I couldn't keep away from this inmate.

It became literally an unbearable situation; I was no longer allowed to go up on the second floor where the majority of people were housed to do any type of detail work. I was contained on the first floor to work with the mentally unstable and health risk inmates. I was stuck down there for three months while the investigation was taking place.

I kept wondering what I had done wrong to warrant the accusation. I couldn't understand it; I still can't. I was a nervous wreck. I lost close to forty pounds in a month. I wasn't eating, I wasn't sleeping, and I wasn't drinking. I shouldn't have been at work; I wouldn't have been of any help if something went down. At one point I had lost so much weight that inmates that were concerned about me were willing to put a contract out on the inmate. Those that knew me knew that this was a bunch of bull. They had their own way of handling this inmate when she got out on the streets. I remember inmates saying, "I get out in one week. I'll be waiting for her when she gets out." I don't know what happened to her. I didn't want to know. They were asking other deputies, "Is she slamming?" In other words, "Is she using drugs?" I had lost so much weight I looked like a skeleton.

During my accusation period, every lesbian there backed away from me—guilt-by-association. The people that supported me were straight. When my supporters wanted to talk to me, they would pass me and say, "Meet me in five minutes." They would not talk to me in public. They were afraid of the senior deputies. A few of the senior deputies that were very powerful were trying to alienate me from the rest of my colleagues. My friends felt like, "We'll meet you off to the side and tell you that we're rooting for you."

I have a feeling that one particular lesbian officer was behind this smear campaign. I wouldn't be a bit surprised if she dropped a dime to the captain and said I was gay. If I had been heterosexual, I don't even think there would have been an investigation. I feel as though I was outed to the captain, and the captain said, "If she's a lesbian then it's really quite possible that she does have some affectional feelings for this inmate, and maybe we should investigate."

The majority of the newer officers were all on my side. Even a lot of the inmates were outraged at what was going on. The deputies that had been in the jail system for five or six or seven years were all against me. Part of it was because I came in as the darling officer. After my first eval, my sergeants thought they were about to see me as the first African-American female captain. They really had high hopes. I could handle myself very well, I was very professional in carrying out my responsibilities and duties, and I was very good. I have a feeling there was some jealousy, as much as I hate to say that.

Then, on New Year's Eve, I was taking care of an inmate that we knew was violent. We were supposed to have two or three of us take her out of her cell, walk her to a shower area where she was to take a shower, then walk her back to her jail cell, and lock her up. I called to have someone come down and help me with her. Two deputies showed up; I was behind the inmate, and the two deputies were behind me. The woman started to walk toward the shower area very slowly and deliberately; then without warning, she turned around and the next thing I knew, I was up against the wall. Knowing that I had two deputies behind me, I expected some help but they were gone. I was pinned up against the wall. She was choking the hell out of me, she kept banging me up against the wall, and all I could do was to feel around on the wall because I knew that there had to be a panic button. When you hit the panic button, it rang in the main system control area. I could hear over the intercom, "Nine, nine, nine; deputy down; first floor." That means it's an emergency; all available people head toward the given location. I could hear the pitter-patter of feet running down the hall. They were able to grab the woman off me but it took five or six deputies to do it; she was incredibly strong. My sergeant said, "What happened? Where was your backup?" All I could do was say, "I don't know." The next day, I resigned. I left feeling as though it was my fault. There was a lot of shame and a lot of guilt. It was probably the worst time in my life. I just did not understand what was going on. What had I done that was so awful? I really began to take a second look at the career. I began to doubt everything that I thought the profession was.

There was an investigation which was going very well in my favor, but it was never completed because I quit. It's sitting there in limbo, so there's always the question. If you go back and talk to the investigators, they will tell you, "We don't have anything on her to warrant any type of disciplinary action up to and including termination. What we have is a stupid deputy who was trying to be too kind." But the question will always be, "Then why did you quit?"

I had been given a union-appointed representative to help fight this case, and he thought I was not even going to be reprimanded. He thought they would find that there was no foundation for the allegation. He wanted me to fight; he wanted me to sue the county. He said, "This is the only way we're going to be able to fight homophobia; hit them in the pocketbook." But I was just too hurt. I was the darling one moment and hated the next. I was not willing to do that.

It got to the point that although I had the backing of half of my coworkers, the other half were so antagonistic that I felt, "These are the officers that will hit the streets before I will. They'll be the ones that will have to be my backup." And I didn't trust them. If I could not trust them to support me in the jail, I couldn't trust them out in the field. I decided I couldn't stick it out. I had sergeants that wanted me to hang in there; they said they could transfer me to another division if need be. My representative told me to hang in there, but I knew these officers would not forget, and I'd have to face them out on the street one day. It was too dangerous to do that. I realized that I didn't need that in my life. I didn't care how much money I was going to make; it was time to get out. If that hadn't occurred I'd probably still be there.

Law enforcement is a great career for gays and lesbians if they can handle coming out. In time, agencies will come to accept gays and lesbians in law enforcement. It's hard, though; you have got to be willing to take some risks. You've got to be willing to get slapped around.

I think it's necessary in every profession that gays and lesbians come out. We have to. As long as we remain in the closet, the straight community thinks we don't exist. But we're their next door neighbors, we're their best friends, we're their teachers, we're their sons and daughters, we're their sergeants and captains, we're their deputies, and we're their police officers. We're the ones that protect them, and they need to know that.

Ken

Department: San Francisco (CA) Sheriff's Department
Age: 40
Rank: Deputy Sheriff
Job: Classification
Years in Law Enforcement: 10

A sturdy man with salt and pepper hair, Ken has seen a lot of changes in the atmosphere of the SFSD for gay and lesbian deputies. Wearing a 1993 San Francisco Pride t-shirt and dark grey jeans, he spent an afternoon in a Castro apartment recounting his experiences.

E ver since I can remember, I wanted to go into law enforcement. My father was a fireman, and I liked the idea of being a cop, of helping people, protecting people, and taking care of people. Growing up, I always tried to help people; if I saw someone being picked on in school, I would come to their rescue. That was always my thing in life. I hated sports—I was real uncoordinated. I hated hunting, because I couldn't see killing something. I liked to sew and play with dolls when I was real little, I liked cooking and cleaning house; and I also wanted to be a cop.

I realized when I was ten that I was different. At school, people said, "faggot" or "sissy," because I didn't act the same as they did. I came from a Pentecostal background, and I was afraid of what I was feeling. I repressed everything. From ten until twenty-four, I went through life praying every night that God would change me and make me normal, or kill me. Finally, I woke up one morning and said, "He hasn't changed me, he hasn't killed me—I must be normal."

I came from a rather abusive family, not physically, but mentally. I went through life hearing my mother tell me she wished she'd never had me. I kept trying to buy her love, and finally when it didn't work, I said, "That's it—I'm out of here." I was anxious to get out of my house, so after high school I joined the Army.

After six years in the Army, and at the age of twenty-four, I met a man and had my first sexual experience. I decided it was time to get out of the Army. I went back and told them I was gay and wanted out. When I first told them, they said, "What are we going to do? You're going to have a lot of problems when word gets out." I said, "Not as many as you will. I'm a sergeant. I'm in charge of all these people. Who's going to want to work for me if you let them know I'm gay?" He said, "Oh, yeah. We'll keep it quiet."

It took about three months, but I got an honorable discharge. When my discharge finally came, the first-sergeant came in, held out his hand, and said, "Congratulations. A promotion came in, and your discharge came in. If you change your mind, we'll give you a promotion and tear up everything about you being gay. You proved to us that homosexuals aren't what we thought they were." I said, "No. I want out." In the military, they were very selective in their witch hunts. If they liked you, it was fine; they'd let you stay in right up until time to reenlist for retirement. There were a lot of gay people in the military— I didn't associate with them but everyone knew they were gay, and that was '71 to '77.

After the military, I was a bartender for awhile until they started hiring in the sheriff's department. I was in the sheriff's department about eight months before going to the academy. While I was at the academy, I sat there for two weeks hearing derogatory things about Blacks and about San Francisco. I finally stood up and said, "I happen to be one of those faggots from San Francisco, and I'm tired of this." All the people sitting around me wanted to move, and I said, "You don't have any problem. I like real men, not boys." The instructors were the ones telling the jokes, but when my fellow cadets found out I was gay it was like, "Oh, my God. We don't want to be around him." But by the end of the class, we had a big party, they all had their arms around me, and we had a great time. Later, my training officer told me, "While you were in the academy, I got calls from the people in charge saying you had really opened their eyes about gays."

When I first started working, I started to go back into the felony wing, and one straight, Black deputy told me, "I have to warn you that when you go back there, they're going to say everything they can to get to you. If you have a comeback, good. If you don't, keep walking, because if they know it upsets you, they'll keep on." So I walked in, and one of them said, "Hey, faggot. Come over here and suck on this German helmet." I said, "If you don't have twelve inches, don't waste my time. I like men, not boys." I made everyone laugh. Immediately, word went around that a gay officer was here, but you couldn't upset him.

One time, we had eighty inmates in the hallway outside of my office. They kept crowding around my door, I kept telling them to move, and finally I got up and physically moved them. I started back in my office, and this one Latino kid says, "You fucking faggot." I turned around, picked him up by the shirt, held him up against the wall, and said, "This faggot could break you with one hand if he wanted to." I dropped him, turned around, and walked back in the office. For three months after that it was, "Yes, sir, yes, sir, how are you, sir?" You have to let them know that, "Yeah, I'm gay. Calling me a faggot doesn't mean anything to me. I've heard it all my life. Call me faggot. Call me queer. I don't care." Then it's all right.

I had a lot of positive experiences when I was first with the department. Other gay deputies had problems, but I didn't. We had a gay officer that blew his brains out when he found out he had AIDS and was sick. It was really rough in the beginning, because we didn't know anything about AIDS. We had another deputy that had AIDS and worked on the sixth floor of the Hall of Justice. When people found out, they would get up and walk out of the lunchroom when he came in, or they would pick up the phones, wipe them down with alcohol, and put gloves on whenever they were around him. They just really made him feel like shit. They wrote a petition to not have to work with him. I worked on the seventh floor and talked about it to everyone I worked with. When the petition came upstairs for people to sign, they tore up the copies and threw them away. I wrote a rebuttal saying all of us weren't that ignorant. Within a half an hour after I'd written the rebuttal, thirty-five people I worked with—all of them heterosexual—signed it.

Shortly after that, I found out my lover had AIDS. That was in '83, and he was sick for five years. He was infected when I met him, but we didn't know it at the time. We didn't use condoms or anything, but, knock on wood, I'm still negative. My co-workers were very supportive; I never had a problem. If something happened, they let me go immediately to take care of things. The day he was diagnosed with pneumocystis, he called me at work and said, "We have to talk.

I'm dying." I walked up to the lieutenant, he could see it on my face, and he said, "Go. I don't know what it is, but go." Those people were very supportive. That was a different generation ago. My lover died in '88, the day of our eighth anniversary.

A year after he died, I became very bitter. I had a lot of anger I couldn't deal with, so I left the department for two years. I was bitter at the world. I became a hermit in the deserts of West Texas until I could deal with everything. Then I came back; I've been back four years, and I've had more trouble this time. The atmosphere has changed; there's a lot of reverse racism and homophobia in our department now, but things are better in terms of AIDS awareness.

I don't worry about getting AIDS. I think there are people that are predisposed to illnesses, and I don't think I'm predisposed. Maybe I will get it; maybe I will convert. I don't think I will. It's not that I'm not safe, but I have no fear of the disease at all. At the time my first lover was going through his bouts in the hospital, I'd go to visit him after work, and they'd say, "You can't go in without a mask." It was like, "I've been with him for six years. You're not going to tell me to put a mask on now." Or I'd be walking down the hall and another AIDS patient would have fallen, wet himself, and be calling for a nurse. I'd pick him up, and the nurse would say, "You can't do that without gloves." And it's like, "What am I supposed to do—say, 'Wait, I'll go find some gloves?' The guy is laying there suffering."

I've done things that my coworkers wouldn't do—they thought I was nuts when we had an inmate who had slit his wrists. He had arterial bleeding that was hitting the ceiling, and I put my bare hand over it and applied direct pressure. They said, "You're nuts. You should have put gloves on." I said, "He would have bled out." They said, "So?" I said, "I've been around AIDS a long time. Once I get him treated, all I've got to do is wash my hands, and I'm fine." When he got to the hospital, they said he would have bled out had I not applied direct pressure.

To me it's a continual education of the people I work with. I've had new deputies that I would be training, and they'd say, "I like working everywhere except down there with the homosexuals." At the time, they didn't know I was gay. And I would say, "You should be very careful what you say about working with people, because you don't know who you're talking to." "Why? You're not one." I said, "Oh, yes, I am." Then, within a week or two it's like, "You guys aren't bad at all." It's a challenge to continually educate people, and hopefully I've changed a few people's views.

Most of the gays in our department are very much overachievers. I really don't know why that is. I only know of one gay deputy out of fifty or sixty in my ten years in our department who really wasn't very diligent. I don't know if it's to prove we can do the job not only as good but better. We *can* do it better. The gay people I've encountered, with the exception of one, are not lazy; they look for things to do to stay busy. Even when I was in the military, the gay people were overachievers and always got awards. Maybe it's because we have pride in ourselves.

My present lover is HIV-positive. I had to come to terms with that when I started to go out again. There was a three year period after my lover died that I didn't go out or do anything. When I decided I was going to date again, I went and got tested, and I was negative. I've been tested regularly since. I had to decide, "Am I going to cheat myself or someone else out of love because I'm afraid of an illness?" I had to come to terms with whether or not I could deal with going through it again. I decided it wouldn't be fair to myself or a potential lover to not take that chance. I try not to think about it, though. So far, he's healthy; I put the fear in the back of my mind.

In my free time, I usually go to the Castro and have a beer or two. I don't pack off duty, because if I'm drinking, I don't want a gun. If I have to shoot someone and there's alcohol in my system, how am I going to justify that? I see people I know in the street all the time; my friends are amazed by it. We'll be walking, and someone will come up and shake my hand. My friends will say, "You don't have a gun. Doesn't that worry you?" "No. I don't abuse people." I don't know if it's because I went through a life of abuse, but I don't abuse people; I treat everyone as equal as I can. I'm not there as a judge or a jury, and I'm not there to punish them. That's not my job. I try to treat everyone like a human being and the way I would like to be treated. If they respect me, I respect them, and I will do what I can to help them. My job is to keep them safe and to make sure they do their time in a safe environment.

I recommend law enforcement to anyone that has the desire. You should never hide what you are. Some people probably would find it very difficult— lesbians seem to be more accepted than very effeminate males. I love what I'm doing. I plan on being there until I die.

Danita Reagan

Department: San Francisco (CA) Sheriff's Department
Age: 37
Rank: Deputy Sheriff
Job: Dorm Supervisor
Years in Law Enforcement: 8

A sensitive and articulate woman, Danita works "both sides of the desk:" she works full time as a deputy sheriff and is in her second year of law school. Dressed in a black polo shirt and black jeans on a sunny, fall day in the Castro, she talked about her experiences working in the jails of San Francisco.

I think I was born a dyke. When I was very young, I got to dress in blue jeans, tank tops, and black, high-top, PF Fliers. I never did the things my sisters did; I was always out running around with the boys. I remember going to people's houses and hearing, "You have five girls, no boys?" and having one of my parents say, "We don't need any boys. We have Dani." So you tell me, did they dress me in jeans because they knew I didn't have any interest in dresses or did they want to socialize one of their daughters to be able to take out the trash?

The first time I remember thinking about law enforcement I was fifteen or sixteen. We had a problem with some biker guys harassing one of my sister's boyfriends. I was driving, and one of them threw a bottle at my car. I told my mother, and she, of course, called the police. The police came to the house, showed me all the pictures of the people that were in the gang, and asked me to identify the guy. Jokingly, the cop said I should be a cop.

I was going to be a psychologist when I grew up, but I got tired of being a poor college student, so I started working in a gas station. I got to wear a uniform, and that was kind of fun. Then I got caught up in the work industry and did a bunch of non-traditional jobs for women like construction. Through my girlfriend, I met one of the cops in Palo Alto, and she started talking to me about being a cop. I thought, "Maybe I ought to try this," so I started applying. In law enforcement, you don't just go to an interview and get hired. There's this traumatic, dramatic series of intrusive procedures you have to go through. I applied to a lot of different departments, and I finally was hired by the San Francisco Sheriff's Department.

Knowing I was a lesbian created no concerns for me going into law enforcement. It just felt like I wouldn't have to worry about what to wear, I could have my hair short, I could do things I'd be interested in doing, and I could wear pants. It seemed to fit with my personality and how I liked doing things. I would have joined the military, but I would not lie about being queer. If someone's going to hire me, especially in a job where you're going to be out there in public, they're going to hire me for who I am and what I stand for. That has to be okay, 'cause if it's not then I don't want the job.

The academy was very intrusive. I went to the San Francisco Police Department Academy, and I placed first in my class; I was thirty years old at the time. There were men in there who were twenty one years old, and they would piss me off because they were so full of themselves. My classmate, David, was in all the newspapers as being the first gay man known to have AIDS in a police academy. We had all kinds of physical things we had to do as well as the book-work, and he and I ended up being partners. I remember we were standing alphabetically, and he was two lines away from me. They said, "We're going to do this exercise. Pick a partner." It was like this slow motion type activity where I saw everyone in the room moving as far away from David as they could. As everyone was moving away, I was moving towards him since he and I were the only two queers in the class. It was horrible. When he died, I spoke at his funeral about how we got through the academy together. The academy was a wonderful experience and a horrible experience all at the same time.

One of the people in the class said something once about David being gay, and I turned to him and said, "You never can tell who you're going to be working with on any particular shift. It just might turn out some day that the only people on your shift are going to be gay. There's going to be a time when a lot of shit's going to come down, and some queer might be the one to save your fucking ass. You need to think about that." To this day, though, he and I are practically best friends. One time he said, "I always remember what you said to me. You know what? You're right."

I was out in the academy. I look like a dyke; I would talk about it if it became apparent, but my agenda was not queer consciousness raising. My agenda was to get through the academy. I had a pretty good rapport with everybody and was never picked on or discriminated against. I think they might have been afraid to, 'cause everybody was watching because of David's being in the news. But also I think a lot of it had to do with how I carried myself.

After the academy I went to County Jail One, an intake facility. It's the melting pot, as we call it. Everyone who's arrested in San Francisco goes there for booking. It's also a holding area for people waiting for arraignment. You see people at their worst—you see cops at their worst, and you see the public at their worst. We took care of everything people needed in order to be legally booked and held for arraignment.

People come in to the jail under the influence of every kind of substance imaginable and are very scary. We have to search people, 'cause you need to make sure they don't have drugs or weapons on them. Doing strip searches is very intrusive. If people are in there for a felony arrest, you have them remove all their clothing, and you do a visual check. You never touch anyone. It's a hard thing to do. You do fifteen to twenty of those a night, then you go home to your girlfriend, and she says, "Hi, honey, I missed you, let's make love," and you want to run to the other side of the room because you've had enough. It was a really hard thing to get to the point where you could separate it or get rid of all the negative things it brought up for you, 'cause it wasn't pretty. It's a very professional, hard part of your job. They're cursing you out saying, "You god damn bull dyke; all you want to do is see me naked," and you're thinking, "I hope I can hold my breath long enough so I don't have to smell this woman who's been living on the street for three weeks." It's horrific.

I worked there for close to two years. Then I worked in the classification division where we were responsible for the housing of inmates and making sure predatory-type people were not housed with people who were in jail for the first time for something very minor. We also had a gay men's dormitory. I would go through these questions, "Do you have any enemies? Do you have this? Do you have that? Are you gay?" You'd ask them to everybody. And if they would even hesitate, I'd explain, "We have this tank where we house the gay men, unless they're very predatory, because we don't want people in our custody injured." They'd say, "Yeah, I'm gay, but nobody knows." I'd say, "Nobody's going to know on the outside that you're in here. This is for your protection."

My attitude is a lot different than a lot of people I know. I do not feel it is my job to punish people; the penal code says being incarcerated is the punishment. I don't go in there with an attitude like I have to be the bitch from hell. I go in there with a very positive attitude and as a role model. I go in there being someone they can talk to, and I have no doubt in my mind that they can do everything I ask them to do. I have reasonable expectations that are not hard to follow, and they do. I have a good sense of humor. I'm real with people; I don't put on a persona with my uniform. I am Deputy Reagan in a uniform and out. I'm the same person.

I think I have my job because I am a lesbian. Several years ago, the sheriff went out into the gay community and started recruiting people. I applied as a lesbian, and at every stage of the process, I said I was a lesbian. I think it was his intention to make sure the community of San Francisco was represented. He wanted to make sure he hired gays and lesbians, as well as African-Americans, Filipinos, Samoans, Chinese, Japanese, and you name it.

I work with so many other gay and lesbian officers, I haven't had to worry about not getting backed up. I have a great shift. If something like that were to rear its head, the sheriff would come down on people so fast their heads would spin. I don't think it would be tolerated. The philosophies come from the top. If you're the person in charge and you don't want things like that to happen, you say, "These things will not happen."

A big stress for gay cops is this overachiever thing that happens. We are very tuned in to how we think the straights see us; we want them to see us as very competent and effective, if not even superior, in our work. God forbid you should be average. But the thing is, most of the people I know who are gays and lesbians do really well in the department. I don't know if it's because they push themselves or just that we're dynamically superior.

Some of the real old timers would probably balk more at me being a woman than a dyke, and they would probably have more of a problem working with some of the gay men than with a lesbian. But being a lesbian has come in handy, since San Francisco has a very large gay population. Gay and lesbian people get arrested all the time, especially when there are mass arrests for demonstrations like ACT UP. Practically every person arrested is queer and people still have this assumption that "cop or deputy" equals "straight, White male." So when they come in and see a bunch of gay guys and me hanging out ready to book them, fingerprint them, house them, or bring them blankets, they think, "Oh yeah, this is San Francisco." It makes a difference.

In the women's dorms, obviously, the women know I'm a dyke. Most of the women that have been in and out of jail have at one time or another had a jail-house romance with another woman. It's part of the power struggle that goes on, and we try to keep that to a minimum. One of the things they might use is flirtation to see if they can get me to bite. That always amuses me. They're very provocative in their manner and in the way they speak, saying things that are right on the line. They know that I know exactly what they're doing. They're trying to use the fact that I like women so they can get some special treatment.

There're jail lesbians and then there're lesbians who are lesbians on the out-side. Some of the women will have a woman while they're inside, and then once they get out, they go back with their man. The women who consider themselves lesbians outside of jail will expect somehow that I know how it is and that I should cut them some slack because the world's hard and they're being discriminated against because they're lesbian. There were these two women in one dorm who were trying to get this little jail house romance going, and we had to split them up and put one in one dorm and one in the other. They were mad because we wouldn't let them go out to a program at the same time, because they couldn't seem to manage to behave appropriately. They thought I should know how it was. I said, "Yeah, I know how it is to behave appropriately. The problem is you don't." That's not exactly what they wanted to hear.

Early on it was hard because people in the community thought I was selling out to the patriarchy; I was now a daughter of the patriarchy. As far as the les-bian community was concerned, I had nothing in common with them. They weren't interested in me; I was an aberration. And then we started marching in the gay pride day parade and walking down Market Street in uniform with hundreds of thousands of people cheering for us; then it makes you think, "Yeah, it is okay. They do accept me."

I still think there's a dichotomy; every time there's a humongous demon-stration and I have to be out there helping to arrest people, search them, and put them on the busses, all people think is, "How could we do that? How could queers do that?" But if we weren't doing it, who would be? Somebody a lot ugli-er, I think. Somebody who would probably beat a man to death in order to get a piece of crack out of his hand. Somebody's got to do it, and I think I'm a much better person for the job.

When I'm going out on a date, I always think of what would happen "if." What would happen if I went to one of the sex clubs, and they got raided. How would that look? Or, I could have ten people see me in that sex club that I know because I booked them in at jail or I've been their dorm deputy. How would that look? If I was anybody else, I could go and do whatever I wanted. There are horror stories of cops getting involved with someone and finding out later that they've been dealing drugs. You want to be really careful, and even when you're really careful, terrible things can happen that effect your credibility.

Working in law enforcement can be very hard on your psyche. Like I said, you see people at their worst, and it can effect how you look at life. Sometimes some very sad things happen with women in jail. In order to cope, you have to put up a wall or a barrier. You have to protect yourself because you have to go back in there the next day. When you come out of that environment, you don't just snap and say, "I'm all better now. I can be a real person." Sometimes you flow back into being yourself and being able to communicate with people, and sometimes whatever has happened really pushed some of your own buttons so you don't want anybody else close to you.

Who knows what the future holds? I saw a picture of all the sheriffs from California, and it was a bunch of White guys. I looked at that, and I said, "There's something wrong with this picture." I knew none of them were gay. Our sheriff stands out because I know him; it was the only kind face in that big White picture. And, he's the only attorney out of that whole group. It may be his legal education that makes him progressive, intelligent, informed, and humanitarian. Maybe the same type of education might do something for me—not necessarily make me sheriff, but make me a benefit to the department in some type of supervisory position.

I want to do things in my life so I'm not living on the dark side, and so I don't think that all life is dark. Law school reminds me of the other elements of our world, that there are people who can function in our world, and function very well. Law school is a balance in my life to keep me from tilting. You have to have something other than crime and jail in your life; otherwise, that's all you'll see.

Being a deputy is a good job, it's a good career, and you can stay in for twenty years, get all your benefits, and retire. I really encourage gays and lesbians to get involved in law enforcement. Being a cop is a way to be involved. You can do a lot in law enforcement. If you can effect one person's life while they're incarcerated and have them have a positive experience instead of something that is totally devastating, then you've done your job. If each of us in our lifetime did that, this world would be a very different place.

R. P.

Department: Bottineau County and Cass County (ND)
Sheriff's Departments
Age: 39
Rank: Sergeant
Job: Correctional Officer Supervisor
Years in Law Enforcement: 10

Growing up gay in rural North Dakota was a tough start for R. P. One morning before the start of a weekend fishing trip, she relaxed in her living room and talked about finding her niche as a deputy sheriff.

From my earliest memories I wanted to be a police officer or a mailman; I loved uniforms. I remember being really small, being underneath my highchair, and pretending I was driving a car and being a police officer. I must've been three or four years old. When I was a teenager in Minot, my grandmother had a good friend who was a deputy sheriff. She was a woman, and I'd never really known that women could be police officers—they were supposed to be nurses, secretaries, or teachers. I thought, "If she can do it, I can do it, too."

In 1979, I got an opportunity to work in the Bottineau Sheriff's Office as a dispatcher and jailer. I took the job, and six months later I applied as deputy sheriff. In Bottineau we had the sheriff, the chief deputy, five deputies working the city of Bottineau itself, and three deputies out in the county. That's a lot of ground for eight deputies—Bottineau's a big county. We'd have one person work the city of Bottineau on nightshift, and backup was at least ten minutes away 'cause the person had to get dressed and get out there. I know from personal experience that even a minute is too late.

Nobody on the department knew I was gay, but they'd be really stupid if they didn't have any suspicions. I lived by myself, was getting into my thirties, didn't have any boyfriends, never dated, didn't wear make-up, and wasn't exactly the girly-girl kind of person. They knew most of my friends were women. The one male friend I had was gay, so they had to be pretty dense not to know it.

They'd make fun of gay people, "They don't have any right to teach school, they shouldn't be in the military, and, heaven forbid, they shouldn't be in law enforcement." I'd get into some pretty good battles because I'd defend. I didn't care what they thought. Besides, what were they going to do? They weren't going to come and egg my house. It was just total prejudice, bias, ignorance, and derogatory name-calling. It would incite me. I felt absolutely out of place.

When I first started, I had to prove myself. I was the first one out of the car, I was the first one to somebody's door, and I was the first one inside of a building. I wanted to let them know I wasn't afraid, they could count on me for backup, and I was a solid officer. I was the only woman deputy on the road; in fact I was the first woman, and there haven't been any since. I got one comment from a deputy—a total bozo—who said something about, "I'll get out of the car if you give me a kiss." I shut him down, "If you ever say anything like that to me again, your ass is going to be out of here." He must've believed me, 'cause it never came up again.

Towards the end of my time in Bottineau, I was more visible as a lesbian. I don't know if that had anything to do with my not getting backup one night when I needed it. I was the only one working—after two o'clock in Bottineau, you're the only one out. There were two guys: one was a guy we'd had trouble with forever, and the other had threatened me—I'd picked him up for DUI and different stuff, and he said the next time I stopped him he was going to shoot me. About two months before that, a good friend of theirs pulled a gun on a deputy at two o'clock in the morning. I had just gotten off duty and was over at another deputy's house, and we were listening to his scanner. We were no more than forty-five seconds away from where he stopped him. The guy pointed a gun at the deputy, but the deputy got it away. They were fighting, and the deputy drew his gun, shot, and killed him. By the time I got there under a minute later, it was all over. These two guys blamed us for it. They figured it was a set-up, that we'd lured him out there to kill him.

So there I was one night about three o'clock in the morning, I stopped a vehicle, and who was it but these two guys. I asked for backup and nobody came. In fact, a woman who was looking out her window called the sheriff's office and said, "You have a deputy out there who's in trouble and needs some help." Fortunately, though, I thought, "Discretion is the better part of valor," and rather than see somebody else get hurt or killed—especially myself—I backed off. I got back in my car and drove away. I still have a lot of shame about that, 'cause you're not supposed to do that. You're not supposed to let them go. It's hard for me to talk about.

I'd already given my resignation, so it didn't have anything to do with my quitting law enforcement. I figured that, after six years of being out on the road and dealing with people like those guys, that was the first time I'd really been frightened for myself. I'd had scary situations before but not like that. I felt somebody was going to get hurt that night, and I didn't want it to be me. Nine bucks an hour wasn't worth it. In the long run, retreating lets you do more and better law enforcement over a long period of time, rather than being dead out of hatred.

I got out of law enforcement for five years and then got back into it. I'm working in the Cass County Jail now. I don't want to be out on the road again. The road is boring, mostly. You're either really bored or adrenaline-filled; there's no happy medium. You're just waiting for the next call to come through and it's anxiety. Six years of dealing with drunks and domestics is plenty for me. It's hard working to put them behind bars and having some lawyer plea bargain them down. I'd rather have them behind bars.

At first, it wasn't hard to be closeted. I was too excited with my new job, making a place for me in the department, working a lot, and learning as much as I could. But after a while it got to be difficult, especially when I started seeing someone. People who know about me now are lesbian themselves or else are very open. I do get into a few fights with the guys when they call the guys, "faggots." We go around and around about that, but for the most part, it's been alright.

If somebody at work came up and asked me point blank if I'm gay, I'd say, "Yeah." I'm not afraid of it anymore. If they want to fire me for it, go ahead. I'm too old and too tired to care anymore. It would be very unlikely that I'd lose my job if I came out, but anything's possible. The majority of people at work don't know, but my partner comes down to the jail with my lunch, and I talk about her and her boys as my family. I'm very open about that. Nobody's ever said anything. For the most part, people would not care if they knew about me. It would be commented on for a little while, but then it'd be forgotten, because I don't think it matters that much to them.

I don't have any fears for safety or backup in here. Everybody is gung-ho; most of the officers in corrections want to get out in the road, so they want all the action they can get. We can book in twenty-three people and have to wrestle with all of them one night, and they're going to call it a good night. I'm going to call it the night from hell. If they hated an officer's guts, they'd still go in and help that officer, because they like the excitement.

We get called all kinds of names by the inmates because they're angry and drunk, and they don't want to be where they are. They look at us as having power and them as having none. Sometimes you run across somebody who doesn't like women, and in here, woman have the power to lock them up. They act out in strange ways. We get called a lot of names, particularly if you look like a dyke, and I look like a dyke.

I'm going to stay in law enforcement as far as I can see into the future. I love it. It's a great career. The pay sucks, the hours suck, but it gets into your blood, and you can't get out of it. It makes me feel good about myself. I'd recommend that to anybody.

James M. Leahey

Department: Massachusetts Department of Corrections–Concord
Age: 32
Rank: Correction Officer
Job: Head Cook, Food Service
Years in Law Enforcement: 5

A powerfully built man with an unassuming manner, Jim was on medical leave from his job as a correction officer due to harassment. Sitting at his dining room table surrounded by newspaper clipping accounts of his case, he recounted the incidents that led him to leave law enforcement.

I was in the Navy from 1980 through 1989. Nobody in the service ever knew about me being gay. I got out because my father was dying of Lou Gehrig's, and I wanted to be around the house. I was unemployed, and my father suggested I try out the prisons. I started checking out all the institutions, was accepted, and was hired in June of '90. I went through the academy and was given the highest physical training scores award. The day of graduation, we went to the hospital to visit my father, and he died that evening. I took bereavement the first week, and then I returned to my job at MCI–Bridgewater. I put in a hardship transfer to get closer to home so I could be near my mother. I transferred to MCI–Concord in February of '91. I worked in the kitchen—food service. It was my trade in the military. I was a kitchen guard.

I had always wanted an earring. I had seen people at work wearing them, and these guys were married. I thought, "I want an earring," so I went and got one. I went to work, and the next thing you know I was picked on. A lieutenant started really picking on me about it. He would say, "Jimmy must be gay because he's got an earring." So I would turn around and say, "Why don't you say that to the lieutenant over there who's got two of them." They'd say, "He's married." Big deal. I saw a lot of officers with them, so I didn't think anything of it. Then the food service director told me to leave it at home and not wear it. I asked a couple officers, "Can the food service director tell me to leave this at home?" And they said, "No." So I told him, "You can't tell me to take it out of my ear. It's not in the rule book so I can wear it." He turned around and said, "I don't care what you do in private, being a fag or whatever, but you're going to leave it at home."

I met some people at an AA meeting, and someone asked me to go to pride day. I wanted to go so I used a personal day. I was really scared. When I got there I met two lesbians from MCI–Shirley who said, "They can't do anything to us. They can't fire us." So we grabbed a banner and walked. The next day it was all over the place that I was gay and at the march. They said, "You never take a day off. You must have been at the fag parade." I said, "I was with my family. What are you talking about?" I covered it up, but they didn't believe me.

I would go to the gym before work, and when I got to work I took vitamins with my lunch. They'd call them "homo pills." They started joking around, and next thing you know, this officer was telling the inmates to whip their dicks out at me; they took their penises out underneath their aprons. It was a big joke in the kitchen. I was humiliated. I'd be walking around the kitchen and the officer would say to an inmate, "Show him." He'd lift his apron, and there it was sticking out. I documented everything they did, and after a certain point I went to my food service director and told him, "I have no respect from these guys." I couldn't even do a pat search when they left the kitchen to make sure they weren't stealing anything. The food service director accused me of grabbing them in places I shouldn't. The inmates were afraid of me touching them. They would make jokes, "You ain't touching me," or, "You can touch *me*." I just hated it. So I told the guy that was there with me, "You do it. I'm not doing it." Or else I'd just let them go. I wouldn't touch them. I didn't want to be accused.

There were other things that happened. They locked me in rooms and inmates did things to me which are still difficult to talk about. Someone attached a picture of a woman's body with my face on it to my time card. The day of the election with Ross Perot and Clinton running for president, I came into work and this lieutenant made some jokes about, "Perot doesn't like you fags anyway." When he said that, he grabbed my ass and my balls. Everybody in the office started laughing. They thought it was a big joke. I said, "If you ever touch me there again I'm going to kill you." He tapped my ass and said, "I know you were in San Francisco when you were gone on vacation. I hope you took care of that ass for me, that you didn't do anything bad." Then we were in the chow line serving the inmates, and he walked by me and grabbed my ass again in front of all the inmates. That's when things started getting out of hand.

I had a phone call from a guy I was dating. We had a P.A. system in the kitchen that went into the dining rooms, and I was watching over some of the inmates cleaning up. A guy got on the P.A. system and said (in a falsetto voice), "Jimmy, telephone. Your boyfriend's on the phone." Then he said something to the effect of, "Are you cum-drunk today? How do you like it there?" Inmates loved that stuff, and they figured, "If an officer's doing this to him, we can do it." So inmates wouldn't respond to me; they would never listen to me.

I told the superintendent, and his words to me were, "This stuff happens all the time. Go back to work. Imagine if you were a woman." I didn't get any-where. That's when I went to GLAAD—Gay and Lesbian Alliance Against Defamation—and we brought it back to the superintendent. He said, "We've been doing our own investigation. We have discovered that the P.A. system incident was true and that inmates were whipping their penises out at Mr. Leahey. We're going to take care of that."

Somebody leaked my story to the newspapers and said that I was filing a five million dollar lawsuit against the department administration at Concord, which wasn't true. If it was, I'd be happy today. It was a big headline that says, "State disciplines three workers for harassment of gay prison guard." One guy was fired for having the inmates whip their penises out at me. Another was sus-pended for six months without pay, busted to a correction officer, and trans-ferred to another institution for sexual harassment of a female officer, not for what he did to me. He kept his job, and he was the one that did the touching and grabbing. Working in the kitchen where there're knives and stuff, I'm con-stantly afraid of what's going to happen, not just with the inmates, but with the officers, too. There were signs up for a fundraiser for the officer to help him pay his bills.

I went back to work after everything was settled and done, I did my job, and a lieutenant said, "Watch your back; they're after you. They're going to get you." He was being honest with me. Next thing you know, an inmate wrote a letter to the superintendent saying I sexually harassed him. I wasn't told about it until a court hearing with the clerk magistrate. I went to court, and they threw it out. Then three or four months later I had a hearing because the inmate wanted to take it higher. We were in front of a judge, and he said he had witnesses. Then another inmate filed a charge against me because the newspapers said I had five million dollars. He filed a charge against me for assault and battery. He said I hit him. I never hit him. So I was in court again, and this was within a month of the other hearing. I went into work the next day, and I said, "Are there any more charges on me?" "Well, yeah. The same inmate is saying you sexually harassed him."

One day the superintendent called me and said, "We're transferring you. You have an hour to decide where you want to go." They wanted to send me to Shirley, because Shirley's well known for having a lot of gay people. It felt like I was going to be segregated. I chose not to go. I wanted to stay where I was. He said, "You can't. If you stay here we can't be responsible for anything that happens to you." I said, "But you will be if anything happens."

I went to work on November 4 of '93 and had a nervous breakdown because I was just tired of it—going to court for the two inmates and the officers who were trying to set me up and frame me because I had their fellow officers fired or transferred. So I called the stress unit, and they told me to see my doctor. Now, I am sitting at home on 60 percent pay, and I can't return to work. I've done nothing wrong but be gay. I never wanted anybody hurt. I told them from the beginning that all I wanted was for the touching, grabbing, and making me feel really low about myself to stop. I feel like I was raped. I have nightmares every night.

I didn't want this to happen to any of the guys—I still don't, but where's the balance? I have to stand up for myself. Returning to work is impossible for me. I liked my job. I'd like to be able to go back. They promised me it would be an environment that would be safe for me, but they didn't come through. I did nothing wrong. That's what I don't understand. So what do I do? I have no other education. I don't want this to happen to somebody else.

Lena Van Dyke

Department: New Jersey Department of Corrections
Age: 43
Rank: Sergeant
Job: Compound Sergeant
Years in Law Enforcement: 10

A woman with a hearty laugh, Lena's philosophy is, "If you're going to be one, advertise." So, she changed her last name to "Van Dyke," her pick-up truck tags say "G-Pride," the tags on her and her partner's car say "WOMYN," their checks have pink triangles on them, and every once in a while she shakes up Millville, NJ by getting out her "Lesbian Money" stamp, stamping all her money, and going shopping.

My ex-husband was a police officer. I wanted to get into police work but because his male ego would not allow it I got into security. I was an armed security guard at the nuclear generating station. That was my way of inching into policework, and the beginning of the end of our marriage. Then I worked in security at a local glass house; from there, I went to the prison. I would have rather gone into police work as a regular street officer but I was thirty-two or thirty-three and getting a little too old for police work. We have two prisons here, it was a good opportunity—good money and good benefits, and it's as close as I could get to law enforcement.

I came from a very bad childhood where I was sexually, physically, and mentally abused. When I was three and four years old, my father used to kick me

160

down the stairs. My mother left him when I was five. Then I had a step-father who was very violent. My mother caught him fondling my breasts one time and beat the shit out of me. When I left home at eighteen he left my mother, broke into my apartment, and raped me. I had a lot of things to overcome because as a victim of incest you feel that it's your fault. And back in the '50s and early '60s it wasn't talked about. So all of my life there's been an abusive background. I think law enforcement was something that could make me feel good about myself. I could bring myself out of my family. I could be a survivor and someone that people could look up to and say, "She pulled herself out of the gutter."

I got married when I was twenty-one, and when my husband got into law enforcement I thought, "I really would like to do this." He said, "Absolutely not," because he didn't want the competition. When I went through the police academy, I scored higher on the range than he did, and the guys all rode him about it.

I took the test for the department of corrections, scored decently on it—I think I scored a ninety—and was passed over. A guy and I had exactly the same score, and he started to work at the prison on July 7. I started the eighteenth of December; I was hired with people who scored in the seventies. They didn't want to hire women at the time, so they were passing us by. The week after I was hired, they were hiring people who hadn't even taken the test.

When I first went in, a lot of areas were closed to females, and I just did general assignment stuff. The last two years before I made sergeant I was the accreditation manager—I was writing policies and procedures for the institution. Then in '90 I made sergeant. For the last 2½ years I've been the compound sergeant on second shift.

We have no cells in our jail. The inmates have free reign and can walk all over the place except during count-time. It's like walking a beat. I have several officers under me, and we maintain control of 652 inmates. If there's a fight or anything, we respond. It's basically a medium security prison, but we have medium and maximum inmates.

I was thirty-eight years old when I discovered I was a lesbian. I didn't have the growing up with all of the fears, so when my lover and I got together, I wanted to shout it from the rooftop. I think that makes a big difference. We have been together for four years; this is my first relationship. Now I look back and see I have been a lesbian all my life. I've been married twice, but I was never fully happy until now. We were good friends, we fell in love, and it's the most wonderful thing that's ever happened to me. We have been together since.

I was on sick leave when my lover and I got together. The day I went back to work, I went to the chief's office and said, "You're going to hear rumors about me, and I'm here to tell you they're true. You got a problem with it?" He said, "No." I said, "Good; glad to hear that." I had a couple friends who I didn't want to hear about me from rumors because rumors are vicious. One of them was a minister's wife, and I said, "I got to talk to you; I don't want you to hear this the wrong way." We talked, and she said, "You've never looked so good; you've never looked so happy." I've been lucky; I have friends that really care about me as a person.

We got married in Washington and had a big reception the following week here in town. We sent out formal wedding invitations, and it was really great. We had more straight people at our reception than gay people. For a straight couple to come said a lot for the men and women I work with. I was afraid to dance with my lover because I didn't want to make anybody feel uncomfortable, but we did. Then our daughters cut in and danced with us. There wasn't a dry eye in the whole place; it was real emotional. After that, everybody danced and had themselves a good time. I got all good reports from work. When I came back to work, people who weren't invited were saying, "I heard you had a great time."

When we were in Washington, one of the officers was in the officer's dining room at work spouting off about me—very negative, derogatory remarks with sexual content. There were inmates in the area. Now, you can make jokes, and I can deal with it, but when you're vicious and vindictive, I'm not going to take it, especially in front of inmates. So I went to the union and told them to put a leash on him. I told them I was filing an affirmative action complaint and going for his job the next time I heard anything from his mouth. And I will.

At the academy, we learned, "Fair, firm, and consistent." I may bullshit with the gay inmates, but when it comes down, you've got to do the same thing with everybody. Inmates know they can come talk to me if they got a problem. I really haven't had too much trouble; every once in a while you'll get some inmates that are trying to make names for themselves and will make a few comments behind your back, but I don't respond, 'cause as soon you turn around and make a big deal out of it, they know they've got you.

We marched in the first gay pride parade in Asbury Park, and there was an article about it in the New Jersey magazine. I got a phone call telling me to be careful 'cause I had worn my department of corrections baseball cap—internal affairs was going to bring me up on charges for wearing part of my uniform. I was all ready to start taking pictures of guys playing ball and in the mall with their hats on, but they knew they couldn't win. That was not a pleasant.

I was told I shouldn't tell anybody I was lesbian. I don't understand why. They said, "If you want to get anywhere, you can't tell anybody you're a lesbian." I said, "I can't not tell anybody I'm a lesbian." I demand and am entitled to the same validation that everybody else has in a relationship. My partner had a heart attack; I can't begin to explain how good it was to have people come up to me and say, "How's your partner?" the same way they would come up to somebody else and say, "How's your husband; how's your wife?" To me that meant more than anything, because they validated our relationship whether they approved or not.

I never considered not coming out at work. One night I was almost an hour late because an officer and I sat and talked about homosexuality and how important it is to be out. I said, "You work with your partner five days a week. If something happens to your wife, you can say, 'I'm really worried about my wife.' If you're having a bad day you can talk about it. If you go to a prison function, you have the right to dance to your song and hold hands. We don't have that right. Little things that you take for granted, I don't have. That's what's so important about being out—the fact that I can say, 'I'm really worried about my partner.' We have the same job, but I'm denied the benefits that you have, and it's not right. She shouldn't be working right now, but because I can't put her on my hospitalization she has to go to work just to be covered under hospitalization. If you die, your wife is entitled to your survivor benefits and your social security. Yeah, she is entitled to my pension, my life insurance, and my deferred compensation, but she's not entitled to my social security benefits, and she may not get the same respect that your wife would have if something happened to you. If something happened to you, somebody would go to your house and get her. If you're in the hospital, they'd transport her back and forth to the hospital. That's not going to happen for closeted people."

We need to be who we are. If you're ashamed of who you are, how do you expect other people to respect you? How do you expect them not to think you're wrong. If you're so afraid, so closeted, and so embarrassed, then you can't expect other people to give you respect; you don't give it to yourself. That's one thing that I do—I respect my relationship, and I respect my partner. If being gay is who you are, then you better give it everything you've got. I give everything that I have to being a correctional sergeant, I give everything I have to being a woman, and I give everything I have to being a lesbian. You have to be what you are.

Stephen St. Laurent

Department: Massachusetts Department of
Corrections–Framingham
Age: 36
Rank: Lieutenant
Job: Shift Lieutenant
Years in Law Enforcement: 12 1/2

A corrections officer for more than twelve years, Stephen works at the Massachusetts Correctional Institution at Framingham. He lives in a brownstone overlooking a park in Boston's South End with his four pound, miniature, Yorkshire terrier, Winston.

I never had a lifelong dream of being a cop. I never sat on my daddy's knee and said, "I want to be a policeman." It was something that came out of necessity. When I got out of high school, I worked in the factories. In 1981, I was involved in a bunch of financial problems, and I wasn't making enough money. I was twenty-four when I started working for the department, and I've been there almost thirteen years now.

As a young kid, I was attracted to boys. I was brought up Catholic, and being gay was an absolute aberration. I always thought that there was something wrong with me. I had a lot of self-esteem problems because of my thoughts. My first real sexual experience with a man was probably a year before I got married.

I was engaged at the time. I figured if I got married and had a life like everyone else, I'd be like everyone else. That didn't happen. The thoughts never went away and the guilt built. I resorted big-time to drugs and alcohol. Within six or seven years, I was a raging alcoholic.

It wasn't too hard to hide being gay. For twelve years I was married and living the life that everybody else thought I was supposed to be living—partying with the boys every night and raising hell just like all the other macho bullshit things that everybody does. I was the party animal, and they never really questioned me.

I don't think being gay played a big part in my decision to go into corrections. Subconsciously, I almost think it was buying insurance that I wasn't gay, because it was this macho job—"No fags are in there. I can play the role of the straight macho guy. Nobody'll ever suspect me." Looking back on it I was big time into proving to myself that I wasn't gay. My whole lifestyle was bullshit. It was all a farce. It was all somebody else. I ran with all the tough guys, hung around in all the tough bars, and got into the brawls and the fights and all that crap. I always knew that deep down inside it wasn't me.

In 1987, I was a sergeant, and I was driving around cruising and was arrested for drunk driving and possession of drugs. I was still married, and I thought my life was over. I knew the police knew what I was doing, but they never mentioned anything. Correction officers and policemen don't get arrested. I thought my career and my life were over. It ended up on the front page of the newspaper, "Local correction officer arrested on drunk driving and drug charges." Fortunately, through an employee assistance program at work, I was given the ultimatum, "Either go for treatment or you're going to get fired." I was in in-patient treatment for thirty days. I came out, and I've been sober ever since.

What made me find myself was, without a doubt, sobriety. If I wouldn't have gotten sober, I'd still be sitting in a bar, and I'd probably be dead. Sobriety's what got me clear enough to realize I was worth saving. It wasn't until I got sober that I felt like I was a good person. Never had any hope. Never had any dreams. I have dreams today. Since getting sober in '87, I've lived three lives compared to the life I had before.

After three years of sobriety, I realized there were a lot of other things in my life I had to change. I was thirty years old, and I had never lived a life for me. I had always lived for somebody else, doing the things I thought everybody else wanted me to do—living everybody else's dreams. Never once had I done anything for me. That's when I decided I was going to divorce my wife, come out as a gay man, and let the chips fall where they may. But I would be able to look in the mirror.

I divorced my wife, and much to my surprise, I divorced my family, too. I did not come out at that time—I didn't want to do that to my wife. I wanted to make a clean divorce and deal with all those issues afterward. It didn't take long for me to realize I had to change a lot more than the marriage. I decided I was going to move to the city, so I moved to Boston.

The way I came out at work is a great story. I was basically living the gay man's life here in Boston, but I had never actually come out at work. Talking about gay issues with people at work was a big taboo, but I was getting to the point where I knew I would eventually tell people. I was reading the local gay newspaper and there was an article about a gay police officer who was starting Gay Officers Action League (GOAL) of New England. I wrote him a letter and ended up going to the first meeting. It was great to see the handful of people who were there. I remember walking in and they were talking about the same issues that I had been struggling with my whole life. I felt freedom, like I was okay; and like I wasn't as fucked up as I had always thought I was.

I got involved with GOAL a little bit at a time by going to meetings and stuff. Then came gay pride, and GOAL was marching in gay pride in Boston. I struggled with the idea of marching with them. I finally decided, "It doesn't matter, there will be a few people in Boston that'll see me. I don't care. Let them talk." I really didn't think too much about it.

The next morning my AA sponsor called me on the phone, and said, "Great picture, Steve. You better go buy the paper." I said, "What's he talking about?" So I went down the street, and bought the *Boston Globe*. Lo and behold on the front page of the Metro section of the Sunday *Globe* was an eight by ten color picture of me carrying the Gay Officers Action League banner. I remember saying to myself, "If this isn't fate, nothing is." I thought my career was over. I had a good friend that I was out to at work, and she called me. She was like, "What the fuck did you do? They're running pictures of this thing on the copy machine all day long. They're all over the jail, and everybody's talking." I said, "It's done. There's nothing I can do about it." I thought I would never be able to work again. I thought I'd be harassed right out the front door. I thought, "The inmates will never give me any respect again."

The ride to work was the longest ride in my life. But nobody said a word about it. Not a soul, not even the inmates. Come to find out my captain had gone around and told everyone that he would fire the first person he saw harassing me about what was in the newspaper. He called me in his office and told me, "If anyone says anything to you about what's gone on this weekend, I want to know about it, and I will fire them on the spot. The bottom line is you have always done a good job for me. You've always had my respect, and that hasn't changed. As long as you continue to do that, we'll never have a problem."

The same thing happened with the inmates. They didn't give a shit either. They couldn't have cared less. A lot of inmates came up to me and said, "Jesus Christ, you've got balls." They gave me a lot of respect for that.

I have a lot of respect from my officers and my sergeants. They really respect the fact that I'm honest about my sexuality. I've had some people say, "They wouldn't dare mess with you, because you're a lieutenant." I don't buy that. I know a lot of lieutenants who happen to be straight that are messed with constantly, because they're no good. They treat me just like I should be treated. I have no complaints with the department of corrections as far as how I've been treated. The assholes distanced themselves, and my true friends came up to me and said, "Steve, I don't care." The biggest issue they had was, "Why didn't you tell me before?" It bothered them that they had to find out in the newspaper. But I was afraid to tell them. I was afraid to lose their friendship. I never took any abuse from anyone. All those fears that I had my whole career were in my head, and they never materialized.

It was not too long after that that I applied for the lieutenant's position. I'll never forget when I went for my interview with the superintendent, and her first comment to me was, "Mr. St. Laurent, you're rather famous these days, aren't you?" I started laughing. The interesting thing was, she thought that it was a big asset for me. She said, "I need somebody with your diversity in my institution. I really respect your honesty and your integrity. Your record with the department is great. You're here to do your job, and you don't care what people think. I like that in you." And I got the job. Coming out and going through all that actually played a big part in me getting promoted. It was an interesting twist.

I teach at the academy and we talk about gays and lesbians in the work place. The rookies love it. I think a lot of them have questions and concerns but are afraid to voice them, especially in a regimented, academy setting. I walk in, they all jump to attention and salute, and then I start talking about gays and lesbians. It's been good for me 'cause I feel like I'm making some changes in people, and bringing out issues that were never talked about before. People didn't even say the word "gay" in the department of corrections ten years ago. The best thing it can do is promote some discussion with these people in order to have them think about what they're doing. If I can save another officer from having to put up with gay jokes, then that's good.

I want people to know that it's possible to come out at work and not have to go through hell. I know some people have gone through absolute hell—some of them are good friends of mine. Officers have been bashed. People have gone through nightmarish stories. People think that every time somebody comes out they're going to go through an absolute hell. They don't. I'm living proof. I was treated very well, and my hat is off to the department. They never messed with me. It's got a lot to do with my performance and being a good officer. I was treated with the respect that I deserved.

I believe I can do anything I want today because I have self confidence. There's nothing holding me back. Nobody can stop me. I'm past my radical stage. I have a lot of acceptance about things now. If anybody ever bothered me about being gay I would fight them just as hard as ever, but I don't feel like I'm carrying a flag anymore. I'm not as much of an activist as I was. I've done a lot of work, and I want to chill out. I do wonder, "Am I letting my brothers down?" I don't hide anything from anybody, and I never will. If someone asks me, I'd tell them, but I don't feel like I need to march in and say "I'm a gay man, and I'm the only openly gay officer in the Massachusetts Department of Corrections." I guess I'm to the point where I want to be known as Steve St. Laurent. And that's good.

Carroll Hunter

Department: New York City (NY) Department of Correction
Age: 52
Rank: Deputy Director (Retired)
Job: Guidance and Counseling
Years in Law Enforcement: 10

Carroll has a bachelor's degree in Black Studies from Lehman College and a master's degree in guidance and counseling from Hunter College. Having retired from full-time service in 1990, he has since been elected president of the thousand member, New York chapter of Gay Officers Action League (GOAL). Four days after hosting "Together in Pride," the first national conference for lesbian and gay criminal justice workers, and a day after Stonewall 25, he curled up on his living room couch and told his story.

As far back as I can remember, I was interested in criminal justice; not necessarily police work, but probation, parole, and correction. I always liked the idea of cops and robbers, and I never really wanted to do anything else. I had some other fascinations here and there, like all other kids—one time I wanted to be an actor or a ballet dancer, but when I became an adult, I knew I wanted to be in criminal justice. Law enforcement was something I wanted to do, but I didn't think they would let me do it because I was gay. I always knew I was capable, but I didn't know if they would give me the chance.

I'm an African-American, and we live in a country that's stratified by caste, class, and color. Because of that, I'm a member of an underclass. In large urban areas, the members of the underclass are the people that make up the prison population. Jails are places for people that cannot make bail, for people that are members of the underclass—never mind who's guilty or who's innocent. I wanted to work with them; I wanted to help people that "looked like me." As it worked out, the people that looked like me varied place to place. If you go through the jails in Anchorage, Alaska, they're all Eskimos. If you go through the jails in North Dakota, they're all American Indians. In San Diego, they're all Mexicans, and in New York, they're Blacks and Puerto Ricans. Who the "nigger" is depends on where you live. So, when I say I want to help "my" people, my people are all people.

I come from a Caribbean background—my people are from Jamaica and they are incredibly homophobic. Violently so—they have been known to kill people. I had a lot of trouble as a little kid because I didn't do the things my other brothers did. But as I got older, I also knew that I wasn't going to be a victim. I was always the kind of person that if you got in my face, I'd knock you down. Nobody was going to abuse me, nobody was going to take advantage of me. I'd go down to Jamaica as a teenager, and I was constantly in fights. There is nothing in the world more devastating for a heterosexual man than to be beaten up by a queen!

I was a gay activist in an all boy's high school. The boys would pick on and beat up gay people, so I banded us together. If you picked on one you had to fight all of us. I got them to be really rough and tumble, and it frightened the management; it scared them to death. They threw me out of high school my senior year because I was a gay activist.

While I was in undergraduate school, I took a course called, "Field Work in the Black Community," where you were sent to work in an agency. The first day of class, the teacher told me she was going to send me to Riker's Island here in New York, the world's largest correctional facility. She said, "Go out there and teach elementary Black Studies to adolescent inmates." When she said that to me, it was like somebody said, "For the rest of your life, every day is going to be Christmas." After the second or third week, the deputy warden asked me if I wanted to work for the department of correction, and I said, "Yes."

I wasn't hired as a teacher—I was hired as a correctional counselor. Eventually I was promoted to Deputy Director of Counseling Services for the whole agency—I had 125 social workers and counselors working for me. I came up through the ranks over a period of ten years. I had to garner the respect of a lot of straight people that worked with me and, as I got promoted, under me. What I did was what a lot of gay people that work in criminal justice do—gay people get the job and hit the ground running. They don't go in acting like, "It's just another job, and I'm going to try to skate by." Gay people can't do that. You've got one strike against you because you're gay, and if they look at you and think you're ineffective, you don't know what you're doing, or you don't care, they can really get on your case. But if you go in there and jump through those hoops backwards, they don't bother you. People do have problems, but as long as you keep your eyes focused on the prize, as long as you do a good job, they won't bother you. In all my years working for correction and as president of GOAL, they haven't bothered me. But, you can't be in the closet.

Being in the closet is the most self defeating thing you can do, 'cause then people know what buttons to push. When you're out, you don't hear the fag jokes any more. Every once in a while, some new inmates would come in, and I might have to hear it, but I would set them straight very quickly. At first I would ignore it, but sometimes I'd be coming down the hall, and they'd make sounds like construction workers make when they see women walking down the street. When they did things like that, I called them into my office and jumped on them verbally. The White inmates never did it, but Black and Hispanic inmates would. I'd lay a guilt trip on them, "What the hell's the matter with you? Don't you see I'm a Black man just like you? Where the hell is your respect?"

I always felt an affinity toward the gay inmates. Gay male inmates are looked at as clowns, comic relief, and objects of humor. They're not looked at as though they have special counseling needs. When I was just a fledgling counselor, all I could do was make sure the inmates got a phone call to their lawyer, or make sure they got to the clinic if they were sick. That was not counseling; that was stamping out little fires. As I moved up the ranks, I made sure I put programs together so the counselors would determine what needs the inmates had and how to rectify those needs while they were there. We did an incredibly good job in the rehabilitative effort.

As far as my physical safety was concerned, there were some harrowing times. It was a hot, dirty, dangerous environment, and sometimes I was scared. I remember the first riot I was in. I was in a housing area in one of the oldest jails. These cell blocks were huge—you're on the bottom, you look up, there's three or four stories, and it's all open. There's hundreds and hundreds of people in these cell blocks. I would go into the housing area to do different counseling things. I walked in there, and this big, strapping inmate was standing over me like the "Incredible Hulk." He didn't say anything but he was standing near me like something was going to happen. All of a sudden, a television set came flying through the air, it hit the ground, and pandemonium broke out. The inmates started assaulting two correction officers, and the riot button was pushed. This big, hulking inmate walked right up to me, put his hand on my chest, pushed me into the wall, and said, "Nobody's going to bother you Mr. Hunter. You just stand right there." All of this happened within the space of fifteen seconds. When it was over, they were mopping blood off the floor, and nothing happened to me. The inmates will protect you if you're a stand-up guy, and I was an inmate advocate. I was scared then, and I was scared a couple of other times. I saw some terribly violent things out there.

I always kept a picture of my lover on the desk, and I had a huge, black lambda painted on the wall. Sometimes inmates would try to compromise me by making passes at me. I would always tell them in no uncertain terms, "Unless you're in this picture with me, don't bother. Take it some place else." Sometimes it would get violent. I've had inmates come into my office, stand in front of me, and flex their muscles. I pushed them out of my office, "What the hell's the matter with you? Give that sex stuff to somebody else. That's not what I'm here for."

My lover was an extremely successful architect, engineer, and interior designer—we worked in two entirely different environments. I would be in a riot one day, and get into a Leer jet with him that night to go to some wealthy estate in Florida to help him do an interior design. So I had a good release—I didn't bring the job home with me. A lot of the officers, gay and straight, bring the job home with them. They're a cop all the time—even when they're not on duty, they've got that gun. You're in an environment where you have to be consistent, firm, and fair all the time. If you're not careful you can bring those behavior patterns home with you, and they can get in the way of your relationship. You walk around the jail, and you're telling people what to do all day long. Then you come home at night, and you have to be able to turn that off.

I'm African-American and my partner was White. Sometimes there were difficulties because we were different colors. There were never any problems in the gay community—gay people didn't give a shit, it was the straight people. We'd go out for dinner, and he would always be given the check. We would always travel first class in a plane. I remember once we were going to Egypt, we got on the plane, and one flight attendant came up to me and said, "May I see your ticket?" She didn't ask him. About three minutes later, another flight attendant came up and did the same thing. Because we live in a society that's racist, and because my partner worked in such a glamorous realm, I was always in places where Black people weren't expected to be seen, like riding in the

Concorde or in the Presidential Suite of the QE II. He took me to all kinds of incredible places, but we never had any trouble with gay people.

My lover and I were together for twenty years, and he got stomach cancer four years ago. We were in St. Thomas on vacation, and he got sick. He got sick in November and died in February. It was awful. We were going to grow old together. I retired because I wanted to be at his side for the last few months of his life. It was four years ago, and when I talk about him, it was like yesterday. We had saved a lot of money and made a lot of good investments, so I didn't have to work anymore. I decided I would spend the rest of my life working with gay and lesbian people in criminal justice to advance our issues, needs, and concerns.

My major regret is that I wasted ten years of my life before getting in to criminal justice. I would have been very happy to be there for twenty instead of just ten. I miss making the contribution to the rehabilitative effort on a full-time basis. What I don't miss is getting out of bed at five-thirty in the morning to get over there. I can't say I miss the people because I'm around them all the time. Being the president of GOAL is like a full-time job, so it's not as though I'm out of the business. The only thing I do miss is direct, hands-on rehabilitative stuff with the inmates. I miss that very much.

My proudest accomplishment ever was the "Together in Pride" conference. We never thought there would be a time when you could get gay and lesbian criminal justice people together in caucus. It was something that was unheard of, so bringing that concept from fantasy to reality was really important. We worked very hard to put it together. This gay pride was the proudest of all. First of all, we wanted gay people in criminal justice to know they're not alone. We wanted them to know there is a network out there that they can plug into for nurturance, support, and encouragement. We also wanted all gay people to get a psychological shot in the arm by going up the escalator at One Police Plaza and seeing the gay pride display.

A stress for gay people who work in criminal justice is that gay people, particularly the guys, are fascinated with uniforms. They look at us in mysterious sexual terms. Sometimes people are attracted to you because of that, not because of who you are. I've been propositioned because of the uniform, and to me, it's an immediate turnoff. Personally, I would rather be propositioned because of my brains. The fact that I work in criminal justice is not a sexual thing at all, and if people come on to me that way, they're putting me down. Not all of our officers look at it that way. There are some people in the organization that really are into the uniforms and the handcuffs. I'm not sexually attracted to people in uniforms. A man in a nine-hundred dollar suit and a Hermes tie? Oh, pitter patter!

The more gay and lesbian people there are in criminal justice, the more our political needs, issues, and concerns are going to be addressed. I also think gay and lesbian people add a certain amount of humanity to the criminal justice world. Criminal justice traditionally attracts authoritarian personalities, and in a collective sense, I don't think gay people in criminal justice have that. I think we lend a certain humanity to it.

I think visibility is the most important thing for all of us. It's only in numbers that we benefit—they realize there's not just one or two of us. I think all gay people should be out and I encourage them to come out. People who aren't out get on my nerves. Usually people that are not out do not make contributions to the effort—they are so busy hiding that they're not there to give us any support at all. What offends me the most is that we all know that the day will come when gay people will be treated just like every body else, when we're going to be able to sit down at the banquet of our accomplishments. But on that day, you'd better watch out because when the dinner bell is called, those that have hidden like frightened, little mice are going to be the first ones to run to the table, and they just might knock you down in the process. I really don't like people that are in the closet. They're scared of me. I am a firm believer in outing—in a heartbeat. People that are in the closet and don't want to make a contribution steer a wide path away from Carroll Hunter, 'cause I don't give them no rhythm.

Part Three: Adjudication

P rosecutors/district attorneys, defense attorneys, and
judges work in *adjudication*. Depending on the jurisdiction,
district attorneys or prosecutors are either appointed or elected
to their positions. In most instances, the district attorney hires
deputies or assistants who represent the state and are responsible
for, among other things, determining which cases should be
pursued through the criminal justice system, negotiating
appropriate plea bargain agreements, and prosecuting those
cases that go to trial. Defense attorneys represent the accused
in all phases of the process. Finally, judges preside over
courtrooms making sure laws and correct procedure are
followed, and in some cases, judges render decisions and
sentence the convicted. Safety and backup are of less concern
with these professionals, but good working relationships with
and respect from other criminal justice professionals are crucial
for doing one's job effectively.

David Rubin

Department: Office of the San Diego County (CA)
District Attorney
Age: 35
Rank and Job: Deputy District Attorney
Years in Law Enforcement: 7

His "pride and joy" a red convertible, Dave works for the San Diego County District Attorney's Office. One warm and sunny "winter" day near Balboa Park in San Diego, he talked about how it has been for him as the first openly gay criminal justice worker in Southern California.

I graduated from U.C.-Berkeley as an undergraduate with a double major in film and political economics. This is not what you call real marketable material. I had gone to LA with a boyfriend, and I wanted to work in LA but while there, I realized I didn't have the personality for it.

My late father had been a lawyer, and I had grown up around lawyers. Let's face it, with those two degrees I wasn't going to go to medical school, I wasn't going to do anything technical, and I wasn't going to go to engineering or business school, so I kind of backed into law. Criminal law is most exciting for people like me with attention spans of twenty seconds or less; the average life of a case in criminal law is probably four months or less versus a civil case which can go on for years.

I had done an internship at the D.A.'s office in San Francisco, and I really enjoyed it. When the D.A.'s office in San Diego came and recruited, I signed up, did the interview, and got a job with them as a law clerk. I took the bar, did the clerkship, and then was hired as a deputy district attorney.

I made a commitment to myself that I would never be an "in the closet" professional. Period. Anywhere. Anytime. I'm not going to get promotions and have them hinging upon, "I'm out or not out." If they don't want to hire me, fine. I'd rather know that up front.

Being gay didn't come up in the job interview. I remember thinking, "What am I going to do if it comes up?" and deciding I was going to tell them. But it didn't come up. I was out, though, the first day at work. I was waiting to go in to get my assignment, and the secretary said, "Are you single?" I said, "Yes." She said, "We'll have to find you some nice, single woman to marry." I said, "I'm gay so it should be a man. But anything you can do is appreciated. I don't know anybody in San Diego." About an hour later I was meeting with the guy for whom I was going to clerk, and he was on the phone to his wife. They were trying to fix up a single person, and he said to me, "Are you married?" I said, "I am gay." He said, mishearing me, "You're engaged?" I repeated, "No, I'm gay." He said, "Oh." That was it. I was out from day one.

I was the first openly gay law enforcement official of any kind in southern California. The district attorney was going to make sure that this was not a problem. My first assignment was working in a unit downtown; I think there was some sensitivity in my being placed there; that is, near where the district attorney himself worked. I think it was, "Let's keep him here. That way, if anything happens, I'm right here." I think it also was a message to others that, "The D.A. expects this is going to be just fine." I think he was worried about what kind of harassment I might get, and that came from rumors about how some deputies felt about hiring someone who was openly gay. My first supervisor later told me, "There was some sensitivity in finding a supervisor that would not hassle you and would give you a good start." And that was exactly what happened. Once my first assignment was up and everyone saw that the world didn't end and the sky didn't fall in, the D.A. said, "We're going to send him off on a regular branch assignment."

When I asked to be transferred back downtown to the child abuse unit in 1989, it was controversial. People associate gay/lesbian with molesters, perverts, and pedophiles; to have an openly gay deputy in that position was controversial, but the district attorney didn't see it like that. His attitude was, "David's doing his work, he does good work, he's handled controversial cases in the East

County branch office, he'll handle them down here, and that's the end of that discussion."

I had a case involving a day care center in a home. This guy had molested two or three of the kids, and he wound up pleading to a lot of years. Before sentencing he wrote a letter to his elderly cousin saying, "I am being prosecuted for all these things, but the D.A.'s a homosexual, and no one seems to care about that." She called me up and said, "He's been saying some really nasty things such as, 'You're a homosexual.'" This was the first time that a defendant was going to play with this. It became clear to me that he was going to make this an issue at the sentencing hearing. The issue for me was that the hearing was going to be televised, so I needed to have a good response when he discussed my being gay. I called the "front office" and explained, "I need a good way of dealing with this." We kicked around some ideas, like, "Why is he dwelling on the prosecutor when he's the one who's out there molesting girls?" When it came time for the hearing, he didn't say a thing. That was the only time my being gay ever came up, and the office really stood with me.

Colleagues have been pretty respectful when face to face with me. No one's really said anything anti-gay to me. I've been in the field before with officers who didn't know who I was or didn't know I was gay, and they have said things. I've had to say, "We don't use the word 'faggot' when we're on duty, now do we." But pretty much, people have been very professional. Within the office, people have gotten more relaxed. When I first got there, there were people who wouldn't talk to me. On the other hand, there were people who were very warm and supportive and wanted to make sure that I felt comfortable. It runs the range. Over the years, more people have warmed and let their prejudice go, which is why being out is so important. In all fairness, I've had more run-ins with defense attorneys. Everyone thinks the defense bar is so hip, but that is just a stereotype. I was once doing a settlement conference, and this guy said, "Have you heard they call Hillcrest (San Diego's gay neighborhood) the 'Swish Alps'?" and a whole series of gay jokes. I remember turning to a defense attorney colleague of his who knew me and saying, "Do you want to handle this or should I?" He said, "I'll handle it." The defense attorney who knew me took the other one outside. They came back in, and the first attorney apologized; that was the end of it. The nice thing about being out is your associates can handle some of the homophobia for you. They say, "That was really uncool. This guy's gay, and we don't do that," and that's the end of it, so I don't have to deal with it alone.

People in the closet have tremendous stresses. They've got the stress of having to not reveal who they are. They've got to listen to homophobic remarks and not react. Gay cops are afraid of not getting "cover" or of people doing stuff to them. I don't have that; being out of the closet, I don't have that kind of problem. Mine's more of a white-collar situation; I'm an attorney. It's more just not being socially accepted. While people are cordial at work, you don't tend to bond with them the way they bond with each other. There's a sort of we/they situation. You don't wind up getting invited to their houses very much. The fact that you're "other" and you're not really going to be accepted socially by them on some level can be a little stressful.

I've also been concerned that when I go into court with a case a judge is going to mess up my case with bad rulings because I'm gay. I've had judges razz me a little bit more than they should or not treat me as respectfully as they could have in front of the public because they don't like me. They'll be rude, they'll talk in a curt tone of voice, or they may be more solicitous of the opposing counsel or not even look at me. That's the kind of thing that stresses me. I pretty much know the bench now. We all know what everyone's limits are and everyone tries to get along, but in the beginning, you're always worried because you don't want people's bigotry taken out on your victims or you don't want cops to not take you seriously.

The gay community is going to be naturally suspicious of law enforcement. The law enforcement community has always looked a little askance at lesbians and gays, but the experience in San Diego County has been pretty positive. You get vocal aspects of both communities who can make things a little uncomfortable.

What are the major concerns of the middle of the road, white-collar gay/lesbian community? I'm really not worried about if people can go to the park for sex or not; I don't worry about entrapment. My feeling is, "Stay out of the park. Take it home." The top issues in the gay/lesbian community are: One, we're worried about being able to get health care benefits to cover partners. My lesbian friends apparently have a higher degree of breast cancer, and they need to have their domestic partners covered. My partner's glasses are three hundred bucks a pair because he's got bad eye sight. If I get them on my vision plan, I could get them for under a hundred. Two, we can't get married and get those tax breaks, and we've been together for years. Three, we're really worried about education, and four, we're getting eaten up by taxes that don't seem to be paying for very much any more. I'm paying more in taxes and getting less in services. Those are our big issues. What are the big issues for heterosexuals? I'll bet they're the same. Isn't that funny? We have a lot more in common than in distinction.

I don't want to have people look at me and say, "What you do in your private life is your business." Sexual orientation is not about my private life. Sexual orientation is very public. Some of my straight colleagues wear wedding rings. They've got pictures of their kids on their desks. They're advertising. They're broadcasting their sexual orientation. If we change the language of the discourse about sexual orientation, we'll change the associations non-gay people have of the community. When you say gay/lesbian to most people, right now they think "sex." We need to change that association to gay/lesbian equals cop, gay/lesbian equals prosecutor, gay/lesbian equals health care problem, gay/lesbian equals mortgages, gay/lesbian equals kids, gay/lesbian equals Boy Scouts, and all that stuff.

I don't think any of us who are gay in law enforcement are kidding ourselves. We know that behind our backs or behind closed doors people are saying things that are prejudiced and bigoted. I think the perception is that it's very bad to be blatantly bigoted. We've increased the transaction cost and driven the bigots behind the closed doors, and we've come out. If we don't feel like we have completely won everyone over, at least we have started to make it taboo to be openly homophobic.

Albert J. Mrozik, Jr.

Department: Cities of Newark, Asbury Park, and Ocean Gate, New Jersey
Age: 39
Job: Municipal Prosecutor; Municipal Court Judge
Years in Law Enforcement: 7

Bert is New Jersey's first openly gay municipal court judge. A week after taking the bench, he talked about his career as a prosecutor and a judge while dining on pizza in the living room of his two story home in Asbury Park.

I grew up in New York City in a place called Richmond Hill. Back then, policemen were an integral part of the community. As a child, I remember the policeman coming around the house to check to make sure the back door was locked. He was a pretty caring individual. I never really thought much about entering the law enforcement field because from the time I was very small, I had been geared to become to doctor. When I was about nine, my cousin married a physician, and I was geared to take over his practice.

I entered Columbia College in 1971. In my junior year, they had a program called "interns in public service," which was offered in New Jersey during the summer. It was a part-time summer job to go out and work in the municipalities in the state government to see what it was like. I applied and got chosen by the Ocean Gate Police Department. They said, "You're going to be a policeman in Ocean Gate for the summer." I was not really thrilled with Columbia because it was a very difficult school, and when it came time for me to go back, I opted to sign up with the police department. For about a year I was a policeman in Ocean Gate.

I went back to Columbia and thought I was going to go to medical school. I applied to medical and dental school but couldn't get in because my grades weren't high enough. After that I became a paralegal at a very big, prestigious firm in New York City. I worked there for four years, and then decided to go to law school at the University of Denver in Colorado. A few years later, an opportunity came up for me to be an assistant prosecutor for the city of Newark. I've done that since 1987.

I am very out on the job. There's nobody who doesn't know I'm gay in the city of Newark. Have I been treated very differently? That's hard to answer. I'm very friendly with a lot of the policemen I've known for a very long period of time. I extend myself for them all the time, and they do the same thing for me. They kind of bust my chops—they're always making gay jokes or asking me out on dates. There was one very good looking policeman who blew his brains out around two years ago. He constantly used to tease me, but I got along with him. I was never really offended by that.

There are six police departments that I deal with, and I've never had a problem with them. As a matter of fact, last year I was invited for the first time to a state police Christmas party. I was pretty impressed that the state police, who I considered to be very homophobic, invited me to their party. At the party, there were a couple of cracks made by the lieutenant about people of different orientations and, "Who wants to sit next to Bert?" It was a little bizarre. It was the first time they had something like that to deal with.

I know the state police is very homophobic because back in 1990, I joined Gay Officers Action League (GOAL) in New York. About that time there was an article in the newspaper about a state trooper who lost his trial to regain his job with the state police. Apparently this trooper was off-duty and spotted in a beauty salon getting make-up and a wig. He became involved with GOAL too, and I did an amicus brief for him on behalf of GOAL. That was my coming out to the legal world. The judge who handled the case was partner at a law firm for which I had clerked. Let me tell you, he got very shabby treatment both from the state police and from the court system. They decided they didn't want somebody who dressed in drag to work as a state trooper, so they called him into the barracks and said to him, "You have a choice—you can either resign or we will investigate this matter very thoroughly." That was pretty clever because they actually had no charges to file against him. What he had done was done off-duty, privately in a beauty salon. It was really unfortunate because, as far as I'm concerned, they had no business delving into his personal life. In any event, we went on appeal for that, and the appeal got denied. We went up to the Supreme Court, and I had a very good shot of overturning the judge's decision based on privacy laws. The other screwy thing about it is that the guy who represented the state police is gay. He indicated to me that back in August of '91, the Governor issued an executive order that, "No department may discriminate against anyone because of their sexual orientation," among other things. The state police asked to be excused from that executive order; that's how homophobic they are. I wanted to amend the record to show exactly the mental state of the state police when they fired him. I filed that motion to amend the transcript, and four days later, the appeal got dismissed. I guess they were afraid of blowing the cover on the state police. That was really unfortunate. He really did get screwed.

The lesson from that is that law enforcement people are very gossipy, and people who are very closeted always tend to do really stupid things. That's the problem with a lot of gay law enforcement people—they're always so busy trying to hide what they are and who they are. In the city of Newark, I hired a gay city attorney who's also a prosecutor. During the interview I said to him, "Are you gay?" I thought he was going to drop dead. He said, "What does that have to do with anything?" I said, "I'm gay, too. I was just inquiring." He got the job, and he's running around at work creating the impression that he's straight. Is this screwed up? It's so obvious when you look at him.

As prosecutor I've really never had a problem. They deal with me very well. There's maybe two or three people that really have a resentment toward me as a result of my sexual orientation. They're very cold or callous, or they don't say hello all the time. I'm a pretty friendly person; in Newark, everybody knows me, and everyone says hello with a few exceptions. I'm definitely out of the closet because last summer we had the first gay pride parade in Asbury Park. A friend of mine who's a reporter wanted to do an article on gay law enforcement people. It wound up in a New Jersey monthly magazine which is very widely distributed, and my picture was in it. As a matter of fact, the first day it got released one of the court clerks sent me a copy of it. That probably did not hinder me at work either because they knew that they really couldn't touch me.

I was talking to a lieutenant at my police department here in Asbury Park, and I said, "Had I remained a policeman, I'd be able to retire next year at more money than what I make full-time now. The only difference is, I'd probably still be in the closet." He said, "I think that's true." So many of the policeman I know are tortured constantly. They're not even out, but it's suspected. I'm in a better position than most people; now I'm at the top position in law enforcement. As a prosecutor, I'm in a better position than a policeman because all I have to do is say, "This one is giving me a hard time," and he really could be in for a lot of trouble. I'm more like management, so I have less fear.

It's been pretty good working here in Asbury Park; I just started being municipal court judge in town. I am absolutely the first openly gay judge in New Jersey: municipal courts, superior court, supreme court. I wouldn't be municipal court judge in Asbury Park if I weren't gay. Being gay has never really helped me get a job with the exception of this one. It's a political appointment. I was gay, I lived in town, and they needed someone from the gay community. They felt somewhat indebted to the gay community for sticking it out here because everyone else has left Asbury Park. I guess this is their thank you.

The police department here in Asbury Park, though it's not homophobic because it deals with the gay community all the time, is typical for most small town departments. They're really not all that open. As far as my sexual orientation being a judge is concerned, I'm going to make that more of an issue than the department will. I'm not entirely sure what's going to sensitize them to the concerns of the gay community. It's too new to me; I've only been over there a couple times.

I had a meeting with the tactical narcotics team 'cause we have a very large drug problem here in Asbury Park. The first meeting I had with the prosecutor was after five. I drive a motorcycle so I went in jeans and a shirt that says, "Visible, equal and proud." I wanted to make sure there was no misunderstanding, and everything went real well. Nobody made mention of it, but I was speaking with one of them a couple days later, and I said, "Have you had any training?" In my mind's-eye I was thinking of high-intensity drug training offered by the Alcohol, Tobacco and Firearms Bureau. But he says, "Oh no, we had sexual orientation training." I thought that was really funny. I guess he knows it's on my mind; it's certainly on his mind.

An attorney in town went up to someone I know very well in the neighborhood and said, "I understand Asbury Park has a gay flavor these days. You have a gay judge." That was a little bit out of line. So she said to him, "Asbury Park has had a very gay flavor for a long period of time. If you worked here for ten years, how come you never noticed it?" I've heard some other comments from the merchants; nobody knows who I am, but they know I'm gay. I'm waiting for one of the defenders to comment on it. I'm not entirely sure what I'm going to do. I'm probably going to send them to another judge for a contempt hearing 'cause it really is irrelevant. Justice should be blind.

The gay community has a problem with law enforcement in that they view law enforcement as part of the problem. When you're gay and you're with law enforcement, they automatically assume that you're on the other side, that you're really against them. It puts you in very peculiar position. There's an assumption that you make the laws, not that you enforce the laws, and that you're really part of the problem and part of the homophobia.

I feel terrible when I have to sentence someone I know to be gay on criminal charges. I had a bar owner appear before me in court, and I had to send the case away. If I did what I should have done, she would've hated me. If I felt sorry for her and didn't, everyone would have said I did it because she's a dyke. So I had to steer away from it.

I've really gone out of my way to help the gay community; I really shouldn't do that because I have to be fair and just, but the system in unfair and unjust, and I will do my best to rectify that. Police officers, judges, and prosecutors have a lot of discretion. They can decide to do things or not do things. That's where the straight community takes advantage of the gay community if they're homophobic. A policeman will write a ticket for somebody just because they're gay whereas they'd let a straight person out of it. If judges have an idea defendants are gay, they may give them harsher sentences. Even up at the beach, the people who get the summonses for lewd behavior are gay people. But let me tell you, I've been on that beach many times. I've seen straight people acting worse than any member of the gay community, and they don't get summonses. Maybe I can help make up for that.

Marcy L. Kahn

Department: New York State Supreme Court
Age: 44
Job: Justice
Years in Law Enforcement: 8

The Supreme Court in New York is the trial court of general jurisdiction. At her home in New York City on a Saturday morning, Marcy talked about her involvement in the lesbian and gay community which, in part, has culminated in her election as one of the first two openly lesbian Supreme Court Justices in the state of New York.

Before I set off to law school, I was told by someone whom I respected greatly that I could not be both a lesbian and a lawyer and that I would have to make a choice. I didn't really have any evidence to contradict that. I didn't know any gay lawyers when I was in law school or in college deciding to be a lawyer. But I felt that being a lawyer would be the best protection I could have for protecting my civil rights and the civil rights of others. I think being gay influenced my decision to be a lawyer more than it influenced my decision to be a judge.

There were no openly lesbian or gay judges around in the early 1970s when I went to law school, and in many states, being openly gay or lesbian was grounds for being disqualified from admission to the bar. It was acknowledged as a permissible basis for excluding very well qualified people who were at the top of their law school classes, had never committed a crime, and had always paid their taxes from serving as lawyers in the state of New York. So it didn't occur to me to become a judge before I went to law school. When I went to law school at New York University, there were about half a dozen of us lesbian or gay law students. I was the only lesbian law student that was willing to self-identify. We organized the first gay law students group at NYU. It was not of the same order as gay students' groups are today at graduate and undergraduate schools. We met in secret, we did not let the school administration know of our existence, we certainly were not willing to let our professors know of our sexual orientation, and we met chiefly to give each other support and follow the progress in litigating for the right to be admitted to the bar in this state without regard to sexual orientation. We held each other's hands through law school for three years not knowing whether or not we would ever be allowed to pursue our chosen profession.

After I had passed the bar, I went before my interviewer on the character committee, and I was very anxious about it. I knew I had to disclose that I was living with a woman. I didn't feel I had to say anything more than I was living with her, but she was not a law student and one might wonder. I was shown into the room, and there was this very elderly man who invited me to sit down. He kept looking over my paperwork, and I thought, "Oh, God; he's going to ask me about living with this woman. What am I going to say?" He looked up and said, "I see you worked for my friend so-and-so in his law firm during your law school years." I said, "Yes, I did." He said, "He's a wonderful guy. I'm just going to send your application right along. Good luck." That was it. So because as a law student I clerked for a lawyer who had been a mentee to this very prominent former judge, I was of good character, and I was approved. Boy was I shocked to be part of the old boy network in New York City.

I wanted to work in public service when I graduated from law school, and one of the jobs that I was interested in was being an anti-corruption prosecutor prosecuting corruption in the New York City criminal justice system—corrupt police officers, district attorneys, lawyers, and judges. The office was interested in me, I thought I interviewed well, and I was very excited about it, but I was very worried because I knew they were going to do a background check on me. I was very worried that if they found out I was a lesbian, I would be denied the job. I was not familiar with background checks at that time, so I spoke to a sympathetic professor about my problem who said, "Don't be silly. They don't think women can be homosexual. They're not going to even consider that question with regard to you, so don't worry about it." I got the job and became a prosecutor. I think she was probably right. Lesbians, at least in the mid-'70s, were not perceived of as much of a threat.

At a smaller firm where I was a partner, I had a lot of autonomy. I was also active in a small lesbian and gay religious organization in the early 1980s, and they approached me at one point saying that they were going to be evicted from their office space and could I represent them in landlord-tenant court. I got involved and met some of the political leaders from the gay community, and pretty soon I was heading a confederation of representatives from about fifty gay and lesbian groups in an effort to secure the building as a community center for the lesbian and gay community. I was the lead negotiator with the city of New York to buy the building from the city for that use; I worked with some other gay leaders who were much more politically savvy than I and others who were very prominent within the gay and lesbian community. We managed to prevent the city from selling the building, keep the sub-tenants from being evicted, and secure the right to buy the building. To do that we had to raise $150,000 within three weeks to put up as a downpayment, and in 1983, the New York City gay community had never put together that kind of money. We managed to raise the money and get the building, and now, of course, it's the New York City Lesbian and Gay Community Services Center; it provides services to five thousand people a week.

When I was able to be out at the law firm in 1983, it was very liberating. I could relax much more. It was much more comfortable. When I came out, I had one partner at the firm who was pretty shaken up. He and I, his wife, and my partner had been going to bar dinners and firm dinners together for a long time. Everywhere I would go, he would see my partner, but somehow it didn't register with him until someone said the three-letter word to him. He was shaken up. So I took him to lunch, and we had a talk. He had been very supportive of me at the firm previously, and he said something like, "The firm had a gay client once," or something like that. It was clear to me that he did not know the other gay people who were working at the firm, and he certainly did not know how many of the firm's clients were gay. I just reminded him I was the same person who had been his partner for the previous three years. I was not any different just because he now knew I was gay.

There was a little resistance, though. For example, I was honored by the gay business group at a fundraising dinner. Typically, when one of their partners was in such a situation, the law firm would buy a table at the dinner. One of my partners actively protested the firm buying a table at the Greater Gotham Business Council's Annual Dinner. Although a couple of my partners did attend the dinner, the firm declined to pay for a table.

After we got the center rolling, I was obligated to return to full-time law practice at my firm. I did, but it made me want to consider returning to the public sector or the public interest sector. And over the course of the next couple of years, I lost a number of my friends to AIDS and really felt that it was time for me to make a change in how I was putting my professional energies to use. At the same time, I found myself feeling less in need of being an advocate and more interested in being an adjudicator. There were openings on the Criminal Court of the city of New York, the lower criminal court in the city. It's an appointed judgeship, and people were being urged to apply; so I did. There had never been a lesbian appointed to that court before. I had some significant support from the gay community because of my work on the community center, I was a member of the national board of directors of Lambda Legal Defense and Education Fund, and I had organized New York City law firms' gay and lesbian partners to volunteer their services for Lambda. And, I guess city hall felt the time was right to name a lesbian to that court, so I was appointed.

I served from 1987 through 1992 as a judge of the Criminal Court. In 1993, I was designated by the administrative judge for New York City to serve on an acting basis in the higher court. He named me an acting supreme court justice. At the beginning of 1995, I took office as an elected supreme court justice. I had to run for that office, which I started to do in 1991. I was the first lesbian to run for state supreme court justice in this state. Campaigning involved attempting to secure the support of the Democratic Party in New York City. While there was a great deal of enthusiasm for my candidacy in some quarters, and I was very gratified to have the entire lesbian and gay community in New York behind me, there were still some pockets of opposition and resistance to my election. I had one political leader from Manhattan tell me that she liked me very much, she was sure I was well-qualified, but she couldn't possibly support me because her religion dictated that I was unqualified for the bench based upon my homosexuality. Fortunately for me her constituents did not see it that way. After running for four years, I was elected, and I'm now the first lesbian to serve on the criminal term of the New York State Supreme Court.

During the campaign, everyone talked about the candidates, and the first thing anyone would say about me was, "She's gay." Some people would say, "Why do we have to know that about you? Who cares who you sleep with?" You have to explain to people without threatening them that I would like to keep my personal life private, too, but, unfortunately, we live in a society where powerful people consider people such as myself to be not normal, not qualified to hold certain types of employment, or not entitled to the same employee benefits or the same civil rights as everybody else. It's very important that everyone know that many of their neighbors, relatives, and friends happen to be gay and lesbian people, and they have to consider whether they want to deny employee benefits, civil rights, and employment opportunities to them. The other reason I gave for why it's important for a gay public official to be open about who she is, is that there are thousands of gay and lesbian kids growing up in this country right now who are thinking about their futures and trying to decide whether they have futures. There is a very high suicide rate among them, and it is very important that they see that they can be anything they want to be if they put their mind to it. It's very important that they have role models. I didn't, and I know how I suffered because of that.

Generally, the non-judicial staff and my colleagues have been very supportive. Every once in a while some stupid person makes an idiotic comment. A court clerk once told me that in his view I was not entitled to be a judge because I was a homosexual. He refined poor judgment to a high art and was not typical. We now have a couple dozen gay judges here in New York City. I know that straight colleagues of mine have given extra thought to decisions involving gay and lesbian and AIDS-related issues by virtue of our presence on the court. I think our presence has made a real difference.

Knowing a gay person; sitting down to coffee with her every day; attending the judicial seminar with him every year; seeing him go into the office next to yours; knowing he handled a particular part of the court last month, you're doing it this month, and you're both really equally qualified to do that work; hearing him or her talk about important life issues, their commitment to their partner, their need to have family leave when the partner becomes seriously ill; seeing they're living their lives the same way you live yours with the same kinds of concerns that you have makes us more familiar, more personal, more human, and easier to understand. It makes our issues more real and more comprehensible.

When people are willing to be public about their sexual orientation and assume public office, it really does change things. There's a lot of support for people everywhere in this country doing that now; there are national organizations of gay public officials, gay judges, and gay law enforcement people. Right now the New York City Gay Judges Association is negotiating with the state court administration to provide some sort of tele-video equipment to enable one of our colleagues with AIDS to work from home, and the reaction from the court administration has been very positive. I don't have to educate them about their obligations under the Americans with Disabilities Act. They are very well aware of that. Whenever a group is able to organize and identify itself, the issues get heard and addressed more than if people are not pulling together.

The judiciary is a wonderful job; it's very challenging and very rewarding. It has involved financial sacrifices having left a partnership at a major law firm, but I wouldn't trade it for anything. I find the work fascinating, interesting, and challenging. You have to have the right sort of temperament or you won't enjoy it. If you really want to be an advocate, you should not seek a career on the bench. You have to know your own strengths and follow them. Until the mid-1980s I never had a clue that I had an option of being a judge, and I'm just delighted.

Jerry R. Birdwell

Department: Criminal District Court #195, Dallas, Texas
Age: 52
Job: District Court Judge (Former)
Years in Law Enforcement: 7 months

Texas born and raised, Jerry was appointed to the state court by then-Governor Ann Richards. Seven months later, he lost his bid for re-election. On a Saturday afternoon at his home in Lake Tahoe, California he talked about the "trials and tribulations" of being an openly gay public official in Dallas, Texas.

I became interested in politics at a very early age. I was active in high school politics, and when I got out, Congressman Jim Wright took me to Washington, D.C. as a White House intern during the Kennedy administration. I worked in the White House, with the Defense Department at the Pentagon, and then on Capitol Hill in congressional offices until my twenty-first birthday. Then I returned to Texas and announced for public office where I was defeated in a run-off election.

When I got out of law school I went to Dallas to practice law and had a couple of criminal cases right off the bat. I had always enjoyed the courtroom, thoroughly enjoyed the cases, and was very successful in criminal law.

When you get out of law school, people ask the question, "When are you going to get married?" It was easy to say, "I'm just out of school, and I can't afford it." So I passed it off for a number of years. Pretty soon, though, that old dog don't hunt no longer! I led a very active life in the gay community and didn't hide anything. I practiced law with a couple of straight lawyers, never hid, and never dated women. I'm sure there was talk around the courthouse that I might be gay, but nobody came up to me and called me "faggot" or anything like that. Subconsciously I was always working a little bit harder because I felt that I had to do the best I could to be successful, be at the top, and win my cases. I had to do all this because if people were to find out I was gay, it would be an equalizer.

Being gay wasn't discussed with me until probably 1988. Certain friends knew, but it wasn't openly discussed. At that time a district judge in Dallas tried a guy in his court for the murder of a gay man. He made the comment when he sentenced the defendant, "It's just a queer that he killed; it was no big deal, be it a prostitute, queer, or some low-life," and he didn't give him a very stiff sentence. This outraged the gay community. One afternoon I looked out the window and saw all these people marching in front of the courthouse holding up signs. I had just walked out of the courtroom, was standing there in a three-piece suit with my briefcase, and thought, "This is it; I'm getting ready to make a statement. I'm upset about this. What he did was wrong, and I'm going to do something about it." So I went out there and marched. The other people were in shorts and jeans, and I was in a blue suit so the tv cameras focused on me. There were judges standing there watching us march, and it made me feel real good.

The story on the protest ran on CNN and mentioned me. That afternoon, another judge, probably the most redneck district judge that we have in Dallas, was staying in my home in Lake Tahoe, California. He and his girlfriend had gone there to ski. That afternoon he came in, reared back in the chair, turned on CNN, and heard "Dallas, Texas courthouse." Of course it perked his ears. He was a very close friend of the judge that had given the light sentence. He came back to Dallas, and the following week I was at the courthouse walking down the hallway, and I heard his old, gruff voice yelling at me, "Birdwell!" I thought, "Oh shit, I know what this is about." So I walked in, I shut the door, and he said, "Saw you on television! People have asked me if you're gay, and I didn't know." I said, "He should never have made that statement about giving a defendant a light sentence because he killed a gay person. It was absolutely, totally wrong. Something should be done. That has no place in the judiciary. I will do everything in my power to see that something's done." Of course, he tried to calm me down.

The gay community proceeded to file a petition with the judicial qualifications board; I made sure that I was the first one to sign that petition. The judge fought it every way he could. In the end they didn't remove him from the bench, but the board did sanction him saying, "If you do it again, you leave the bench." So I felt very good about it. Of course I was never allowed back into his courtroom, and from that point on, everybody knew that I was gay.

After Governor Ann Richards was elected, I made an application for one of the benches. When I went to Austin for the interview, I interviewed with the secretary of state, the governor's attorney, and a couple of other people in her office. They asked, "Is there anything about you that would embarrass the governor?" I said, "You better know now that I'm gay." They said, "We already knew that." I said, "Other than that, there's nothing." I met with the governor's appointment secretary, and she said, "You will be getting a call from the governor within two weeks. Don't say anything until that happens." In about two weeks I got a call from a friend who said, "The governor just made a call to another attorney; you didn't get the appointment." I wondered what happened. The next appointment came up, my name was on the list, and I missed that one also. I knew another one was getting ready to come up, and by this time there was a new appointment secretary. I got the appointment through him.

In the interim, the redneck district judge who had been in my Tahoe home and I became much closer friends. When I was appointed to the bench in May of '92, I called the courthouse and talked to him and said, "I just got my call from the governor's office; they are faxing the oath to me. I want to come down and have you swear me in." He said, "Why don't you do it this way? Call some of your friends, have them come out to your house, I'll come out and swear you in out there, and we'll have a little party." So I got on the phone and called my friends and my parents. They came up to my home, and the judge swore me in.

When word got out that I had been appointed, the Republican Party heard that I had been sworn in at my home. They called a press conference and claimed that I had been sworn in in secrecy at my home, and that I had all these gay people around me. They said that I should leave the bench because I was breaking the law every day. They made a big issue of it. Bear in mind, the judge who suggested the location and swore me in was a Republican. They held press conference after press conference demanding my departure from the bench. I had people picket outside the courtroom.

The man who was the president of the anti-abortion group Operation Rescue stayed on me. Any time we held a press conference or a meeting, he would come, preach from the Bible, tell me what a sinner and how awful I was, and tell me I was going to hell. It was awful. It was unbelievable what he would say. Every day I was on the bench they had someone in my courtroom trying to find something I did wrong. They always used the fact that I was gay and said that I had to leave the bench because I was breaking the sodomy laws of Texas. It got really awful, but I knew that I was right and that as an American citizen I had every right to serve. Being gay doesn't disqualify me at all. That's what kept me going. I knew what I was doing was correct.

I was always on my toes to make sure that nothing went wrong and that I followed the law. If there was any question, I would be off the bench looking up the law rather than guessing. I wanted to make sure I was right because I knew I had people in the courtroom observing me. They were there strictly to find something wrong. Having somebody in the courtroom constantly over your shoulder hoping that you will say one word they can pounce on and use on the news is stressful.

My fellow judges treated me very well, and I was close to several of them. After the Republican county chairman had his press conference demanding my resignation, the judges said, "Keep your chin up, and don't let it bother you. Just get in there and do your job."

When I was appointed, I was immediately thrown into a campaign for my re-election. We live in a quiet neighborhood where I've lived for seventeen years. During the campaign, I had campaign workers come by the house, and we put signs together out back. People would come along at night and vandalize automobiles—break the windows out, slash the tires, and spraypaint the cars. It got so bad that during the last two weeks of the campaign, my lover and I had protection around the clock because we were getting threats against our lives. They would say they were going to get us, "Faggots; you need to die," and stuff like that. People would have my campaign bumper stickers on their cars, and they would find "Fag" written on the bumper sticker with a big, black marker.

One of my childhood friends wanted do what he could for the campaign. He said, "I'll put up your eight by twelve signs, and that'll be my contribution to your campaign." He put all these signs up, and they kept being spray-painted with "homo" or "fag," or torn up. He had one place in particular that he really liked, and the sign there was getting torn up one night, the next night it had "homo" on it, and the next night it had "fag." It became an issue with him, and he said, "I'm going to sit up and catch him." One morning I got a call, and he said, "Birdwell, I'm on the mobile phone, and I'm chasing the guy. I caught him doing it, he jumped into his car and took off, and I'm following him. I've already called the police." I stayed on the phone with him as he followed the guy through town. Finally the guy pulled in front of a house, got out of his car, ran up to the front door, and knocked. Another guy let him in. At this time I had off-duty police officers and sheriff's deputies that I personally hired to sit out in our driveway, so I went out to the car, he ran the tag, and it belonged to a company. He ran the street address, and nothing came back. Then he ran a voter registration and found out it was the home of the president of the Texas chapter of Operation Rescue.

Eventually the guy came out and wanted to know what my friend wanted. He said, "If I go back and take care of everything, will you not do anything to me?" My friend said, "I won't, but I can't tell you what Birdwell's going to do." I said, "I can tell you what I'm going to do; I intend to file charges against him." When they got back to where he'd torn the signs down, the kid told the police officer what he had done, and the police department wouldn't even take a complaint. Finally I got it to go to the grand jury, and the grand jury filed on him. The case was just recently disposed of.

In the election I got about 48½ percent of the vote. Of course, that wasn't quite enough so I was defeated. The good part was that I got more votes than any of the Democrats that were defeated, so you can't really say it was a gay issue that killed it. Even though I know I lost a lot of votes because of the gay issue, there were other Democrats who lost getting forty-six or forty-seven percent of the vote. You could say that it was more of a Democratic issue that defeated me rather than a gay issue.

After the election, I went back to private practice. As far as what I do in the future, I'm just going to have to wait and see. It looks like Dallas is getting more and more conservative, and I don't know whether I'd be wasting my time trying to run again.

If every gay person would just stand up, we could change the attitude of America in a very short period of time. A lot of people don't like us because of our image. When you turn on the news and see the gay pride parade with somebody going down the street on rollerskates in a tutu with a parasol, that does not project the image we need. If we were to change that image, we'd have a chance to change the attitudes about the community. A lot of gay lawyers and judges won't come out. I've had them tell me, "I wish I had the guts and could come out and not be defeated." But they're afraid. Just because nothing happened to me doesn't mean that it won't happen. I can understand, but by same token, I can assure you that I am much happier being out and open than they are being closeted and on the bench. I don't have any fear. They do, and I feel sorry for them.

Part Four:
Special Forces

A number of criminal justice functions are required both to keep the system running and to serve special functions. For example, recruitment, training, background investigation, and personnel officers keep a steady flow of well trained officers ready to go as more senior officers are promoted, relocate, or retire. Community liaisons and community services officers serve as linkages between communities and police departments in efforts to improve relationships, and dispatchers organize the communications between incoming calls for service and officers on the street and among the officers. The criminal justice system could not function without the services of these professionals and those in similar positions. While typically not exposed to the same dangers and hazards as their counterparts on the streets, these professionals are still concerned about fitting in, advancing their careers, and being able to do their jobs without harassment.

Edgar Rodriguez

Department: New York City (NY) Police Department
Age: 35
Rank: Sergeant
Job: Recruitment
Years in Law Enforcement: 13

A compact man with bright hazel eyes and a crew cut, Edgar is in command of the department's recruitment section and, in his off-duty hours, is active in GOAL, the Gay Officers Action League. Relaxing at home in his Manhattan apartment one evening, he talked about how it hasn't always been easy being Puerto Rican and gay in the NYPD.

I wanted to be a cop or a doctor ever since I was a kid—my heroes were police officers and doctors. A neighbor had a friend who was a police officer. They used to get together, and I used to hang around them and listen. He was a really big, tall, gentle man—full of confidence—who symbolized what I saw on tv. I was pretty excited about the possibilities of becoming a cop one day.

I had a lot of fears growing up; as a child I was picked on for being small and quiet, I was afraid of the dark, I was afraid of fighting, and as I got older, I wanted to try to find ways of challenging my fears. So when the opportunity to take the police test came along, I thought, "This is something I always wanted to do and definitely another way to challenge my fears." So I took the police test, and before I knew it I was in the academy. I also wanted to work in a field that would give me real life experience. I got more than I bargained for. I saw things about life and people that most others never could imagine.

When I first came into the department, I looked like I was sixteen or seventeen. I was so young-looking the guys saw me as a kid and took me under their wing. I got really good training from them. I began to feel like "one of the guys." However, I was reminded very quickly that I was different because I was Puerto Rican. My first precinct was predominantly White male but the community was Black and Hispanic. Over time it became very clear to me that my ethnicity and my cultural background played a very strong role in how people perceived me. There was one time when I stepped into an RMP (radio motor patrol car) with a cop, and he didn't know I was Puerto Rican—he didn't know my last name. He said, "I hate this precinct. It's full of niggers and spics." I looked at him, he looked at me, and then he looked at my name plate. He began to stammer and stumble over his words, "I don't mean all of them—only the bad ones." That's the kind of mentality that existed with some of the cops.

After several years I transferred to the SPECDA unit which is the School Program to Educate and Control Drug Abuse. It was a great opportunity. I educated children throughout the city about drugs and alcohol, peer pressure, and self-esteem issues. It allowed me to interact with thousands of inner city kids, and share my life with them. I recognized how important my presence was for some of the kids, especially the Latino kids. I started to become active in GOAL and as I began to understand more about lesbian and gay issues, I learned that the highest rate of suicide was among lesbian and gay youth. It started tearing at me because I began to realize that my being in the closet was perpetuating this situation. I thought, "Here I am a role model for all these kids...how about the lesbian and gay kids?" I remember teaching a sixth grade class, and I saw a kid who was probably gay. I thought, "This kid needs to know that I'm gay," but at this time in my life, there was no way I could tell him.

At the same time, the recruitment unit in the police department wanted to recruit lesbian and gay people into the police force. They wanted to make a recruitment poster and GOAL asked me to pose for it. I was still closeted, but when I thought about the kids who needed a role model, I knew I had to do it. I was photographed with three other New York City cops, a Riker's Island Corrections Supervisor, the lesbian and gay liaison for the Manhattan District Attorney's Office, and eleven leaders of the lesbian and gay community.

One time, I had an argument with a cop at the office who suspected I might be bisexual. She began to yell horrific gay slurs, and at the end, she said, "Not only are you a faggot, but you're not even a proud faggot 'cause you're such a fucking closet case!" When she said that she took me down. Although I felt I was proud of myself and understood that I had some acceptable reasons why I felt I had to remain closeted, I still harbored a sense of shame remaining in the closet, and when she said that, I realized I wasn't totally proud of myself.

I left work early that day and, on the way home, broke down and cried. I talked with a friend about what happened and got some good advice. With that I decided to go back to the office, let her know that what she said really hurt me, remind her about the department's strict, official policies regarding the use of ethnic or cultural slurs, and request an apology. I was also going to come out. The next day, I did just that, and after a long and personal dialogue between us, she apologized, and I felt relieved, "It's out in the open now."

She told the whole office, and the next day, an African-American officer in my unit who I deeply respected for his intellect and good nature said, "I heard you were gay. I'm a musician, and there are a lot of gay people I deal with. I don't understand this thing. Can you explain it to me?" I sat there for two hours and told him my story, what I knew about lesbian and gay people, and my pain. When I was done, he looked at me and said, "With all your suffering and pain of having to live such an important part of your life in secrecy, I really give you a lot of credit for coming in here every day with a smile. I really respect you," and he shook my hand. At that moment, it hit me; I realized that there is hope. I saw a light of hope in that conversation that made me realize that I could educate the world, that I could reach people with my story. That's when I began my quest to educate people about lesbian and gay issues and to come out and be a role model for kids.

A week or two later, I was promoted to sergeant and coincidentally sent to the Sixth Precinct—Greenwich Village! I recognized that being a gay, Puerto Rican sergeant was going to be a difficult situation because of racism and homophobia. I also knew it was going to affect the way some people perceived my authority, my intelligence, and my ability to supervise.

When I first got to the Village, nobody knew I was gay—nothing came up that would let anybody know my sexual orientation. I was getting along with the cops really well. But, then the recruitment poster came out. The first person to see the poster was the property clerk, and I guess he decided that it was everybody's property because that's who he showed it to. The news spread like wildfire.

Then people saw me differently. They never really got a chance to get to know "Edgar, the cop" or "Edgar, the person." They only saw "Edgar, the gay sergeant." I'd walk in and people would stare at me. It was very difficult. At the same time, I became more of an activist. I got involved in media—tv and newspaper articles—and the cops resented that because they would get phone calls at the precinct saying, "You've got a fucking faggot working there!" The cops would be embarrassed by having a gay man working with them. They wanted me to be invisible to the community or silent like most of the other lesbian and gay officers. You know, like "Don't ask, don't tell." They responded to an article in the paper about me with a letter to the editor saying, "... we are opposed to the undue criticism brought upon us by the public we serve, due to the comments made by a newly appointed supervisor....the assumptions of a psychologist stating that 15 percent of the police department is gay is an insult to the straight officers who may be unduly subject to insults and allegations." About a third of the precinct signed the letter. If you took out the word "gay" and substituted "African-American," "Asian," or "Latino," you could see the bigotry in that letter. It really was very difficult for me. Ironically, the cops who wrote this didn't realize that at least 15 percent of that precinct was and still is gay and lesbian. They just never new it, and some probably never will.

There were a lot of times when my authority was usurped because I was gay. When I gave orders regarding certain things, some cops would do it reluctantly, saying, "He only wants us to do it 'cause it's for the gay people." They'd complain to the supervisors, and some things I was trying to do in the community were all knocked down. I would've accomplished so much more in that precinct, not only for the lesbian and gay community, but for the community at large, if that wasn't occurring. There was a lieutenant in that precinct who was very homophobic. He hated me from day one. The first time I talked to him he told me that if his son was gay he would disown him. He treated me like shit, made my life miserable, and was my boss. There were times when I tried to discipline cops who weren't doing their jobs or were discourteous to me, and he would get in the way. I never got the support I needed from him as my supervisor. The way he treated me and his lack of respect set the tone for others in the command.

One day another very homophobic lieutenant went crazy on me saying he was looking for me and couldn't find me. He failed to recognize that I was on meal. I was up in the sergeant's lounge where we were allowed to be for our meal period. He called me into the lieutenant's locker room and talked to me in a way that no one has ever talked to me. He berated me worse than I've ever heard. I was never so close to exploding on someone; I was never so humiliated. There was another lieutenant in the locker room who was so mortified that he told the lieutenant to stop. I was professional—I knew how he felt about gay people, and I knew why he was responding to me that way. I regret I didn't say what was on my mind, but I've always been respectful of rank even if I don't respect the individual. I come from the old school of policing where you're not insubordinate unless they're making you do something illegal.

While there were cops who resented me, there were also a lot of cops and bosses who were my allies, especially some of the sergeants, lieutenants, and cops that had experienced some form of discrimination on the job themselves. A lot of my friends would tell me the rumors they heard. One rumor was, "All Sergeant Rodriguez does is drive around and look at guys." I knew I was under a microscope when I came out and knew I would have to be above-board unlike other cops. Not only that, I'm very professional. That's always been my style of policing.

An interesting parallel was there were people in groups like ACT UP and Queer Nation who hated my guts 'cause I was a cop. There are some who think I'm selling the community short by being a police officer because I assist the whole structure in oppressing gay people. I can understand their perspective, but I truly feel that my presence helps to change the attitudes of others in our society and change the direction of how the police department responds to lesbian, gay, bisexual, and transgender people. At the same time, I was a hero for many people 'cause I represented a new level of power in a structure that oppressed them. I also represented a bridge for them to go and get help when needed. For five years, lesbian and gay people in that precinct that were victimized came to me, and they would never have come forward otherwise.

As much as I wanted to do more in that precinct, I realized I was reaching a stalemate. I couldn't do as much because of people getting in my way, so I left there and went to the recruitment section. So there I am, the cop who posed for the gay recruitment poster in command of the recruitment section. I work to improve the police department by guiding it towards recruiting the best police candidates while increasing its diversity. Working there thus far has been quite a learning experience and challenge. Most of the officers that work with me as well as the supervisors I am accountable to seem to view me with little or no prejudice.

Not too long ago, the Gay Officers Action League organized a convention in Puerto Rico, and Puerto Rican police officers were asked about their perspective on hiring gay and lesbian people. The head of recruitment said, "We don't hire criminals, people of ill repute, or homosexuals." A sergeant also said that gays would be ineffective, too effeminate, and too weak to take on responsibility for policing. That caused a little fire storm in the lesbian and gay community. We were invited on a local tv show with a lesbian bar owner to speak about these issues. The debate was won by the lesbian and gay panel who did really well. That night, the bar owner threw a welcoming party for the lesbian members of GOAL at her club. At 1:30 in the morning, the bar was raided by the police. A SWAT team raided the bar with shotguns and automatic weapons. It was very clear that their goal was to intimidate and harass. It was really disgraceful and unprofessional how they had pulled the welcome mat from under us. As a Puerto Rican, I was really ashamed and embarrassed. I expected that professional courtesy would transcend their homophobia, and it didn't.

The next day we held some press conferences. Interestingly enough, one of the things that had been alleged was that lesbian and gay people were ineffective and weak. However, our members were at the beach one morning when a straight couple went out swimming and started to drown. According to witnesses, the Puerto Rican cop stood by and did nothing, but a gay cop swam out and pulled these people to safety. It was very profound, especially in the middle of the debate.

The trip turned out to be very inspiring because with each oppressive or repressive thing that was done or said, we grew together and galvanized with the lesbian and gay community in Puerto Rico. We celebrated our unity there, and there was a lot of really strong energy in the air. It was like a second Stonewall.

I'm really kind of afraid for my future because it seems that laying low and being quiet helps me progress in the police department. They don't like anybody they perceive as being a loose cannon. I'm not a loose cannon, but sometimes I feel that they're really afraid I might become one. Most gay cops who go places in the department are the quiet ones who don't get heavily involved in the politics of discrimination and community activism, and that bothers me. It's like you have to be a good faggot to get around—silent and invisible. So it seems as if I kept quiet, never said a word, and never got into the media, I'd get places. But now because of Puerto Rico, I'm re-energized and want to get even more involved. Now, more than ever, I recognize the importance and the accomplishments of being visible and a role model to others. So many cops have come out because of my visibility. However, I also want to rise up in the ranks and be a high-ranking officer. I know that when given the opportunity, I always accomplish my goals. Whatever my fate, I will continue to help bring positive change and improve the police department for all communities, and only time, the collective efforts of many, and the politics of our administration will tell how much will be accomplished towards this means.

I try not to view anyone as an enemy even those people who might try to harm me. I recognize the realities of the ignorance that exists in the department, but there are a lot of really good cops out here. As hard as things may have been, I have a tremendous sense of satisfaction and achievement, and there have been a lot of good times. I'm very proud of being gay, of being Puerto Rican, and I'm very proud of being a New York City police officer.

Sharon Lubinski

Department: Minneapolis (MN) Police Department
Age: 41
Rank: Sergeant
Job: Police Academy Supervisor
Years in Law Enforcement: 16

After working on patrol for many years, Sharon recently transferred to the training unit and now supervises the police academy. Late one afternoon over coffee, she talked about her path from growing up very closeted in rural Wisconsin to being the first openly lesbian police sergeant in the Minneapolis Police Department.

I had no career inclinations to go into law enforcement. I graduated from University of Wisconsin in Madison and had a bachelor's degree in International Relations. I saw an ad in the paper for deputy sheriff and thought it sounded like a challenging job where I wouldn't be tied to a desk. I applied and got the job. I had always had fairly non-traditional jobs—I was always a tom boy. I worked a donut machine in high school and drove a cab in college.

I started off in 1978 in the Dane County Sheriff's Department in Madison, Wisconsin. I stayed for eight and a half years, and then fell in love with a woman who happened to be in Minneapolis. I decided I wanted to make the move and applied to Minneapolis so I could be up here with her. So at age thirty-four, I went back through a basic academy which is akin to boot camp. I got thrown to the floor mats by twenty-one year olds fresh out of the military which was really a rotten experience. But in terms of my personal life and long term goals, it was well worth the change. I'm still with the same partner.

When I applied for the job, I was conducting myself in a very closeted way. As with many closeted gays and lesbians, we think if we're not doing anything overtly gay and lesbian, nobody else knows. It's a fallacy. When I was in the sheriff's department I don't recall being really worried until one of my field training officers strongly implied that if I really wanted to get out of field training and become a full fledged officer I needed to prove I wasn't a lesbian. That hit me like a ton of bricks. I had been playing the game of not bringing my partner to any sort of department functions or events, always changing pronouns from she to he, and going to great lengths to avoid that kind of information coming out. Yet he still said that. That absolutely shocked me, and I was terrified. It meant that I had been denying myself all these things and they knew anyway.

Being closeted was draining, at times terrifying, and a false sense of security in many ways. I don't believe in outing anybody—it's a very private decision—but being on the other side of this big barrier called the closet, I feel the difference. There is a certain energy that is wasted on being in the closet. It's also humiliating because when you're closeted you're probably not going to speak up for yourself or other gays and lesbians. So in the past before I was out, if somebody would say something really negative or homophobic about a faggot or a dyke or make their wrist go limp, I'd keep my mouth shut. Later on you hate yourself because you've allowed that to happen. But you want so very much to be accepted, you don't want to be rejected, you don't want to ruin your career, and you don't want to put yourself in danger. There's some sort of inner humiliation that comes from not speaking up when I know I should have. In many ways you think they already know about you, and that's infuriating because they know you're powerless. When they do those behaviors they want to keep you down; they want to make sure they've got one over on you. We're one of the last acceptable prejudices. These days at least in this department, you don't see people saying outwardly negative things about African-Americans but it's still acceptable to joke about "faggots."

It became increasingly terrible to stay closeted. As you get to certain age, you think, "This is just bullshit. Why do I want to conduct my life this way? Why do I want to keep hiding? Why do I want to use my energy this way? Why don't I have my partner come to department ceremonies with me as my partner and not as my roommate?" My decision to come out was really many years in coming. A few years ago, an internal pressure built to the point where I could not ignore it. I had a number of pretty serious conversations with my partner, 'cause once I came out, she came out. She really didn't want me to do it. Finally I just couldn't stand it anymore. I'd seen reports that if people know somebody who's gay, they seem to have more understanding and acceptance. I was already a sergeant on the department, I worked with a lot of neighborhood groups, I'd been in the papers for community policing, and I felt like if I came out publicly, maybe I could set a good example and change a few minds. I felt like there should be some gays and lesbians who come out of their own volition, of their own choice, because there is a negative message if the only time someone who is gay or lesbian comes out is when they lose their job, lose their child, or get kicked out of the military. I really felt like somebody should come out just 'cause they wanted to, and I decided to be very public about it and go to the media. It was one thing to go to the chief or to my supervisor and say that I'm out, but think of all the gays and lesbians in Minneapolis who could feel a little better about the police because they knew there was a lesbian on the police department.

I knew that there was power in numbers, so I decided to see if other gay and lesbian friends wanted to come out with me. I really didn't want to do it alone, but I would have. We had some gay cops come over to the house and did some planning. Step one was to walk in and say, "Hi, Chief. I'm a lesbian," but then what do you do after that? I really wanted to start a task force to deal with this issue so a few of us decided to come out to the chief as a group and ask him to accept in concept a task force to deal with gay and lesbian issues.

The chief did not know what we were going to do or who was going to come and visit him. He knew we were going to talk about gay and lesbian issues and some of his employees were going to come along, but he didn't know who. It was scary 'cause once you crossed that threshold into the chief's office, that was it; there was no going back. The meeting went extremely well. He agreed in concept to carry forth on the task force, and at the end of the meeting he gave me a hug. It's not every day of the week that that happens.

Once I made the decision to come out it wasn't scary at all, and I never looked back. The scariest part was really making that "bungee jump," when you really have to put your absolute trust in your equipment, your background, or your life, and you have to trust that once you jump off that platform you're going to be alive when the jump is done. So the scary part was making the decision. I feel much safer now that I'm out. I'm known as a lesbian, and people can take me or leave me whereas before you never quite knew how they were going to react to you.

When I went to my precinct the day after it came out in the paper, I was really nervous about people's reactions to me. I noticed people looking at me, but they weren't talking to me. I talked to my partner, and she said, "They're probably waiting for you to make some kind of reaction; they're cuing off of you." So the next day, I was joking and kidding about it and bringing it up on my own. Then people were much more at ease. I think they were waiting to see how I reacted. I can't tell you how many cops said it was a really good thing—conservative cops and cops of all ranks. For the most part, cops were very congratulatory and happy about it. I know there were a lot of people who said stuff behind my back but they never said it to my face. But for the most part people are just fine with it.

The reactions of closeted gay officers has not been good. It's guilt-by-association, and they don't want to be seen with you. It's too bad they're that afraid that they reject one of their own. I'm not outing them. In many ways some of the harshest and most hurtful reaction has been from some closeted gay people. From the gay community there's been enthusiasm, acceptance and congratulations, and a sense of relief that they know there's somebody here. Six months after I came out we had our first police employment recruiting booth at the pride festival, and we were enthusiastically received.

I was more concerned about backup before I came out. Quite frankly, if some act of discrimination happened to me, or if I didn't get backed up, before I came out, I could not say it happened because I'm gay. I couldn't invoke the local ordinance to say there's been some discrimination against me. But now, I feel much more protected because I can use the ordinance if that's what's going on. So to me, putting my neck out made me feel much safer. I feel much better now 'cause I know who my friends are. If anything, once I came out people were making a point of backing me up. I had a young, macho cop come up to me shortly after I came out, and he said, "Sarge, if somebody doesn't back you up, I'll be there." Safety is an issue of real concern for anybody who's gay, but in my personal experience I have not, knowingly, not been backed up.

I don't think I ever will be fully accepted by either the gay community or the police community. Being a woman and being an officer, or being a Black person and being an officer, I think you get those same awful feelings—you're never fully accepted by either. You feel like you don't belong to either one. It makes me kind of sad sometimes, especially when you have some pretty pure motives. You want the gay community to be able to trust the police, you want the police to be able to do the best they can for the gay community, and there's suspicion by both groups that, "You must be a traitor in our midst." One person in the gay community went so far as to publish an article about me entitled, "Sleeping With the Enemy."

I have never had a moment of regret. It sure as hell hasn't been a particularly easy year, but the rewards of being out are so much more than the negative. Everyone needs to weigh the price of the closet, but you're probably a lot more out than you think you are. It's hard to say this, but gays and lesbians who are not out play into that dirty little secret—if you're not talking about it, there must be something wrong with it. I know it's scary, but you need to think that through. I'm so glad I came out.

Lee Jensen

Department: San Francisco (CA) Police Department
Age: 42
Rank: Police Officer
Job: Training Officer
Years in Law Enforcement: 13 1/2

Lee is the first openly gay training officer at the San Francisco Police Department Academy and the vice president of the Golden State Peace Officers Association. A slight man with brown hair, brown eyes, and a mustache, he was casually dressed in a black t-shirt and black jeans. At the time of the interview he was on medical leave recovering from an AIDS-related illness.

W hen I was in high school, I thought, "Maybe I'll try out for the California Highway Patrol (CHP)." Then in driver ed classes, they show you CHP movies of all the bodies that have gotten in accidents, and I said, "I don't want to see that." After college, I got a job at Metropolitan Life Insurance paying medical claims. After a couple of years I thought, "I am not geared for sitting behind a desk eight hours a day, five days a week. This crap isn't cutting it." I was in a bar, and a sergeant in the sheriff's department came in handing out notices that the police department was taking applications, and gays and lesbians were more than welcome to apply. I thought, "Hot shit," and I filled out the application. It went from there, and I've been doing it ever since.

April, 1980 is when I went into the academy. In my class there were six of us that were gay: three men and three women. At that time, the department was starting a new academy class of forty people every six weeks, and there was at least four gays or lesbians in every class. Now I am at the police academy as one of the training officers for recruit classes. Hopefully I can curb some of their bad attitudes and habits before it gets them or somebody else in trouble. To the best of my knowledge, I'm the first gay or lesbian officer to be in that capacity.

I was out when I applied for the San Francisco Police Department, and sexual orientation really wasn't an issue in the academy. If any of the training officers had an issue with it, they kept it to themselves. By the time we got out of the academy and went to our field training stations, pretty much everybody knew who the gay and lesbian officers were—the police department is no different than any place else as far as gossip and the grapevine.

During the field training program where you're actually in uniform out on the street with a senior officer, I didn't experience any derogatory words directed at me. However, there were a number of officers at the station that anytime I came near them they walked a different direction or they completely ignored me. If I tried to ask them something they would be real curt. But that was not the majority of the officers; there were only seven or eight of them that would be that way.

I didn't have any real problems until I got to my first assignment. On the radio there's words for the alphabet like Mary for "M" and queen for "Q." I was running a plate, there happened to be the letter "Q" at the end, and I said, "Robert Tom Queen," or something like that. Somebody came back on the air, "Queen, like you?" At that time, I thought, "Just consider the source, ignore it—some brain dead, Irish-Catholic pud that doesn't have the cajones to say it to my face." I had a suspicion who it was, but he muffled his voice so I really couldn't tell. Then in my mailbox at the station, I found the queen of hearts playing card.

Then there was an incident down in one of the alleys. I was standing there after hours talking to a sergeant and a deputy from the sheriff's department who were both sitting there cruising. One of the police department patrol units came by and told us, "You can't stay here." We were like, "We're all law enforcement officers; we're just standing here talking." And this first-rate, asshole said, "I don't care who the fuck you are, get out of here." He was one of those that was well known for being a homophobe. So we started moving as they came back around. Somehow it got around that I was in a car in the alley doing lewd and lascivious activities. It just happened that I was on vacation when the god-awful rumors started coming out. Things were being written all over the bathroom walls. Luckily my sergeant couldn't believe any of this was true, so he went around cleaning it all off. When I got back from vacation, I told him, "I was in the alley, but I was standing on the sidewalk with another officer and two deputies. We were just talking about things that were going on in our departments. We weren't doing anything." He said, "That's what I thought. You've worked for me for the last six months, and I know you better than to do something like that." Pretty much everything was blown over by the time I got back from vacation; I thought, "Thank God."

Four or five years ago, I had my star number on my locker at work. The last number happens to be an eight. By the eight somebody put "IDS" for AIDS. Then there was something about fags written on the wall in one of the stalls in the men's bathroom. We had an idea of who put it there—there was one officer who left the station who was extremely homophobic and stupid as ditch water. As soon as he came back, all this nonsense started. We can't prove that it was him, but we found it rather interesting that all the shit was taking place within a few days of him coming back. He has been heard to say anti-gay things, and he also doesn't have a whole lot of respect for Blacks and Asians. He's pretty much a racist. There were a few other people that were extremely homophobic. Everybody knows who they were, and everybody kept their eyes on them.

Most of the people at the station don't care about my being gay. All they look at is, "Can I trust you to back me up and save my butt if the proverbial shit hits the fan?" That's the crux of it right there. Even some of the straight officers will joke with you. They feel comfortable to say things, so it's a good atmosphere. There's one who's very straight and religious. She was on her way to the shopping center to get something to eat, and I said, "You going to get yourself a boyfriend while you're down there?" She laughed and said, "No, but I'll get you one." She teases every now and then.

The majority of the officers in our department believe, "You may be a fag, and I don't agree with your lifestyle, but at the same time, you are a police officer, and that's what we have to look at first. Even though I don't particularly like things that you do, we have to count on and work with each other." There are those who wouldn't do diddley squat for you off-duty, even if you were drowning. But most of them really don't care—as long as you don't shove it in their face.

In the department, my partner knew about my HIV status. She needed to know, "If I get punched out, and I'm bleeding all over, you'd better damn well put on some rubber gloves or make sure you don't get it on you." Later on when I went to another assignment, I had to tell the sergeant I was working with. He didn't let it bother him one bit. At that time I had an enlarged spleen, so if we got in a fight and I got hit, it could easily start bleeding, and I could die within five to ten minutes. He had to know so if something happened he had to get me to the hospital quickly.

Some people haven't made any big deal about it my being HIV-positive. I have heard from other people that several of our brain dead puds were passing around that I had AIDS. At the time I didn't—I just recently got the diagnosis of having AIDS. Until then, I was doing just fine. A good many of the officers know I have AIDS now because I'm on a medical leave—I've been on medical leave for the last three months. I'm due to go back to work soon. In this department, if somebody has to be out for an extended length of time, any other city or county employee can donate sick time or vacation time to them. I had over two hundred hours of sick time donated to me and that was nice. I got hours from people I would have assumed would never donate time. It proves to me that a lot of the people look at, "He's an officer first, and he's part of our family. He is in need."

I have noticed that a lot of the guys who had been in the department five to ten years when I came in have relaxed and become more tolerant. They have begun to talk to us and treat us like anybody else. By and large a lot of people's attitudes have changed now that they've had all these years to see how gays and lesbians do the job just as good as anybody else. Across the board, there's no difference as far as work ethics, job performance, or mental stability. We're police officers, and we are doing the job. A good many of us have medals of valor; several have a bunch of them.

I've always treated the gays and lesbians on the job as I would treat anybody. If I start cutting all the gays and lesbians slack, then I'm not doing my job properly. I came in to the job to be fair and even across the board—not to give special privileges to people and overlook all the bad things they're doing just because they're gay or lesbian. But in certain situations, I might. I pulled over this person who was obviously an AIDS patient. He had enough problems as it was without me giving him a citation for running a stop sign. So I gave him a short lecture about watching the signs and said, "I don't want to see you in an accident." He was very apologetic.

When it comes to going to a domestic problem between two boyfriends or two girlfriends, gay cops can usually handle those better than straight officers. Sometimes it doesn't matter who you are—all they want to do is shoot each other. You could be the pope walking in there, and it's not going to make any difference. But by and large, when they realize we're gay officers, we can diffuse the situation a little sooner.

Socially, some people are absolutely freaked that you are a cop. There was a young man that I picked up at a bar that I thought, "This is potential lover material." He was intelligent, he was handsome, he could put words together and make a coherent sentence, and he could carry on a conversation. He was a real sweetheart. The first time I took him home he saw my star (in San Francisco we have stars, not badges), I could see he was getting real antsy, and he asked, "This is real?" I said, "Yes." He goes, "Is it yours? Are you really a police officer?" I said, "Yes." He goes, "This is a sting operation, isn't it?" I said "No. I brought you here for me." He was nervous as hell and didn't know what to do. I came to find out later that he came from Dallas, Texas, and the police down there were doing bar raids on a regular basis. One night, the police came in to do a raid, and he and another guy got under the table so they could avoid getting hit by the night sticks. They were arrested for lewd and lascivious conduct in a public place. It was like, "You're damned if you do and damned if you don't."

When I came into this department, being gay was never a consideration. It's always been the coincidental thing. Most of the people don't give a shit if you're gay or lesbian. All they want to know is can they count on you to back them up when the going gets rough.

Shannon and Amy

Department: Minneapolis (MN) Police Department
Ages: 28; 30
Rank: Police Officers
Jobs: Backgrounds Investigator; Drug Abuse Resistance
Education (DARE)
Years in Law Enforcement: 7 1/2; 6 1/2

*Shannon and Amy met six years ago at work on the MPD. At their suburban home with their
three-week-old daughter MacKenzie, they talked about how becoming moms has changed their
perspectives on their jobs as police officers.*

S HANNON: In tenth grade, I got involved with a group called the Explorers. It's a faction through the Boy Scouts for students interested in law enforcement. Through that I decided that law enforcement was something I wanted to go into. I went to a junior college and got my two-year law enforcement degree. I was hired three months after my skills program. When I was hired as a police officer I had already worked for a suburban police department as a community service officer for three and a half years. We handled non-emergency calls, motorist assist, all the animal complaints, and parking enforcement. We were pretty much "go-fers" for the cops but it was a really good experience.

When Minneapolis offered me the job, I knew there was a large gay or lesbian officer population in the city. I felt like I could bury myself and not worry about it. I never considered coming out. I knew I would never come out; there was not a question in my mind that I wouldn't be closeted my whole career. That changed. There's absolutely no doubt in my mind that there were suspicions when I was in rookie school. The guys knew right away: if you weren't sleeping with another guy on the department then you were a dyke. Either you were sleeping around or you were a lesbian.

I worked patrol for six years, and most of the time I was on power shift which was seven-thirty at night 'til three-thirty in the morning. In June of last year I went to the backgrounds unit; we investigate the backgrounds of all our civilian and sworn applicants and make sure they're fit for hire. I've enjoyed being off the street. I was in a serious accident a while back—I got hit by a truck. I had to have two surgeries and was on light duty for over half the year. After that I thought being on patrol was not worth it.

AMY: I went to college at St. Cloud State—that's where I grew up—and started taking some law classes. That's how I got interested in law enforcement. I thought it'd be a fun job. I graduated from college in '87, went to my skills program that summer, and got hired in Minneapolis February of 1988. I went to the academy for two months, then did my field training for five months. I was in patrol for five years, and presently I'm a DARE officer. We go into the fifth grades and teach a seventeen-week curriculum to help kids stay off drugs. We teach them about peer pressure, different ways to say no to drugs, what drugs are, what they can do to you, and the consequences of using them.

I was still in the closet when I was hired. Throughout my five years on patrol there were a few straight officers who I trusted and told. Plus there was a group of gay officers that hung out together, so obviously they knew.

SHANNON: Amy had just come on the police department when I met her and she was still in rookie school. I called another officer over and asked who she was, she told me, and I knew I was destined to meet her. Our police department had a woman's softball team, Amy went out for the team, and we got to know each other then. We've been together ever since—it will be six years next week. Meeting Amy is the one thing on this job that I'll never regret; if it hadn't been for this job I would never have met her. I can be thankful for that.

The precinct I worked in bordered Loring Park—a large gay area—so we went on a lot of gay domestics. The partner that I worked with was also a lesbian. I remember going on gay domestics and the people would almost out you by saying, "You know what I'm talking about; you know how it is; you're one of us." We'd both deny it, "I don't know what you're talking about. We're not hear to discuss us; we're here to take care of your problems." It was almost terrifying. We'd get in the car and think, "Oh, my God, that was close." It was stupid, because everyone in the room knew about us but we would deny it left and right. Then I'd feel stupid. I'd get in the car and think, "That was really dumb." But you didn't want to have these people know because they could hold that over your head if you weren't out. If you were with a different partner one night and the people on the call knew you were gay, they could say something to out you. Before I was out it was very intimidating to go on a gay call.

AMY: If you're not out it's very stressful for fear of being found out. If you go on a call you could be outed by somebody in the community. My biggest fear was going into gay parties where gay people would seek you out and talk to you, and other cops might think, "Why are all these gay people talking to this cop?" I was called to a gay party once, and people came up to me and said, "Hi, sister." There were all these straight cops around, and I wondered, "What are they thinking?" That party made it very uncomfortable for me; it was very stressful.

SHANNON: In roll call there'd be comments about, "I had to go on a call with these fags," and things like that. It was as much my fault as anyone else's because if I didn't stick up for myself as a homosexual, that let the door open for them to go ahead and say things like that. I never did say anything; I sat there, bit my tongue, and let it slide like everyone else. The more people who come out, the more it leaves the door a little bit smaller for people to be able to make comments like that.

AMY: The whole thing to me was discrimination. When you're not out and things happen to you, you don't want to say anything. That makes it hard. All summer long we would go to party calls, and for the most part you'd go there and advise people to shut the party down. If you have to come back two or three times, the third time you'll give people tickets for "loud party ordinance." I've never been in a situation where the first time you go you give out tickets unless the people are being complete assholes. We went to an obviously gay party, and the officer in charge wrote all the people tickets. To me it was like, "Why are you giving them tickets? It's our first call here, everybody's leaving, and there's no problem." My feeling was they got tickets because they were gay, but I don't know for sure. If you see somebody being discriminated against and you're not out, it's very hard to stick up for them or tell the cops to knock it off. But now that I'm out, it's completely different, 'cause people know you're gay, and hopefully they won't do that stuff in front of you.

SHANNON: Amy and I knew our relationship was a lifetime commitment when we decided to come out on the job. I was working with a straight man who had become a real good friend of mine. During that time, Amy and I were trying to get pregnant and have a baby. It was such a big deal in our lives and this guy was such a good friend, so I told him. He was real positive. Also, Amy and I decided that we weren't going to raise a child and say at home, "It's okay that your mommies are gay," and then bring our kid to work to pick up our pay checks and say, "Now don't say anything about having two mommies." We decided that if we were going to have a child, we were going to be out to our families, to our friends, and at work. We were going to raise our child in a perfectly honest environment.

AMY: Coming out had a lot to do with the baby. We didn't want her to be raised with closeted parents. It was an easy way for us to let the Chief and other people on the department know that we were gay. We didn't want to hide it anymore for her sake. We have no regrets about coming out. I couldn't imagine not being out and having to hide. Hiding and being afraid causes so much stress. Now it's like, "This is who we are; accept us or don't."

SHANNON: The opportunity was there when Sharon Lubinski decided to come out. I had a supervisor who came up to me and said "Sharon's going to the chief the day after tomorrow to let him know she's gay; we're trying to get some people to go and show support." I said, "Instead of just a show of support, we may be interested in coming out with her." I came home and discussed it with Amy. Sharon was going to do it publicly. She was going to the newspaper, and we didn't want to go that far. We didn't feel it was the public's business. So Amy and I decided we'd go with her, and we came out to the chief. At the time I had just miscarried our first child, but we knew we were going to try again. So we came out to the chief and told him we considered ourselves to be married, that we were trying to have a baby, and that we would be more than happy to assist him in any way by being a liaison with the community. He was very supportive and positive. I really couldn't ask for more from him. He's treated us very well.

AMY: He didn't really say a lot, but it was very positive. We created a task force, and he supported that a hundred percent. He told us he wouldn't tolerate any discrimination on the department. Ninety-nine percent of the reaction has been positive. There was one incident with our federation. The task force did a survey on the police department asking basically, "What do you think of gay people?" Our federation helped us put it out, and the president signed off on it so we could send it out to the officers. It kind of back-fired because there was a small group of twenty to thirty officers who did not think that our federation should have been involved with helping send out these surveys. They looked at it as we were trying to get special treatment. We went to a federation meeting, and a small group voiced their strong opinion against it saying, "We're all blue, and it doesn't matter." The "all blue" crap doesn't fly. Granted, we all wear the same uniform, but obviously they didn't like gay people. They said, "Why do you have to let your sexuality be known; it has nothing to do with your job." But some of the surveys came back very discriminatory saying, "Fuck you; you're all going to burn in hell," and that kind of thing.

SHANNON: There is a small group of people who bitch about everything, and this was just one more thing to bitch about. They gave the old, "We're all blue." That's such a bunch of bull shit; it would be great if that was the way it was, but it's not. Women get treated differently on the department, Blacks get treated differently, and Hispanics and Indians get treated differently. That's society in general, and the police department isn't any different. They'd say, "There are rules, ordinances, and procedures that protect you." But unless you're out, how can you be protected? How can you prove that you've been discriminated against if someone says, "I didn't know you were gay." It was just a small group of officers though.

When we got involved in the donor insemination program, we asked the doctor, "What do most people do? Are most people honest about how the baby was conceived?" And the doctor said, "You need to be honest, and it shouldn't be something that you're ashamed of. Otherwise, it'll make the child ashamed of where they came from. You need to be honest when people ask you how you did it." So when people asked, "How'd you get pregnant?" we told them. The people who I work with have made jokes, and I've joked back all in good fun. They think it's wonderful that we've had a baby and want to know if we're going to have more. They're happy for us that we're a family.

AMY: We've had a lot of support with the baby. A lot of the female officers will come up and want to know what's going on. Everybody in the DARE office has been supportive. They all congratulated me, and a couple of them gave me cards. Minneapolis is a very liberal city, so we're kind of lucky. But the cops are very, ultra-conservative so we've been very fortunate that we haven't had any problems coming out.

SHANNON: The people I work with are all straight, and they're excellent. They ask about how Amy's doing, with us having the baby, and they've been nothing but supportive. Everyone in my office called me after the baby was born and asked how I was doing, asked me to bring the baby by, and asked if Amy was surviving the late-night feedings. I couldn't ask for better people to work with.

AMY: I'm sure there are quite a few people on the department who don't want gays and lesbians on the department, but I don't deal with any of those people. I'm sure they talk behind our backs, but you get to the point where you're too old to care what other people think. The friends who accept you are what matters, and the people who don't accept you, shit on them. Who cares as long as they don't hurt you or discriminate against you.

SHANNON: I'm sure there's a small group who thinks it's awful that we're raising a child, but I think for the most part people who know us know what type of people we are, know that we'll make great moms, and think that a child's lucky to be raised in this household. There's a lot of kids that aren't wanted, and this is a child who's really wanted.

I plan to go back on the street in September because of the baby. Amy's going to stay on days, and I'm going to go back to a middle watch so we don't have to put the baby in day care. I can't say that I'm excited about going back on the street, but Amy and my priority has got to be the baby. Putting her in a day care for eight or nine hours a day with people we don't know is not something we want to do. Going back on the street is temporary; we'll see how it works out.

AMY: I would like to quit, stay home, and take care of the baby, but we're both at top pay, and we are very secure in our jobs. I don't know if we can do it financially. It wouldn't bother me to quit at all because eventually I will end up going back on the street.

SHANNON: Since having the baby my attitude about being on the street has definitely changed. I'm a safe cop. Officer safety has always been my number one priority. I don't feel I'm invincible anymore, and I think the accident changed my mind on that. I don't want to have my child raised thinking, "I wonder if my mommy's going to come home at night." I don't think that's fair. Maybe we can make sergeant and work inside as investigators. In the seven years that I've been on the department, it's gotten worse on the streets; I have seen it change.

I will stay in law enforcement but I'd like to see Amy get into something else. I think my options are a little more limited because I only have the two-year degree. I cannot see myself going back to get a four-year. I really can't do anything else. I'd like to see myself make sergeant and go in investigations for the rest of my career. But I see myself staying in law enforcement. Right now, I'm a little disheartened. I think a lot of it has to do with wanting to stay home with our new baby. I wish I had more options other than having to go back on the street. I have a different perspective now that we have a child. I want to be there for her, and it scares me to think that something might happen. I guess I need to get my butt together and study hard for the next sergeant's test.

AMY: I wish I could be a part-time cop in Minneapolis and work twenty hours a week. We'll just have to see how this goes with Shannon working the street. I could retire today and be very happy. I never thought I would want to be a housewife, so to speak, but it wouldn't bother me at all. I still like my job, too, but a baby changes your life so much. She's the number one thing. Before it was always yourself and each other; now everything has to be based around her. Our biggest thing is we don't want other people to raise her, so we're trying to figure out ways to get me to stay home; we'll have to see what happens.

SHANNON: The worry about not getting a transfer and things like that because of being out is certainly there. I felt like I had been denied a transfer soon after I came out. There was an opening in the backgrounds unit, and I had put my transfer in. Normally when you put in a transfer, you try to get someone to put in a good word for you. I had two people speak to the supervisor of the unit, and the supervisor turned to one of them and said, "She's one of those, isn't she?" and flipped his wrist limp-wristed. This was like a week after we had come out to the chief. The officer said, "As a matter of fact, she is." And I didn't get the transfer. I knew another opening was going to happen in six months, and I was concerned about my chances of getting it—did I have a chance or was it just stupid for me to even keep my transfer request in because being a lesbian was going to cause a problem? So I went to the chief and said, "I'm really concerned about this. If it was any other cop, you could have a law suit on your hands. There's an ordinance and also state laws that protect me." I think the chief could have croaked when he found out this supervisor did this. I said, "I don't want anything to be done other than for him to be talked to. All I want is a fair chance to get the position." So he talked to the supervisor, and I think he could have just about croaked that he got caught. I did get the transfer. Fortunately, the supervisor retired, and I haven't had to work for him. I wonder how often that happens. And like I said, if I wasn't an openly gay officer, what recourse would I have had? I would have just buried my head in the sand.

AMY: We're lucky that we're both officers. When we both worked the street, if we had a bad night at work, we could come home and talk about it. We could relate to each other. If there was something tragic that happened at work, we could share our feelings with each other, and it would be okay to cry. I can open up to her because she knows what I'm going through. We're very fortunate that we are both cops.

SHANNON: Amy understands if I've had a bad day at work or if I've seen something bad. She understands 'cause she's had those same bad days. If I've dealt with nothing but crap all day or if something happened at court and I didn't win a case because of something stupid, she understands. We worry about if we're going to be okay at work, especially when we work the same shifts. I worry about her constantly, and I know she worries about me. With me going back on the street, she really worries. In that way that's not a positive thing, but emotionally it's been good.

AMY: This job affects you; if you see people being hurt, it doesn't affect you. If you cried at everybody who died or at every tragedy, there's no way you could do this job; you'd be a wreck. You kind of become cold—not to be mean—it's just kind of a defense mechanism you have to put up or you'd drive yourself crazy.

SHANNON: Our coming out has been the best thing for a large majority of people to understand that whatever stereotypes they had on gays and lesbians has changed. The drag queens and the dykes are not the majority. We're normal people that want to go on with our lives and be happy, just like anyone. They're starting to see it.

AMY: Since we've come out, having been on the task force, and with the liaison team, another dimension has been added to the job; we're helping gays and lesbians. When we work the pride festival, we feel proud to be a cop and to be gay. That part of it has always been rewarding. It's just too bad everybody can't be out. If people could only see it from the other side of the fence, they'd see once they're out how much nicer it is. It's so much more relaxed.

Stacey Rabinowitz

Department: New York City (NY) Police Department
Age: 30
Rank: Sergeant
Job: Special Projects, Office of Chief of Personnel
Years in Law Enforcement: 5

On the department for only five years, Stacey's career is on the fast track. Currently working for the chief of personnel, she's already working toward her next promotion. After work one day at a deli near headquarters, she talked about her goals and aspirations for working with the NYPD.

I grew up in Brooklyn. Since I was a little kid, I wanted to be a police officer, but I got dissuaded by my mom. I was really interested in the field of oceanography, but I had trouble with my ears; I couldn't equalize pressure. I tried a few other things while I was in college like physical therapy and realized they weren't for me. So I started taking classes in criminal justice and did really well. I have an associate's degree in criminal justice and a bachelor's in police science.

I became a member of the police department as a cadet in '87. It helped me finish my education. I finished my education in '89, and got promoted to police officer in July of '89.

Being gay, I worried about backup—that I wouldn't get it. I knew I was never going to be part of the "in" crowd; I walked to my own drummer, I had my own beat, so that part didn't bother me. But I worried about backup and being able to work with other people—or having other people be willing to work with me. It's easier for gay women than for gay men. It's a macho job, and gay women who come on the job are generally more macho, more assertive, or maybe a little more aggressive. People have a tendency to see that and have the perception that she can handle herself, where the stereotype of the gay man is somebody very effeminate; how could he be a cop?

In the academy, I was respected for having information. If somebody had a problem, they were coming to me asking, "What's the answer to this?" Who knows what they said behind my back, but at least in front of me I was respected for my intelligence. It was not like I was in the closet, per se. You didn't have time to be personal. The women in my squad were pretty comfortable with me; nobody seemed to have a problem. Everybody was very friendly with me except for one woman in another squad. She covered herself in the locker room. She was wearing a bra, and she still covered herself with a shirt even when I wasn't looking at her. I turned around to try to make her feel more comfortable. I wasn't interested in any of my co-workers; that's not my style. Out of the locker room we would talk—she didn't have a problem with me—but she just felt uncomfortable changing.

When you're on probation, they can fire you for anything. They don't need a cause. When I got into my Field Training Unit (FTU), people would talk, and I'm a talker. I'm not afraid to talk about myself, I want to feel included, and if I feel something's relative I'm going to say it. If people ask me how my weekend was, I'm not going to say, "Fine," and just walk away. So I came out to my co-workers. By then I was already a police officer—I was still on probation, but I was not a recruit. We were one step higher than a peon.

When I was in my (FTU), we worked an ACT UP demonstration. They were going to storm the precinct. I was terrified in the sense that if they had con-fronted us physically, they wouldn't know that I'm a gay person. But it didn't come to pass. Then I worked all the ACT UP demonstrations, and I saw people I knew. We had to take people away when they were being arrested. You do what you have to do, but I felt such a conflict! I guess every ethnic officer goes through that when they have to confront their own; you just deal with it. When I had the uniform on I was a cop first before being gay. In everything else, I'm gay first. The lines are very blurred, but when you're wearing blue, you've got to do what you've got to do. The main thing was protecting myself and my fellow officers; if it came down to that, that's what I would do. Thank God it never came off.

People got to know me and didn't seem to have a problem with my being gay. I didn't have problems getting backup. One thing I find is if you're out, it's harder for them not to show up, because if I'm out and nobody shows up, somebody's going to have to answer. A lot of people on this job have the view that if you're blue, you're blue; it doesn't matter what's underneath the uniform. Maybe they don't like you out of uniform, but they don't have to. Nobody's saying that they have to like you.

When I went to midnights, I was the lowest female on midnights, so I got jerked for that more than for being gay. It was nice working in Chelsea. I remember working with somebody one night who was gay, and every job we handled was gay related. I remember feeling really satisfied because I was able to help people from my community. Then the department was looking for an openly gay officer in Brooklyn to serve as a liaison with the community, so I called and said, "I'd like to do it." Mostly what I did was straighten out messes. I'm a very service-oriented person; we're there to serve the public. I was assigned as a community policing officer, and I worked there for two years. I really enjoyed it. I went to meetings, I gave a lot of speeches, I did a workshop on domestic violence to one of the lesbian groups, and there were a couple of bias incidents that I handled. Unfortunately, a majority of my work was domestic violence related calls amongst gay couples. It's a shame to say that it exists, but we can't hide the fact that it does. A lot of times I got called to handle them.

My first day out, one woman was so happy to see me she came up to me and said, "I'm really glad you're here," but she was afraid to tell me her name. That summed it up. It was a thankless job. There were a lot of times I felt that people should write letters to say thank you. Saying thank you to me doesn't tell my captain how nice a job I did; it doesn't tell the commanding officer of the borough how well I'm doing. One of the things that happens in all communities, not just the gay and lesbian community, is they don't thank their police. Maybe they feel they shouldn't have to, but it does make a difference because the letter stays in the person's jacket.

I was openly gay and got promoted to sergeant. I studied for the test, did really well, and got promoted in the first batch. I had an interesting experience as a new sergeant. When you get assigned to a precinct, you become a squad sergeant; you have eight to ten officers assigned to you, and as a new sergeant they try to test you. I had one come up to me and tell me that the officers were afraid to talk in front of me. I said, "If you're referring to the use of the word 'faggot,' I'm not going to tolerate it. First of all, the job doesn't tolerate the use of derogatory words for anybody, so just as you wouldn't use the word 'nigger,' I'm not going to tolerate the use of the word faggot. If they have a problem with it, I'm sorry, but that's the job policy." If anything, my presence is enforcing job policy, so if they have a problem with it, they have to live with it. I don't know if they would confront somebody else about that; if I was a Black male, would they have said, "We don't feel comfortable because we can't use the word 'nigger' in front of you?" They wouldn't have the audacity to say that. One thing I like about being a supervisor is the fact that I have control. If you're a good supervisor, you can take control and handle things. Like, for instance, if somebody says something offensive, you correct it; you take care of it, whereas a police officer to a police officer doesn't have the same effect. It's not the same.

One time, when I was a police officer, I was in the station house, and one of the sergeants made a reference to, "Get out," meaning, "Get out of the station house." And I said, "I can't get out any more than I am." He started rolling; everybody was just cracking up over it. On the same token, the same supervisor referred to "fannybags" as "fagbags." I said, "Sarge; you mean fannybags?" And he went, "Yeah. That's what I meant." So because I had a sense of humor, and I wasn't always coming down on people for different things, I was able to correct without criticizing. That was fine. He took it.

I got asked to work for the chief of personnel to work on special projects, and I like what I'm doing now. It's nice to be recognized for my mind. I don't want to be just deemed the gay officer; there's a lot more to me than that. This will broaden my career. It lets me see different aspects. I work in the personnel bureau, and there're a lot of issues that I have impact on that relate to everybody.

I'm waiting for the next lieutenant's test; I see myself continuing to move up. I'm not sure how far yet, but the lieutenant's test is the next step. My original ambition was to go as far as I can go. There's a possibility I'll make the rank of captain; after that it's an appointed position. My career could be dead because I'm gay; I don't know. It depends on who's there and what's going on. Those possibilities still exist. But I'm also not afraid to speak up, and that helps.

Norm Hill

Department: Boston (MA) Police Department
Age: 34
Rank: Patrolperson
Job: Liaison to the Gay and Lesbian Community
Years in Law Enforcement: 11

A tall man with a thick Boston accent, Norm is the Boston Police Department Liaison to the Lesbian and Gay Community. On a warm July day in an office in downtown Boston, he talked about being Black and gay on the Boston Police Department.

A ll little boys, and maybe little girls, want either a fire truck or a police car underneath the Christmas tree. I always wanted a police car, and that never went away. For as long as I can remember, I wanted to be a police officer, and I molded my educational and professional career around obtaining that goal. This desire was reinforced by the fact that I had six relatives on the Boston Police Department. On holidays when we would all get together, we would sit around and listen to their police "war stories."

During my junior year of high school, I went through the stages of the recruitment process. Boston was going through an economic crisis that forced the city to cut personnel—lay-off fire and police personnel—and there was a hiring freeze. My recruitment class didn't go in so I decided to go to college. I went to Northeastern University and obtained a bachelor of science in criminal justice. In November of 1982, the police department called.

During the first recruitment process, one of the questions they asked was, was I a homosexual? I answered, "No," even though I was. I was not going to let a question like that prohibit me from entering the police department. I was a model recruit other than the fact that I was gay. I was Black, I scored high, I had a college degree, and I molded my life around becoming a police officer. I was the perfect candidate for this job except for one thing in their eyes—I was gay. I wasn't going to let that stop me. During the second phase of the recruitment process the city of Boston had passed an ordinance prohibiting discrimination, so the sexual orientation question was dropped.

I thought being gay would have a negative effect on my career, so I made double efforts to keep my private life separate from my professional life. Before going into a gay club, I would look up and down the street to make sure there weren't any police cars around and to make sure the club didn't hire a private police detail to guard their front door. All these things had to be considered before I would enter an establishment. My stress level would be so high just getting there that more often than not, I would not have a good time.

I thought that if anyone found out, it would not be good. My feelings were that I would definitely be alone, and I would have no friends. I needed to be one of them to fit in, and in order to be one of them, I had to act like them. If being gay ever came out, I would not be one of them. But once I became a police officer, I found out immediately that even though they didn't know I was gay, I wasn't one of the boys anyway because I was Black.

There were Blacks, and there were Whites—that was clearly identifiable. There weren't any outward acts of discrimination that I experienced; it was very subtle. The White police officers would get the better cars and the better beats. I said to myself, "If this is happening 'cause I'm Black, this is a double whammy for me because I'm Black and gay." The only worse predicament I could be in is Black, gay, and a woman.

I can't hide the color of my skin. However, I could hide the fact that I was gay. I'm not saying it was hard for me to be Black, it's just that the subtle forms of discrimination were more obvious. There are still police officers on this job that do not like the fact that there are Black people, lesbian and gay people, or women on this job. I think that will always be. I have noticed more subtle forms of discrimination from being Black than from being gay.

Not being out was terrible. Sometimes police officers are not the most sensitive people—it's because of what they experience, what they see, and what they observe. Police officers who work the streets are constantly seeing the bad side of life. There're no chances for them to see good people, and they build up barriers to protect themselves. There were times I would be in roll call, and there would be gay jokes and like, "Fuckin' faggots... What are you, gay? What are you, a fag?" Stuff like that. Another time was after the Boston Police softball team decided to take on one of the teams from the gay softball league to foster good feelings between the police and the gay and lesbian community. The gay men absolutely kicked Boston Police ass; they walked all over them. The next day during roll call, the sergeant got up at the podium and said, "I'm absolutely ashamed and disgusted of you old men allowing *them* to beat you. What is this?" He went on and on. There was a grin on my face because they beat them, but I could not express my good feelings. I had an intense feeling of being alone. I thought I was the only one that was gay on the department. I thought I was the only gay cop in the world.

I came out seven years ago. It finally got to a point where the rumors were very strong and people just knew. For the sake of decency and my own morals, I had to sit down with my work partner and tell him. It was hard for me, and I'm sure it was hard for him, too. To this day, no one has ever approached me about it in a negative way. The serious support came from a lot of the Black officers. I imagine that was because they had been discriminated against. I'm sure there's talk behind my back and stuff like that, but so what? They'll talk about me for one minute and talk about someone else the next.

The thing that helped me was I had proven myself as a good officer before people found out who I was. I was a police officer that was respected, and because of that, most people didn't bother me.

Some of the greatest support I received came from a guy by the name of William Celester. At that time he was deputy superintendent in charge of the district I worked in. He's a Black man, and one day out of the blue he called me into his office and said, "I've heard rumors about you." I said, "Yeah. I am gay." And he goes, "I want to bring you under my wing. When I came on this department years ago, there weren't too many Black officers on this job." He considered himself an underdog, and he considered me an underdog. He knew how I felt, so he wanted me under his wing. I became his driver, his aid and his community service officer representing him at community crime watch meetings. The relationship lasted a very long time. He opened doors to me that no one else could have opened; there were meetings with the mayor that were open to me, the police commissioner knew me by first name, and all the commanders in the area knew me because I was gay anyway, but also knew me because of Billy. I owe a lot to him. He and his support made my life easier on this police department.

Being out has been nothing but an advantage for me. Being openly gay brought me closer to Deputy Superintendent Celester. If I had been a regular Joe Smoe in a patrol car, he would not have reached out to me. Now, I am the second openly gay liaison to the gay and lesbian community bridging the gap between the gay and lesbian community and the police department.

When I first was appointed to this position, I thought, "How many meetings could there possibly be? I'm sure I'll have a lot of time to myself." That has not been the case. There's been meeting after meeting after meeting, both day and night. Plus I'm creating a lot of work for myself by trying to be proactive and implementing programs. It's all because I love the police department and love the gay and lesbian community.

Doing this job is like walking on eggshells because you're representing the police department and the gay and lesbian community. There are proposals initiated by the gay and lesbian community that would not benefit the police department, and I have to take a stand against them. There are proposals implemented by the Boston Police Department that would not serve the gay and lesbian community, and I have to take a stand against them, too. It's like being torn in two.

One challenge is the recruitment of openly gay people on this police department. There's strength in numbers, and once we have more gay and lesbian officers on this job, gay and lesbian officers will have more of a voice. Being out of the closet is far less stressful than being in the closet. I've been able to do the things I've wanted to do, I've gone to gay and lesbian parties and functions, and I've been open in the media. It's a wonderful feeling that I can be who I am. I wish every police officer who was gay or lesbian could do the same thing. What a load off my shoulders!

Lea Militello

Department: San Francisco (CA) Police Department
Age: 34
Rank: Police Officer
Job: Patrol
Years in Law Enforcement: 13

For several years, Lea was the San Francisco Police Department's Liaison to the Lesbian and Gay Community. Now back on patrol, she took a break from her beat on a sunny afternoon in October to have lunch and discuss her experiences bridging the lesbian and gay and police communities.

The first time I decided that law enforcement was the career path I wanted was probably junior high or high school. I've always been a hands-on person and an outdoors person. I felt the job afforded me the opportunity to be able to do those sorts of things. I also really enjoy helping people. I went to college and majored in administration of justice. When I graduated, I decided I wanted to try the San Francisco Police Department because it was a larger city. I felt like it would afford me more opportunities because it was a bigger department.

I started the academy when I was twenty-one years old, got out, and worked at various police stations as a patrol officer. Then I went to work in community relations for a while. The chief of police at that time asked me to be on his staff and be his liaison to the lesbian and gay community. Now we have this new chief and I got the boot—I'm back on patrol. I have a foot beat now, and I ride a mountain bike.

I entered the police department thirteen years ago, and it wasn't like now where we have all kinds of training programs and all kinds of policies that are in place. I was a little nervous because being gay was not the norm. You're dealing with a society of law enforcement people that are, for the most part, male oriented and heterosexual; it's a little hard to come leaping out of the closet.

I don't really know whether the things that happened to me in the beginning of my career were because I was a woman or because I was a lesbian, 'cause women were relatively new in the field then. We had several women at the station at the time, and we had some pretty shitty things happen. We used to get dildos with k-y jelly and used condoms in our mail boxes, and the only people that have access to these mailboxes are police officers. The straw that broke the camel's back was when I went to my mailbox and there was a donut bag with a dead rat and a half eaten donut. That was it. I wasn't going to take any more crap. I went in and dumped it on the desk sergeant's desk and said, "You either do something about this or I'm going to get a lawyer and sue the pants off this police department. I shouldn't have to put up with this kind of crap." So they dealt with it, and after that, things were okay.

When I was the liaison, I went to just about every community meeting you can think of. You reach out to see how the police department could do things better, and you go to demonstrations and make sure things don't go awry. I developed the department's AIDS training. Also, because of my position as liaison, I became a national expert on lesbian and gay cultural awareness training for law enforcement. I've taught that to other departments as well and participated in the California statewide program development. A lot of really positive things came out of it. It was a really rewarding job for me and something that I enjoyed. On the same level, I have my life back now, and that feels good. I've been with my partner for eleven years and we have a little guy, a four year old, so it's kind of nice to have my life back and be able to be home once in a while.

The liaison job is a really demanding job, and to be honest, it doesn't reap a whole lot of rewards. Personally it's rewarding, but you have to put up with a lot of crap from the community. There's a faction of our community that seems to feel as though lesbians and gay men really don't have a place in law enforcement. Therefore, when you're attempting to be an intermediary and mediate a situation, it can get hostile and nasty because they don't think you should be doing the job to begin with.

A few years ago, Governor Wilson vetoed a gay rights bill, AB 101. Factions of our community went nuts and completely vandalized the state building. They smashed out all the windows and set offices on fire. Because of the position I had, I knew who some of these people were. As a police officer, it was my job to identify them to assist in the investigation that eventually ended in arrests. I caught a tremendous amount of heat for that. I was called a traitor, "How could you turn in members of your own community?" My feeling is, "The bottom line is, I don't care if you're Black, White, Hispanic, Asian, lesbian, or gay. You're still bound by the laws of this state and the country. If you break a law, your sexual orientation doesn't mean that you should escape the repercussions."

The editor of one of the gay papers put an editorial on the front page that basically said I should be fired from my position because I could no longer do it effectively. In my opinion, the guy is a complete asshole. He doesn't have a clue what it took for me to do my job. I have no respect for the man. He got inundated with letters to the editor telling him that he was way off base, but he didn't print any of them. I got a lot of support from the community, and that was good.

It's only a small faction of the community that's, for lack of a better word, anarchists. A group of them did a videotape that appeared on a public television program basically saying they knew where I lived, and they were going to get me and my family. When you start to threaten somebody I love and my child, that crosses the line. To me, those people need to get a life.

At first the job was more playing catch-up where we constantly had to react to things. People would have problems with specific officers being insensitive, and you had to constantly clean up messes. After a while it got so it became really proactive. Because I put myself out there so much, people would call me if they knew something was going to happen.

I had an office right across from the chief's and he had an extremely open door policy with me—if I had anything I needed to bring to his attention I never had to request a meeting; I could just go in. He had complete confidence in me, and we worked extremely well together. He allowed me to do things like change the AIDS training and develop a different sensitivity training. Together we worked with the United States General Accounting Office when they were doing their study on gays in the military, and as a result I ended up back in Washington testifying before the House Armed Services Committee. I was really sad to see the former chief go 'cause he was a pretty great police chief.

I realize now being back on the street and doing a beat that when I'm off, I can leave this job. I go home, and I spend time with my family, whereas when I had the liaison job, I was always on call, and I would work many late nights. It wears on you after a while, especially when you get your butt kicked and beat up all the time by people who are supposed to be your own community.

My partner asked me if I would go back to being liaison if the chief changed. I don't think so. I've done it, I've been there, and like I said, it's nice to be able to leave it when I go home. I missed a lot of the first couple years of my four year old's life because I was off doing things, and I don't want to miss any more. But, there's a lot of the job I miss. I miss the outreach to the community, and I miss the different things I was able to do with the training. I'm still doing the training for the police department, but I miss working with other departments. I teach an eight-hour, cultural awareness training to incoming recruits and advanced officers. It's a training program that I designed to demystify homosexuality. It breaks down myths and stereotypes, and it allows recruits and officers to get answers to questions that they might have in their own head. It's been pretty successful, and I'm pretty proud of it. Inevitably what happens when I teach this class is that people come to the realization that we're everywhere, it's okay, and it's not so strange.

In the training, I do an ice breaking exercise that's sort of a sentence completion. I pass out blank pieces of paper and I tell the participants that I want their honest responses, but I don't want to know who wrote them. I ask everything from, "If I found out my kid were being taught by a gay teacher I would..." to, "If someone of the same sex made a pass at me I would..." to, "When I think of two people of the same sex making love I feel..." The questions get progressively harder. When I'm done, I pick up papers from half the class, and I have somebody else pick up the other half. We mix them up, we switch, and then we pass the papers back out. Then, I re-ask the questions, and I call on people to read the responses. In every class I've taught, there's been a lesbian or gay person in the class. Most of the people in the classes are not cognizant of the fact that they have gays in their police departments. You get some really homophobic comments, and then the class "gets" it. They see there's some real attitudes permeating in our environment.

The training is a lot more beneficial and a lot more effective taught by a cop. The attitude that you generally come across when non-sworn personnel try to teach a police officer about anything is, "You're not a cop, how the hell would you know?" The important thing in the training is you want to address and break down stereotypes. I have a real diverse group of people that come in to the class from the community. Everybody from transgenders to drag queens to business executives to gay grandmothers. The officers are able to ask any questions and these people will answer them. It's important because the officers get an idea of why people are the way they are, or why they do the things they do. I have an activist come in and talk about demonstrating, and sometimes the discussions get heated, but that's good. The idea is not for me to try to shock people. What I want to do is try to break down some of the stereotypes and to show that we're all members of society; we're not just the outrageous.

One of the bigger stressors we had was when AIDS came on to the scene, and we had our first couple of officers pass away of AIDS. I sensed a real need to do something around AIDS training because the myths that were out there about how one gets AIDS were just ridiculous. It was important that people get educated because you're working in a city that has the second highest number of AIDS patients per capita in the United States. Your police officers have to be educated. For our officers that are now HIV-positive or have AIDS, it's a stressor because you don't always know how somebody's going to react. I can't tell you that every officer is sensitive around that issue because quite frankly they're not, but we've come a long way since we've lost our first officers.

I think the important thing to remember is being gay is really not an issue here. Our department's gone through great pains to make sure of that. We don't have a lot of the problems that other departments across the country have. We have anti-discrimination policies in place that deal specifically with sexual orientation and with people with HIV, AIDS, and ARC. It's a very good policy and people can get punished if they step over the line. That's very good, and departments need that sort of thing. I don't think you can effectively integrate lesbians and gays into law enforcement unless you have the support of the person who's in charge of the department. Unless that person is completely committed to and supportive of integration and is willing to put policies into place, it's not going to happen.

It's my hope that lesbians and gays that choose law enforcement as a career have the same opportunities that I've had and that they're able to do their jobs being who they are. I know that's not the case across the country and there are agencies where somebody wouldn't even think of coming out of the closet; that's unfortunate. I hope everybody can have as great an experience as I have had.

John Graham

Department: San Diego (CA) Police Department
Age: 34
Rank: Police Officer
Job: Community Relations
Years in Law Enforcement: 18

John works out of the Balboa Park Community Relations Storefront for the SDPD. His desk is framed by the Law Enforcement Code of Ethics; various plaques, awards, and commendations; and a March on Washington poster. He's known he was gay since the age of 12 when he had a crush on Lee Majors.

As a kid, I grew up watching *Dragnet* and *Adam 12*, so I had what I felt was knowledge of what police work was all about, and it sounded interesting. My father was a general contractor and always wanted me to take over the company. I watched them work twenty-four hours a day, seven days a week, and they never had a regular paycheck. I said, "I'm never going to do that." I wanted to have job security and something where I could feel a sense of accomplishment.

I started as an El Cajon police cadet at the age of sixteen. I went through about two hundred hours of training, but they only gave us a couple hours of defensive tactics training. Back in '76 when I hit the streets, I was seventeen years old. We carried a baton and handcuffs; that was all. The first time I got into a fight I learned, "This is not fun. You get your uniform ripped, and I don't even get paid for this." I decided the skills they taught in the academy just weren't enough, so I started traveling, taking defensive tactics classes, and building up expertise in that field. I found a lot of agencies didn't train police officers on the use of force, and I envisioned that down the road I would train people about defensive tactics.

In April of 1980, I applied for the California Highway Patrol, the El Cajon Police Department, and the San Diego Police Department. On Friday the thirteenth, June, 1980, I got notices in the mail that I was hired by El Cajon and San Diego Police Departments. I chose San Diego. Coming into the police department in '75, people really had strong feelings against gays and lesbians. A lot of it was out of discomfort and not understanding. There are still what I call "Neanderthals" out there, but, for the most part, officers and departments have changed a lot.

When I had ten years on the police department, I read in the papers that Mitch Grobeson had been discriminated against at the LA Police Department and an FBI agent had been fired. On October 11, National Coming Out Day, I met Mitch Grobeson, Frank Buttino, and a district attorney from the D.A.'s office in San Diego, and we talked. I was still closeted, and I was worried about people seeing me because at that time, I was working public affairs and doing a lot of tv interviews. I thought it was important to come out because of Frank Buttino—here was a person with good record, and they said gays can't work in law enforcement. That's crazy. Part of my own process was learning if we're going to make changes there has to be individuals who are out and open.

I thought about it for a couple of weeks and decided I wanted to come out. I told the chief, "I'd like to come out to show we can do a good job in law enforcement, and we can be visible." He supported me 100 percent, so we set up a press conference. All the news media covered it. I knew most of the reporters because I'd been talking crime prevention, and everybody was really cool about it. I called people the day before the newspaper was going to run the article, and except for one person, everyone was fine, no problems.

I thought, "Once you have a press conference, you're out. It's done and over with, you never have to do it again." Wrong! Coming out is a continuing process. I think it's really important for people to understand that, because I didn't when I came out. I will be in community meetings, and there may be something negative said about gays and lesbians. The way I look, most people look at me and think, "He's married." For many years I was a Republican—I became a Democrat after Governor Wilson vetoed AB 101, the gay rights legislation.

When you say, "My perspective as a gay man...," it can change a meeting real fast. Sometimes I don't tell them, I sit there and listen to them, because then I know who the enemy is. For the most part, I tell people just to get their reaction. They're normally quiet; they don't know what to say.

During the same time we started having some attacks up in the Hillcrest area and Northpark. I started telling people in the Public Affairs Unit, "We've got to watch this." It got to the point of fifty-one attacks in the area, and I told people, "We've really got to do something about this. It's getting to the point where somebody's going to get killed." But nobody was listening. About a week later, a seventeen year old kid was killed going to a coffeeshop, and he was straight. The people who attacked him thought he was gay. The gay and lesbian community mobilized that weekend, there was press coverage, and everybody was screaming, "Why didn't the police department do something? They knew about these attacks."

That Monday morning, I was in the office, a lieutenant came in, and he was laughing about the whole thing. I blew up—not the appropriate thing to do, but when you get too involved in something, you lose your objectivity. We got into a yelling match in front of people. People had never seen me mad—I'm easy-going, but his comments were not appropriate. I actually left because I was likely to do something I'd regret. Later we apologized to each other, and that ended it.

I have experienced a hate crime. It was frustrating to see how the system works—or doesn't work. One time, my partner wanted to go have an ice cream, so I said, "Let's go to the Cove." We parked the car and were starting to walk across the street. There were two men that looked like gay men across the street, and there was a Jaguar. The Jaguar started accelerating, and it was approaching us. This was like two o'clock in the afternoon, we weren't holding hands, we didn't have a t-shirt saying, "My boyfriend's gay," so I felt we were blending in with La Jolla. But the car got closer and closer, there was no where you could run and nothing you could do, and it was coming directly at us. I figured, "We're going to be hit. There's nothing we can do. This is it." As it got really close to us, it swerved to the side, and the passenger said, "Fucking faggot." The car went up the hill, made a U-turn, and came back. The driver stopped by us and said, "Scared you, asshole, didn't I?" So now this was a challenge. I identified myself as a police office and told him to pull over. That scared him, and he drove away. We got the license number, and I called the police department. The police ran the license number, went to the registered owner's house, and caught him there. We were driven there, did a standing curbstone line up, and identified the driver. He was placed under arrest for assault. He was in the military and shipped off to Okinawa so he was never prosecuted. I feel lucky that we weren't hurt. Somebody was looking out for us on that day.

Probably the biggest stress factor is coming out—whether to be in the closet or be out. If you are out, you're always coming out. Also, it's stressful being a role model for future law enforcement—the spotlight is on you because if you do something wrong, you're more or less representing everybody. It shouldn't be that way, but it is. You've got to be really careful in what you do. For other departments and for some individuals, coming out may not be the right thing. You really have to be strong and careful. It's good to have people in the closet, too, because then you get intelligence; you know what's going on. It depends on the person, and it depends on the agency. If you go into bigger, metropolitan agencies, then you're going to have a better time of surviving because you're going to meet such a wide range of officers. If you go with a smaller agency, there's potential for problems there because your smaller communities are going to be more conservative.

It's important that people understand that just because you're gay or lesbian doesn't mean that you have to work in a gay and lesbian community. You should be able to work in any community. It shouldn't matter who the officer is.

Ralf Meier

Department: Arlington County (VA) Police Department
Age: 43
Rank: Patrol Officer
Job: Community Resources Section
Years in Law Enforcement: 8

Ralf emigrated to the U.S. from Germany when he was sixteen years old. After receiving his Ph.D. in clinical psychology, he began a career in public service. A tall man with a slight German accent, he and his partner have been together for seventeen years.

I came over to the U.S. by myself. I told my parents, "Either shape up, or I ship out," and they didn't. I was in an engineering school in Germany, and the government had a program where they would send you to another country for one year as an exchange student. It sounded interesting, and, of course, it was an avenue to get away. My first choice was New Zealand and Australia. I got my second choice which was the U.S., and I ended up in Iowa in July. When I got off the plane, I wanted to go back. It was rough. But once I got into air conditioned cars, I was fine. It must have been a hundred degrees and the humidity must have been a million percent. It was awful. In Germany, when it hit seventy-five we wouldn't have school because it was too hot. I went back to high school in Iowa, finished my senior year, and then went back to Germany. I finished my engineering degree, came back to the U.S., went to college, and stayed.

I got my Ph.D. in '76 in psychology, and the last time I used it was in '78. I was interested in the social work part, but then the bottom dropped out, and I had to get a job. I moved to Washington and got a job with the Howard County Association for Retarded Citizens, as sort of a house counselor type thing. I did that for a while but that just was not satisfactory. Then I saw a job with the fire department, and I really enjoyed that. I cannot sit behind a desk; I need to be out, I need to interact, and I like the element of surprise. You have to use your noodle out there. I got to be senior paramedic fairly rapidly on one of the big, heavy rescue squads. We ran constantly, and it was great fun. Then they didn't promote me because I was White. At that time, D.C. had a real hard time with the promotional system. D.C. is 63 percent Black, and the administration back then had a real problem with promoting White people. That's when the fire fighters association filed suit. It was a real mess, and I decided to get out. So I decided to go into law enforcement. There was no ulterior motive. I had no high flying philosophical ambitions to change the world. The gay issue never came up. In a way, it was like showing people that a gay guy can be a cop. To a degree, that's what I was running with.

I was out when I applied, but I don't walk around with a placard saying, "I'm gay." I do have a lambda sticker and a rainbow flag on my cars. If somebody comes up to me and says, "Are you gay?" I say, "Yes. So what?" I haven't had any problems at all. Apparently there was some minor upheaval before I actually got hired. Somebody let it go that they were going to have a gay officer coming on board. Now this is all hearsay, but management apparently quickly put their foot down and said, "Cut this shit out. If he has any problems, people will get fired." And it stopped right away. I have not had a problem at all. We're a good department.

I've always been of the opinion that your sexuality has nothing to do with your job. So I'm gay. I can do a good job in anything I do. When I applied to the department, I was still naive enough to think that there would be no problem getting hired, and it wasn't even though other people said that it might be. Arlington has been really good. Perhaps they were thinking when they hired me, "We don't really want to, but let's try it and see what happens. Then we can always say, 'Look. Here he is. We have a gay officer.'" And then to their great surprise, "Oh my God, he actually is pretty good. He knows what he's doing." Then somebody upstairs said, "Here's a resource. We may want to use it." I've had some concern with some people. There was one guy who doesn't even acknowledge me. I thought it was me, but then I found out he's like that to everybody. I was getting concerned but that's just the way he is.

I had a call up in one of these huge condominium buildings, and the resident manager was going on about, "All these faggots," and stuff like that. I finally said, "Look. You're talking to one." That made him shut up. So, I do that but I don't go around and say, "Hi, my name is Officer Meier, and by the way, I'm gay."

When a gay issue comes up somebody usually calls me. Either CID people, the deputy chief, or somebody will call me and say, "Ralf, what should we do? What is going on?" They acknowledge they don't have a clue how the subculture operates, so they are using me as a resource. We had a homicide where a night manager got stabbed with a screw driver, and we think it was his ex-lover. So the detective assigned to the case and I went through all the gay bars in D.C. distributing fliers and talking to people. They're aware that I am a resource in the department.

I'm now in the community resources section. We do the schools, the DARE program, neighborhood watches, the bicycle patrol during the summer, civic associations, the media, and public relations. I really miss patrol where you're out there on your own, and you have regular hours. The job now is constant; you never get home on time, and you have night programs. It's a real pain. I would like to go back on patrol but damnit, what are you going to do with a forty-five year old patrol officer? That's the problem.

The gay community either hates you or loves you. They either want to go to bed with you, or they don't want to talk to you. I don't think there's any middle ground. The reaction I usually get is, "Oh, that's nice," and the person is gone, or "Wow! Can I go to bed with you? Can I put your uniform on?" That, of course, turns me off. Law enforcement has not been particularly kind to the gay community. There are some areas that still do raids on gay bars, and Virginia still has a sodomy law. In a way, I'm sort of like an unconvicted felon. Very often, when gay guys or lesbians call, the police take it very lightly; no report would be made, no follow up, no nothing. I can see where all this is coming from. It's the same thing as forty years ago with the Blacks. I really equate those experiences. Myself, I have a definite degree of law; there are certain things that I could care less about, there are certain things that I care about if I have the time, and there are certain things that I will do something about whether or not I have the time. Sex and marijuana smoking fall into the first one; I don't give a shit. So, unless something really serious is associated with that activity, I don't think I would follow up on it. The problem is, if a citizen calls up and says, "These people are doing these things over here, and I want you to do something," then we have to do something. Then we can't ignore it.

My partner wants me to quit. He never was happy with this whole idea, but he understands and supports it. He's tired of the phone ringing at four in the morning, and he realizes I can get hurt. I did get hurt badly two and a half years ago. Some guy made a U-turn in front of me when I was running code going about sixty miles an hour, and I demolished three cars including the cruiser. It took them a while to get me out. I apparently had enough presence of mind to say, "I'm at an accident on Route 50;" then I passed out. The dispatcher thought I was looking at the accident, and tried to get me but couldn't. The crash attracted people from the surrounding houses who saw me passed out. Some woman crawled through the back window of my cruiser, grabbed the radio, and said something like, "9-1-1, 9-1-1, I think this officer's in trouble. I think the officer is unconscious; he was involved in an accident." On the tape, you can hear all the sirens come on like somebody flipped a switch. Finally everybody and their mother showed up including the chief. They cut me out of the car and put me on the stretcher. The chief came over, and I said, "Chief, I'm sorry about the car." He said, "Fuck the car." It had thirty-eight miles on it; it was brand new. My immediate supervisor said, "Do you want us to call your partner?" And I said, "Yes." They tried on their cellular phones all the way to the hospital, and then the hospital finally got in touch with him. I think that showed they really didn't have a hang-up.

It's not all bad. Maybe this is not fair, but I think a lot of gay people are their own worst enemies. They want to be treated differently, better. It's like the guys who think everybody's after them and they don't go through channels. And who would want some of these screaming queens as police officers? I surely don't. You have to be professional. I was asked by one of our recruiting people whether or not they should hire somebody, a gay guy, and I said, "No. The only reason he wants to get in is because he wants to wear the uniform." We can't have those kind of people running around out here. You've got forty-nine shots in your gun and in your clips, and you cannot give somebody that kind of responsibility just because he's into fancy uniforms. Let him drive a metro bus. One of the reasons I get frustrated with some gay officers is because everything is anti-gay even though, "Maybe you people are not doing a good job out there, and that's why they are not liking you. Maybe you're a little bit too pushy on some of these issues. Maybe you should be going through channels like everybody else. Maybe that's what your problem is." Of course, they don't want to hear that.

I refuse to get promoted. I could try, but I don't want to do it. I've come to my senses. Who wants the responsibility? I really don't. They want me up in homicide-robbery, but I don't want to go up there. I don't like the cloak and dagger routine. I like the uniform, and being out in the patrol car. Police work is 90 percent boredom, 5 percent sheer terror, and 5 percent eating.

I'm probably one of the worst people to talk to about all this, 'cause I'm not militant. I demand my rights, and if I perceive I'm not being treated fairly I will really go nuts. I don't perceive somebody being against me behind every action that somebody takes so I'm probably not a good person to talk to about these kind of things.

Bonny Louison

Department: Harvard University (MA) Police Department
Age: 34
Rank: Dispatcher
Job: Group Leader
Years in Law Enforcement: 13

After an accident shattered her dreams of becoming an MP (Military Police officer) in the Marine Corps, Bonny became a dispatcher for the Harvard University Police Department. After completing her shift for the day, she sat in an HUPD conference room dressed in blue jeans and a blue-jean jacket bearing a button which read, "It's a queer thing. You wouldn't understand."

I knew I wanted to be a cop in high school; I was able-bodied then. I was on my way into the Marine Corps to be an MP (Military Police officer), so I could be a state trooper. I had already applied to the Marine Corps, was accepted, and was supposed to go in on my birth date. I broke my back that summer after I graduated which ended my career in the Marine Corps. It was not a good summer.

I went to college as an occupational therapist. I tried to find a job, but couldn't. I saw an advertisement that Harvard was looking for a police dispatcher. I applied and was given the job; they were looking for people with disabilities. The chief said to me, "You're a lesbian, aren't you?" I said, "Yeah, I am."

He said, "There are some rednecks around here. Be careful." I have no idea how the chief knew. I assume he'd seen enough in his own life to be able to pick people out.

For the first two years, I kept pretty quiet and didn't say anything. I didn't come out—I was brought out by another dispatcher whose sister is also a lesbian. The sister happened to mention to the dispatcher that she saw me at the bar one night. The dispatcher decided she would tell everyone. I was scared. I didn't really know what to expect. One of my sergeants called me in and said, "Such and such says you're a lesbian. Are you?" I said, "Of course I am." He said, "That's what I thought." And that was it. That was the end of the discussion.

I think basically what happened was they got to trust me. The whole basis of being a police dispatcher is getting the officers to trust you. After working with people for two years, they realized they could trust me to be there when they needed me. It didn't make any difference whether I was in a wheelchair. It didn't make any difference whether I was a lesbian. It didn't make any difference if I was purple. They just knew they could depend on me, and they couldn't have cared less what else I was. That's pretty much the attitude about everything around here. If you're dependable, they don't care what you are. If you're not dependable, watch out.

The first major problem was the wheelchair since that's something visible everyone had to deal with. In some ways it was harder for people to adjust to the wheelchair than the sexual orientation. I figured they all assumed that I was asexual anyway because of the wheelchair. People were real leery because they assumed that people with disabilities can't do things. Their first reaction was I wouldn't be able to move fast enough—people associate wheelchairs with people who are retarded. Before I was brought into dispatch, other dispatchers had gotten together and tried to blackball me. They didn't want me in the room because they didn't think I could handle it. Basically the chief said, "I don't care what you want; she's in," and people got over it. All of those dispatchers are no longer there, and now I'm in charge. They have found out that I move faster than anybody else in dispatch 'cause I just roll right through things. People have gotten real used to the wheelchair; they have gotten comfortable with it, even when I run over their toes. It took them a while to overcome their stuff around disability. Once they got over that, it was easy.

I get a lot of questions from new people who come through. I do a lot of joking about disability stuff, which gets them to put their walls down. The first things I tell new trainees when they get in the room is, "If you can't tell, I'm disabled, and if you don't hear it from me, eventually you'll hear it from someone else—I'm gay. And the third thing is, I'm your boss. So, deal with it." It's funny, it takes them no time at all to realize I'm no different than they are. I talk about my lover or what we're doing on vacation or they'll talk about their boyfriend or their girlfriend or whatever they're doing, and it's just like normal. Somebody from their family walks into the station and they're accepted. Somebody from my family walks into the station, they're accepted. It doesn't matter who you are here. If you're a member of this department, you're accepted. I had a significant other that died a few years ago, and I was given bereavement time the same as anyone else. Nobody contested it. They just gave me the time I needed.

I spend a lot of time training other police departments and at the academy. I go in uniform; if you have a group of officers sitting in a room dealing with a group of civilians they have a tendency to not listen. When you're dealing with someone else in a uniform, they listen to you differently. The best way to start it off is by saying,"Give me some myths about police officers." "They're all Dunkin' Donuts people. They're all stupid." Then I'll say, "Now tell me some myths that you've heard about homosexuals," and we'll name them. I'll ask them, "Are all the things you say about police officers true?" They'll say, "No." "Are they true for *some* police officers?" "Yes." "Well guess what? It's the same with any group of people."

In the past, the relationship between the gay community and the police was never really bad, there was just a lot of miscommunication. There was an incident that happened seven years ago in the Science Center basement men's room, which is a notorious hang-out. An officer walked into the bathroom to use the facility, and as he was standing there, a man reached over to fondle him. The officer turned to the guy and said, "You picked the biggest guy with the smallest cock and a badge on his belt. What are you doing?" There were seven of them that had been doing a circle jerk. In an attempt to make the arrests discreetly, the officers were going to bring them out the loading dock door. It just so happened that that day, the Science Center was selling computers off the loading dock door. It is university policy that anyone who is arrested has to go out in hand cuffs for the protection of the officers as well as the person who is being arrested. One of the newspapers in the area got involved, and since the names of anyone arrested are public knowledge, the newspaper published the names. Naturally, the police department was blamed for it. A group of gay students went to the president of the university and said, "We need to find a way to deal with this that's more constructive." They came up with a committee of four officers including myself, gay students, gay faculty members, and gay staff members. It kind of left me in a weird position because I was straddling both groups. I sat at the head of the table; all of the straight people sat on one side, and all of the gay people sat on the other side. I went to my officers after that and said, "The next time we have a meeting I would like you to intermix," and they did.

The group opened up after telling coming out stories. Each one of us talked about who we were, how we came out, and what that was like for us. The straight officers talked about who they were, how they grew up, and what their perceptions of gays were. It left a room full of people who, very quickly, learned to trust each other. We took that principle and started doing trainings. We've trained all the security guards and got really good responses. Then we trained the staff, sergeants, lieutenants, chiefs, captains, and then the police officers.

Now, every spring Harvard holds a week of gay education. The police department has held a tea here in the afternoon. We invite the community in to look at the police department and to talk to people. It's been an eye-opener for a lot of people. The relationship with gay students on campus has gotten better and better. We get a lot more calls now about domestic issues between same-sex partners. Students aren't afraid to utilize the police department that should be there to protect them in the first place.

I get to do a lot of work with Harvard students who are coming out. One year there must have been ten baby dykes that came in to the police station to talk about what was going on in their lives and how their parents were dealing with things. It's a very strange place to think of as being safe for the gay community. We had a student who came in to tell me that he had been gay-bashed. I called one of my officers to take a report, who called in a Cambridge police officer to file a civil rights violation. There was no snickering, and it wasn't a joke. The kid came back to me and said, "I felt really taken care of." And that's what he's supposed to feel. That's what we're supposed to be here for.

A lot of officers have come to me one-on-one and said, "I have a question. Can I talk to you about this?" I've had people come to me and say, "I need to talk to you, can we talk in private? My sister and my mother just came out, and I don't quite know what to do about it." I talk to them about their feelings, where they're coming from, where their sister and their mother are coming from, and how it affects them. I had one officer come and tell me that he wanted to know how to support someone in his family that came out; he wanted to make them understand that he still loved and accepted them, whether or not they were gay. So there's been a lot of education. And as a result, we have officers in the department that are no longer afraid to come out.

We've had a lot of dispatchers that are gay, and the dispatchers have always been out. As soon as they realize there's one person in the room that's out, everybody's out. But the officers have always been a little more leery, 'cause you never know who's going to back you up when you really need it. What they've come to find out is that they get their backup and nobody cares. I know back-up problems have been in other departments, but not here.

Initially I didn't realize that I would make a difference. There was one officer who was probably the most difficult person in the world. He was the biggest homophobe I've ever dealt with. It was my first six months as a dispatcher, and every night this man would stop racially mixed gay couples and field interview them. After watching this for six months, I gathered the documents, I went into our Black chief, and I said, "Doesn't it strike you as strange that this officer stops only gay male couples and only field interviews the Black males?" That officer got called in, and they pulled him out of his assignment. He was told, "This type of behavior is not acceptable." Finally, he left the department. On the night he left, he cornered me in the garage and said, "I want you to know you've been the biggest pain in my ass. However, it's been a pleasure working with you because I've learned a lot. I want you to know that in my new depart-ment I won't pick on gays, and I won't let anybody else, either." I sat there with my mouth hanging open and tears filling up in my eyes. The most striking thing to me was realizing that I really educated someone. I'd made enough of a change in his perspective of what gays were that he was going to go some-place else and be different.

The chief has gotten a lot of compliments about how well the officers have handled situations. We had the Gay, Lesbian, and Bisexual Conference here— the year before Yale held it and there were forty arrests. The year we had it, it was three times as large and there were no arrests. I spent the whole weekend doing details with the officers. If there were issues that came up I was there to mediate. I got to spend most of the conference standing with the guys watch-ing the lesbians go by, and having them flirt with me and ignore the guys. It was a lot of fun. It was a good learning experience for the officers, because they had a group of people that were controversial, the controversial people were being picked on by a very anti-gay group of "normal" people, and the officers were protecting the controversial people from the normal people. They got to see a whole different side of things.

Commencement was a stress for me. We had Colin Powell here, and it was very controversial. I spent a month talking to my gay friends and police officers about my role. I felt divided between two communities. Am I going to be betraying one community for the other? Will my officers be concerned that if I'm in dispatch, they won't get the support they need? How do I explain to my gay friends that my officers might arrest them? We worked between the Harvard Gay and Lesbian Caucus, the different gay groups in the area, and the police officers, and we pulled off the day with no arrests and no incidents.

I've had a lot more positive experiences than negative ones. Occasionally you'll have somebody make a gay joke, and then stop and realize that they've made a gay joke, apologize and walk out. You'll see homophobia come to a head every once in a while, but I've really seen it diffused. There was one officer who has a real hard time dealing with gay men. He was rambling on and on one night, and one of the officers said, "I worked in Provincetown for three years, and they're no different than anybody else. What's your problem? Maybe you're so homophobic because you really are one." Shut him right up. I didn't have to say anything.

I had the FBI approach me one year and say, "We'd like you to work for us; because you're a lesbian we know you can get information about your community." I laughed and said, "Get out of my face." And they were like, "No, you don't understand. We know all about you." I said, "I don't care what you know about me—everybody knows about me." They were like, "We know about your friend." "Yeah, everybody knows about my friend. There's nothing you can do to us." They said, "You're well thought of in your parents' hometown. Do your parents know about you?" I said, "Of course they know about me, they know about my friend, they know about all the rest of my friends, and they like all of my friends." The FBI wanted me to do undercover work in the gay community! I laughed and said, "Get out of my face." I never heard from them again.

In a lot of ways, the gay community is close-minded about cops. The gay men don't mind, they figure, "She's just a butch dyke." The lesbian community actually has been harder to deal with than the police officers. When members of the lesbian community find out that I am a police dispatcher, they have a tendency to distance themselves, and say, "She's somebody who can't be trusted." I've done a lot of work for the women's music festivals, and one year, I was the security coordinator. I was in charge of about two hundred women dealing with about two thousand campers. One of the women who was working for me was an off-duty FBI agent. When women found out she was an FBI agent, everybody went crazy, "What is she doing here? She's spying on us." In a lot of ways the women's community has been much harder on us. But then, if the women's community hadn't been hassled by so many different groups of people, they wouldn't have to be so careful all the time. It's taken a long time for the women's community to start realizing that the more of us there are in law enforcement, the safer that community is.

You'll find a lot of officers still aren't out, but there are a lot of us, and more and more are coming out. They come out in their own, sweet time. It's a matter of safety, and it just takes time. Once you're with a department long enough, and once you've established who you are, you're going to find that it doesn't really make any difference what you are. You think nobody in the world could possibly know, but of course, the whole world does know. It always looks like it's going to be much worse than it is. I've seen people come out and it be very hard for them. But most people come out, scratch their heads, and say, "I should have done that years ago." You're going to see a trend of people coming out more openly. People need to realize that the more of us that are in all of the different fields, the more of us that are out, the safer it is for everybody, and the more widely we'll be accepted.

Summary, Conclusions, and Recommendations

The Criminal Justice Community

The foregoing narratives of the worlds of lesbian and gay criminal justice workers reveal that no universal experience exists. Similar themes as well as blatant contradictions pervade their stories. At the same time that these men and women provide documentation of horrendous abuses of lesbian and gay criminal justice workers and the lesbian and gay community at large, they also demonstrate instances of profound, and, sometimes heartwarming, support and respect. What accounts for these different experiences? Why do some lesbian and gay officers have colleagues who risk their lives to back them up while others have their lives jeopardized by colleagues who fail to protect them? Why are some people's careers furthered by coming out of the closet while others' are thwarted? Why do some describe teamwork, congeniality, and inclusion while others recount loneliness, isolation, and bitterness?

No simple or single answers can resolve these questions. The explanations lie in a complex web of influences, some of which relate to the historical context, some of which lie in the work environment, and some of which represent qualities of the individual.

Historical Context

> White men have been able to hold onto the job for so long and pass it
> down through generation after generation. For them to see Black men
> come into the field was something that hurt them so much. Then to see
> women come in.... And now all of a sudden people come out of the
> closet, it's like, "Oh, my God, what's next?" (Gwendolyn Gunter,
> *Minneapolis (MN) Police Department*)

Experiences of homophobia as well as harassment, discrimination, and abuse of lesbians, gay men, and bisexuals are not unique to criminal justice professions; they pervade the workplace (McNaught, 1993) and the general culture (Pharr, 1988). Federal protection for lesbians, gay men, and bisexuals, the most recent version being the Employment Non-discrimination Act—ENDA—languished in Congress in the mid '90s due to lack of support. Until lesbians, gay men, and bisexuals are federally protected, anti-gay violence, victimization, harassment, and discrimination will continue unabated and unchallenged.

Within criminal justice, people of color, women, and open lesbians and gay men have been excluded at various points in history. People of color, and later, women, entered the ranks gingerly and were met with harassment, abuse, and discrimination. Eventually, local and national policies such as the 1964 Civil Rights Act and the 1972 Equal Employment Act were enacted to protect workers, and when mistreatment continued, many victims found satisfaction through the courts. While still not always on an equal par with their White male counterparts, people of color and women have come a long way towards successfully integrating into criminal justice professions.

Open lesbians and gay men remain a decade or more behind. In many cases, they continue to endure harassment and discrimination, and few agencies or municipalities have anti-discrimination policies that include sexual orientation. Those policies that do exist are sporadically enforced. Isolated law-suits have begun to force agencies to end discrimination, but more often than not, discriminatory practices continue. If lesbians and gay men follow in the footsteps of people of color and women, these pioneers will have paved the way for the next generation of out criminal justice workers.

In addition to the historical context, several salient characteristics of organizations and individuals affected the experiences related here. These influences fall into three clusters: location, power, and status.

Location

> My advice to gay cops is to consider your location within the United States, consider what size department you're in, and consider how you're going to feel once your partners know. How are they going to act, and what would you do if they weren't your friend anymore because of your being openly gay? I felt that if these guys were my friends, they were going to be my friends whether I'm gay or straight. (David D'Amico, *New Jersey Department of Corrections*)

Numerous aspects of the organization affect the experiences of lesbian and gay criminal justice workers. The most obvious factor is *size*: in general, lesbian and gay employees had more positive experiences in larger agencies. Diverse attitudes, acceptance, and tolerance were more likely within the thousand-member departments of New York City and San Francisco than in the eight-member department in Pineville, WV. Similarly, *locale* was crucial. It is easier to be openly lesbian or gay, regardless of profession, in San Francisco than in Dallas, Texas or Bottineau and Cass Counties in North Dakota. The *number of openly lesbian and gay officers* in an agency is critical to a positive work environment for lesbian and gay employees. With sufficient numbers, lesbians and gay men become part of the fabric of the workplace and are less likely to be singled out for harassment. A lone lesbian or gay employee is more vulnerable. *Anti-discrimination policies* outline protections for lesbians and gay men, but policies are only valuable if they are supported and *enforced* by the administration. Without the active backing of the "brass," lesbians and gay men cannot successfully integrate into criminal justice fields.

Power

> There are people that I have supervised in the jail that have come up and said, "I saw you on Castro." I'm like, "So? What business is it of yours?" If they come back with anything, I'm like, "First off, I'm the one who is in law enforcement; you're not. Second, you should not be con-

cerned with what I do in my private life." (Michael, *San Francisco (CA) Sheriff's Department*)

The more power and authority these criminal justice workers wielded, the less likely they were to experience harassment and discrimination, and the more able they were to handle it should it occur. Power stems from a number of sources. Those in higher *ranks* were more likely to escape serious abuse, as were those in *positions* of authority. Judges were less likely to be hassled by police officers or district attorneys than the reverse, just as corrections workers were less likely to be harassed by inmates than by coworkers or supervisors. *Personality* is another source of power. The treatment criminal justice workers endure is often related to how they present themselves. Those subscribing to the notion of "Out and proud" succeeded more readily than those who believed in "Lie and deny." Portraying shame and helplessness, or being unwilling to challenge homophobia invited disdain and contempt. Finally, those who had *other options*—that is, those who felt secure in their ability to obtain other suitable employment if need be—were less intimidated on the job. In contrast, those who felt trapped and unable to work elsewhere suffered.

Status

Ten years ago there were still a lot of difficult attitudes toward women. They still exist but they've had to go so underground with them now that 25 percent of the officers are women. It's been a harder road for the minorities in the organization. The race thing is more paramount than the gender thing. (Cheri Maples, *Madison (WI) Police Department*)

Gender played an important role in how accepted lesbians and gay men were in their roles. In general, lesbians did not encounter the level of hostility and virulence that gay men did. The image of criminal justice workers as strong, masculine, and macho is more consistent with stereotypes of lesbians as masculine and "men-want-to-be's" and contrary to stereotypes of gay men which portray them as weak and effeminate. In addition, stereotypes of lesbians as erotic and gay men as HIV/AIDS carriers reinforce existing prejudices.

Criminal justice workers holding *"minority" status* experienced more difficulty than those more closely resembling the White, able-bodied, heterosexual, male stereotype. Anyone with one or more characteristics that deviated from that norm were, and in some cases still are, viewed as outsiders. For many, their more "visible" difference—that is, being female, disabled, or non-White—was more of a barrier than their sexual orientation.

The Lesbian, Gay, and Bisexual Community

> Working in the Castro was really tricky, because on the one hand you had a lot of radical community members that hate police, and that will always hate police, no matter what. It didn't matter how good a job I did or how concerned I was, all they could see was the uniform and the star. I experienced a lot of very mixed messages. The merchants wanted me there to clean up the streets and get rid of the criminals, the more radical end of the community didn't want me there at all, and the mainstream were really thrilled to have a dyke cop on a mountain bike. (Pam Hofsass, *San Francisco (CA) Police Department*)

Reactions from the lesbian and gay community varied tremendously, depending at least in part upon the situation in which lesbian and gay criminal justice workers were encountered. When marching en masse at gay pride parades, they were uniformly well received. When they were encountered at demonstrations, their reception was less positive. In social settings, these men and women received mixed reactions. Some officers were propositioned because of their uniform, while others lost friends and potential dating partners when their professions were disclosed. Perhaps the relationship between the lesbian and gay community and criminal justice is evolving from a more distant and hostile interaction to one that is more respectful and courteous, and the transition is marked by both extremes.

Conclusions

Regardless of the prices they may or may not have paid, most criminal justice personnel who were out of the closet believed that the costs were worthwhile. Some paid little for coming out, while for others the fee exacted may have included their jobs, their privacy, and sometimes nearly their lives. Some of the benefits to coming out accrued to the officers themselves, while other benefits provided for future officers, and for the lesbian, gay, and bisexual movement.

Given the experiences recounted here, why do lesbians and gay men stay in criminal justice careers, and why do many more wish to enter the profession? Not surprisingly, they remain for many of the same reasons most people stay at their jobs—because of the salary, the benefits, the lack of other options, their love for the work, and most importantly, because they have the right to do so.

As do heterosexual citizens, lesbians, gay men, and bisexuals have the right to work in the field of their choice.

Reflections

After listening to over one hundred hours of testimonials, I found myself feeling inspired as well as angry. I was encouraged by the "success stories" where criminal justice workers like Stephen St. Laurent, Danita Reagan, and Sharon Lubinski have been valued because of, and not just in spite of, their sexual orientation. I was heartened by the courage of these everyday people working to make their lives and the lives of others a little more free from injustice. I am saddened by the remaining roadblocks to full equality for all citizens. I am angry that competent and productive employees like Frank Buttino and Jim Blankenship have been denied the opportunity to work in the jobs they love simply because they are gay.

The goal of this book, however, is not simply to outrage the reader. It is not enough to mire in the injustices recounted here. Rather, the goal is to facilitate better understanding between criminal justice and the lesbian and gay community, and to use these stories to galvanize and move us forward in the effort to achieve equality and safe work environments for all, regardless of sexual orientation. These stories are not the end point; they are the foundation upon which the lesbian and gay civil rights movement is built, and every individual, regardless of occupation or sexual orientation, has a role.

Recommendations: A Call to Action

1) If you are a lesbian or gay man interested in pursuing a criminal justice career, choose your agencies wisely. Carefully investigate anti-discrimination policies and the attitudes of the administration, and enter with your eyes open. If possible, develop support systems with other lesbians and gay men and/or supportive heterosexual allies within the agency, and if not possible, create alliances outside the workplace.

2) If you are a lesbian or gay man already in criminal justice, carefully assess the risks involved in coming out. Often the benefits far outweigh the risks, but at times the risks may seem too great. Ask yourself, "Are the risks real?" Only you can determine if coming out is advisable, and you will live with the consequences, both positive and negative, forever.

3) If you are lesbian, gay, or bisexual and not in criminal justice, strongly consider coming out. Examine your fears, and realistically assess the risks. Too many people hold stereotyped views because they erroneously assume they

don't know any lesbians, gay men, and bisexuals. People need to recognize that lesbians, gay men, and bisexuals are their friends, next-door neighbors, classmates, coworkers, bosses, and family members.

4) If you are heterosexual, support your lesbian and gay colleagues by confronting homophobia. Do not tolerate anti-gay jokes and epithets. If they are not already in place, work to establish anti-discrimination policies that include sexual orientation. Homophobia and an anti-gay workplace hurt everyone, not just lesbians, gay men, and bisexuals (Blumenthal, 1993).

5) If you are a registered voter, let your senators and representatives know that you agree with their gay-supportive stances and disagree with their anti-gay positions. Urge them to support a federal anti-discrimination policy that includes sexual orientation. If your congressperson will not do so, work to elect those who will. If you are not a registered voter, register now.

> In the early years, being gay just was not discussed; it's very different today. Now I have a picture of my partner on my wall. I'm not trying to throw it in anybody's face, but I have the right to live my life and take the same pleasures that everybody else does. Another officer thought putting her picture up was a brave thing to do. It's pretty sad that such a benign act as putting up pictures of someone you love is thought of as an act of bravery. (Lori Wieder, *Miami Beach (FL) Police Department*)

The courageous individuals who have revealed their lives, triumphs, bitter defeats, virtues, and flaws, in many ways are ordinary people with everyday concerns. They worry about making a good living, doing a good job, maintaining their safety, and getting along with their coworkers. They worry about not bringing their jobs home from work, and about what provisions would be in place for their life partners should something happen to them on the job. Their worries are no different than those of most American workers; their similarities outweigh their differences. However, because their partners are of the same gender, they are subjected to fear, hatred, exclusion, ridicule, harassment, and abuse.

Being an openly lesbian or gay criminal justice worker represents a feat in and of itself. The stories of these men and women reveal both accomplishments and disappointments. We cannot allow our setbacks to deter us. We must use our defeats to rekindle our commitment and mobilize the movement. Change in the criminal justice system occurs as does change anywhere else: one step—and one person—at a time. If each of us challenged even one act of homophobia a day, our workplaces, our worlds, and our lives would be irrevocably altered, and we would begin the process of eradicating prejudice and creating an atmosphere of equality and true justice for all.

Epilogue

Sandy Austin has returned to work and is assigned to the Diversion Unit.

B.: Since my interview I have become quite sick with the AIDS virus. I've been on disability for eighteen months, and my department has been incredibly supportive. The sergeants, captains, lieutenants, and fellow patrolmen have called repeatedly. To show his concern, the chief took me to lunch. My life is a mess now but I certainly am glad to have been a police officer. I miss it beyond words.

Jim Blankenship is still employed as a manager with an auto dealership. He is also currently working in the Monongalia County Court System with CASA—

Court Appointed Special Advocate. He was sworn into the court as an open gay man. He and his partner are working towards adopting a child.

Frank Buttino is now in a two-year relationship with another man. There are now a number of openly gay FBI agents and support people, and the FBI is hiring openly gay people.

J. D.: I am currently enrolled full time at California State University-Long Beach, majoring in psychology. My long term goals include working in the public policy arena and ultimately achieving the goal of a doctorate in Social Work. I thought I would never want to get back into law enforcement. However, with my current partner's full support, I have given considerable thought to returning to law enforcement. Although I believe that I would make an excellent officer and detective, there are still some ghosts I need to tend to. I feel as though time is on my side; therefore I will continue to process through these old demons and come to some landing within the next year.

Ferenc: My hand was forced and I came out at my precinct. I felt that I was discriminated against based on my sexual orientation. Someone I arrested made a complaint to the Internal Investigation Unit (IIU) that I showed gay pornographic material to his brother during a ride along while I was in uniform and on the job. After an investigation, IIU determined that the complaint was "unfounded," but the damage was already done. The word got out that I was gay. Two weeks later I was removed from a city where I had worked for many years, and which contracts with my department for law enforcement services. The reasons given were somewhat unbelievable—one was that I did not smile at an employee. Within three weeks of my removal, the two lieutenants at my precinct filed two complaints against me. Both of these complaints were investigated and since they did not have merit they were both deemed "non-sustained." I received a lot of support from my sergeants, and I felt that all of this harassment was the result of my perceived sexual orientation. I started to document everything, and eventually I went to my precinct commander and gave him a typed page telling him that I was gay. I wanted to be able to show in any future proceeding against my employer that they knew that I was gay and harassed me because of it. There were no more complaints from the brass after that, and I was slowly eased back into the contract city without comment.

All in all, I am glad that my bubble burst. I was treated fairly at IIU and received lots of support from my supervisor and coworkers. I requested and got permission to attend the gay pride parade in uniform while driving my patrol car in June of '95.

Marc Goodman: I was promoted to the rank of Sergeant-II and am currently assigned to Internal Affairs Division. As the first openly gay investigator in the division's history, I can address issues of police misconduct. Whether cops are innocent or guilty of misconduct, it is my job to work as an investigator to get to the truth of the matter. In the interim, I was the chair of the Second International Conference of Gay and Lesbian Criminal Justice Professionals. I am currently studying for the lieutenant's examination.

John Graham now works out of the Downtown Community Relations Storefront for the San Diego Police Department.

Greg: I've had two changes in job assignments. I worked, temporarily, in investigations. I really enjoyed the work although the environment was very anti-gay. One day after an individual was arrested, he informed the officer he was HIV-positive, and a sergeant assumed that meant he was gay. The person arrested teaches locally, and the sergeant proudly came in to the office to tell us he had called the superintendent of schools to tell him of the "gay teacher with AIDS." One investigator said, "I agree. They should be marked if they have AIDS so we know." I could not stay quiet; I erupted! After I spoke there was dead silence, and I thought I may be in trouble for talking that way to a sergeant. After, I heard some encouragement and some talk from the sergeant wondering why I was "sticking up for gays." Things did get better after the incident.

Also, on a local, radio talk show, one of the lieutenants appeared and a caller asked why the department doesn't have mandatory AIDS testing because there is a gay officer on the force. The lieutenant handled it well and basically told her to mind her own business. After the show, two officers approached me and told me I was talked about on the radio, and then they relayed the story. These officers have not changed how they treat me, so that's a good sign.

I still haven't "come out" at work, but more people know and I don't hide it. The political climate does concern me though. I was unsuccessful in my bid for the North Dakota State Legislature coming in fourth in a field of six for three positions. I definitely will stay involved in the political arena.

Mitch Grobeson: Since returning to the LAPD in 1993, I became the first and only LAPD officer to participate in the LA AIDS Walk-a-thon in LAPD uniform and the highest ranking officer to proudly march in full uniform in LA's 1994 gay pride parade. Currently, I am the only LAPD officer to volunteer his time to numerous Los Angeles AIDS organizations, saving them the expense of coordinating security at fundraisers. I also continued to recruit from the gay and lesbian community, working with over two hundred applicants in 1994 and 1995.

Following my reinstatement, the management of the LAPD refused to comply with the terms of the historic settlement agreement, which forbade discrimination against gay and lesbian employees. In reprisal for my successful lawsuit and despite my continued outstanding record, in January, 1995, I was forced off the department. Because I refused to stop working with and recruiting from the gay and lesbian community, the management of the LAPD have stated they intend to terminate me by November of 1995.

Norm Hill: On February 14, 1995, I was promoted to the rank of sergeant. There is a newly appointed, very progressive police commissioner for the city of Boston. He has turned out to be a great ally to our community by doing such things as ordering the recruitment of gay and lesbian people to become police officers, directing the writing and issuance of a pro-gay and lesbian sexual harassment policy, and implementing a gay, lesbian, and bisexual cultural awareness training program at the Boston Police Academy. He sent me on an all-expense paid trip to attend the Second Annual International Conference of Gay and Lesbian Criminal Justice Professionals held the week of September 4, 1995 in Los Angeles. Is this progress, or what?

One bit of sad news is that I separated from my partner of almost five years. Of all of my memories, this was one of the most painful experiences. I am only now getting used to being single.

Lee Jensen died on January 25, 1995 from complications due to AIDS.

Dorothy Knudson: On August 12, 1995 I was promoted to sergeant and reassigned to the Second District, which is located in the heart of highrise housing projects. So far, so good...

Jim Leahey: I have filed for retirement and am waiting for a hearing. My doctors say I cannot return to work because the environment is dangerous for my safety. I still get phone calls with threats of, "Don't come back to work, fag." One good thing is I never picked up a drink or drug; I've been sober for fourteen years. I am so grateful to AA for keeping me going. I'm hanging in there one day at a time.

Sharon Lubinski was promoted to lieutenant in October of 1994 and is now supervisor of the Research and Development Unit.

Cheri Maples has been promoted to lieutenant and is now in charge of the night shift (11 P.M. to 7 A.M.). She is also attending law school on a part-time basis.

Ralf Meier was forced to retire from duty because of accident-related injuries.

Bert Mrozik: I was chosen to be the Grand Marshall for the New Jersey '95 Lesbian/Gay/Bi Parade in Asbury Park by the New Jersey Lesbian and Gay Coalition, partly because I did not get reappointed as a judge in Asbury Park. Because the City Council did not give a reason for not reappointing me, I assume it must be because of my openness.

Judy Nosworthy: Since the community patrol, I had a serious bicycle accident and was off for ten weeks with a fairly serious head injury. Several assignments later, I applied for one of four positions for deputy chief of this service. I made the first cut to eighteen finalists (out of sixty-eight applicants), and was axed in the final twelve. I would have been the first constable to jump eight ranks, the first openly lesbian officer in Canada to hold a senior rank, and the youngest senior officer in this police service's history. The press loved it. Unfortunately, I did not quite make it.

A week after all of this happened, I was charged, arrested, and held for a Show Cause hearing for an alleged domestic assault involving my spouse. Our relationship was on the rocks, my partner was planning to move out, and after a very heated argument I kicked her out. She went to get the police to accompany her to our home to remove our son. One thing lead to another and, before she realized what was happening, she gave a statement that was more than sufficient to have me charged with assault. I was subsequently suspended from duty. Five court appearances later, my case was sent to the Attorney General's office to be prosecuted. Fortunately, most of my colleagues and superior officers have been very good to me, and, if anything, I think this incident has illustrated that being gay or lesbian does not mean that one does not have the same domestic issues as "straight" families do. I am quite confident that all will come to light in the trial. After the criminal trial, regardless of the outcome, I will be charged under the Police Act with Discreditable Conduct and tried, and then I will appear before the Professional Standards Review. The penalty for a finding of guilt under the Police Act could be termination of employment. Now we live in separate dwellings, and I cannot legally communicate directly with my partner or her family. We will be horribly in debt as a result of the legal fees we have incurred as a result of this episode. We are both, however, committed to putting our relationship back together, regardless of what the judicial system does.

My plan is to get promoted and change the system from within, to make this a gentler, less toxic work environment for everyone, not just for gays and lesbians.

Stacey Rabinowitz: In June of 1995 I received two awards: one from the Brooklyn Borough President for the work I did as liaison in the Seventy-eighth Precinct, and one from the Gay Officers Action League for gathering information on domestic partnership benefits. I currently live in Brooklyn with my partner in our new home.

Sara Raines: Mr. Dumas, our gay and minority positive director, retired. The new director is a woman and seems, so far, to also be committed to fairness in the workplace. I have my fingers crossed. Also, because the U.S. Department of Justice has changed its policy regarding lesbians and gay men, I am going to apply before I get too old. I always wanted to see if I had the qualifications to be FBI so now I will have the chance to do it without wondering if I will be pre-judged.

Danita Reagan is in her last year of law school, and is running Library Services and Recreation Services for County Jail 1. She has taken the promotional exam for sergeant and will be considered for promotion within the next year.

Shannon and Amy: Amy is still a DARE officer and Shannon is back on patrol. We have our fingers crossed that Shannon may be promoted to sergeant sometime next year. Our daughter is growing too quickly, and we're currently trying to add another baby to our family. We hope this will happen soon.

Stacey Simmons: I was asked to teach a class of recruits on hate crimes, sensitivity, and issues and implications of homosexuality in regards to policing at Boston Police Academy in July, 1995. I requested to wear my uniform to instruct the class, and was given a "no" answer by the upper echelon. I was allowed to teach the class, but I couldn't wear my uniform and I had to take a vacation day to do it. When I pressed for a reason, none was given. In September, 1995 I was asked to participate as a member of the Honor Guard presenting the Colors at the opening ceremonies of the Second International Conference of Gay and Lesbian Criminal Justice Professionals. Once again, I was denied the opportunity with no reason given. In the past I have conducted several public awareness functions and have participated in opening ceremonies of the International Association of Women Police conferences. On all of these occasions I asked and received permission to wear the CSP uniform. So I end up having to take vacation days to participate in these situations. Since I can't wear my uniform, I wear a white golf shirt with an embroidered CSP patch on the chest. I let everyone know that I am an out lesbian Connecticut State Trooper and proud of it. Thank God for freedom of speech!

Stephen St. Laurent: In January of 1992 I began a long-distance relationship with a man from northern Virginia. In August of 1993 I resigned from the Massachusetts Department of Corrections to pursue a new career as the Security Manager for a suburban Maryland hospital twenty-two miles from my new home with my partner. After a year and a half of living together, I ended the relationship. I continue to enjoy my new career in the private sector. The environment is very healthy when compared to corrections and the people I work with are very supportive. I have established a new circle of friends in Maryland. I travel back to Boston frequently to visit friends and family; it will always be home for me.

Lena Van Dyke: My partner is now on permanent disability, and I am meeting with the Union Executive Board to see if the union lawyer will support me in a suit against the state to get health benefits for her. I have filed two grievances to that effect. I passed the lieutenant's test number three in the state and number one at our prison.

Pete Zecchini: I am on the road to recovery. In the six months that followed our interview, I had constant thoughts of taking my own life. The final straw at work occurred in December of 1993. A group of officers conspired to keep me from answering any radio calls. Whenever I was dispatched to a call, I was immediately canceled by another officer. I sat in the park most nights doing nothing except for the thoughts of going mad, and being emotionally terrorized by these men. Eventually I walked into my supervisor's office and said, "I'm going home." One day I was watching the "Phil Donahue Show," and a police sergeant named Mitch Grobeson was a guest. He had been fired from the Los Angeles Police Department for being gay. I contacted Mitch, and he flew out to be at my side. He saved my life, and I made it back to work over a month later.

In the fall of 1995, I was transferred to "front desk" duty because police administrators feared for my safety. Three weeks later I was "tear gassed" from an area which was restricted to authorized personnel and specially admitted guests. The fire department had to be called. Two weeks later, I was reassigned back to patrol. Realizing that I would be even less safe on the streets, I reluctantly resigned from the police department. I believe I was discriminated against because my lover of thirteen years is totally disabled with AIDS, and some officers perceived I was HIV-positive. I have begun litigation against the city of Miami Beach in hopes of making some difference. I plan on a future of helping others in similar crisis situations. A group of friends and I are forming a corporation to help others with financial assistance for civil litigation for persons with AIDS and for those who are being discriminated by their employers because of AIDS. We hope we can save other lives and keep people fighting.

Bibliography

A black-and-white issue for the FBI. (1988, July 18). *U.S. News and World Report*, p. 9.

Alex, N. (1969). *Black in blue: A study of the Negro policeman*. New York: Appleton-Century-Crofts.

Alexander, J. I. (1978). *Blue coats: Black skin—The Black experience in the New York City Police Department since 1891*. Hicksville, NY: Exposition.

Balkin, J. (1988). Why policemen don't like policewomen. *Journal of Police Science and Administration, 16*, 29–38.

Bardwell, S. K. (1991, August 6). Police officers in sting posing as gay couples. *Houston Post*, p. A9.

Bartol, C. R., Bergen, G. T., Volckens, J. S., & Knoras, K. M. (1992). Women in small-town policing: Job performance and stress. *Criminal Justice and Behavior*, 19, 240–259.

Batten, T. (1994, September 9). Duxbury officer charged with assault. *Boston Globe*, p. 21.

Bell, D. J. (1982). Policewomen: Myths and reality. *Journal of Police Science and Administration*, 10, 112–120.

Blumenthal, W. J. (Ed.) (1992). *Homophobia: How we all pay the price*. Boston: Beacon.

Bouza, A. V. (1990). *The police mystique: An insider's look at cops, crime, and the criminal justice system*. New York: Plenum.

Boxall, B. (1992a, July 16). ACLU suit accuses police of brutality during gay protest. *Los Angeles Times*, p. B3.

Boxall, B. (1992b, August 6). Williams promises changes in LAPD's attitude on gays. *Los Angeles Times*, p. B3.

Boxall, B., & Torres, V. (1993, February 11). LA settles officers' suit, vows to fight anti-gay bias. *Los Angeles Times*, pp. A1, A28, A29.

Brown, M. C. (1994). The plight of female police: A survey of NW patrolmen. *The Police Chief*, 61, 50–53.

Burke, M. E. (1993). *Coming out of the blue: British police officers talk about their lives in "The Job" as lesbians, gays, and bisexuals*. New York: Cassell.

Campbell, D. (1993, August 31). Gay and lesbian police reveal force of despair. *Guardian*, p. 1.

Charles, M. T. (1981). The performance and socialization of female recruits in the Michigan State Police Training Academy. *Journal of Police Science and Administration*, 9, 209–223.

Chauncey, G. (1994). *Gay New York: Gender, urban culture, and the making of the gay male world, 1890–1940*. New York: Basic.

Corelli, R. (1995). Aiming for respect: Policewomen fight to end sexual harassment on the job. *Maclean's*, 108, 46–48.

Daum, J. M. & Johns, C. M. (1994). Police work from a woman's perspective. *The Police Chief*, 61, 46–49.

D'Emilio, J. (1983). *Sexual politics, sexual communities: The making of a homosexual minority in the United States 1940–1970*. Chicago: University of Chicago.

Dey, I. (1993). *Qualitative data analysis: A user-friendly guide for social sciences*. New York: Routledge.

Dodge, K. S. (1993). "Bashing back": Gay and lesbian street patrols and the criminal justice system. *Law & Inequality: A Journal of Theory and Practice*, 11, 295–368.

Duberman, M. (1991). *About time: Exploring the gay past.* New York: Meridian.

Egan, T. (1992, October 4). Chief of police becomes the target in an Oregon anti-gay campaign. *New York Times*, p. 4.

Ferrell, D. (1991, October 25). Gays decry LAPD's behavior at rally. *Los Angeles Times*, p. B3.

Fired gay FBI agent close to settling discrimination suit. (1993, December 10). *San Francisco Chronicle*, p. A4.

Fosdick, R. B. (1920). *American Police Systems.* New York: Century.

Friedman, L. M. (1985). *A history of American law* (2nd ed.). New York: Simon & Shuster.

Friedman, L. M. (1993). *Crime and punishment in American history.* New York: Basic.

Gallagher, J. (1992, March 10). Judge overturns Dallas's policy on police hiring. *The Advocate*, p. 15.

Gest, T. (1987, March 9). A one-white, one black quota for promotions. *U.S. News and World Report*, p. 8.

Grennan, S. A. (1987). Findings on the role of officer gender in violent encounters with citizens. *Journal of Police Science and Administration*, 15, 78–85.

Griffin, J. L. (1992, May 21). Rodriguez says he won't allow police insensitivity toward gays. *Chicago Tribune*, p. 2C.

Griffin, J. L. (1993, August 25). Primary label for gay police officers is cop. *Chicago Tribune*, p. 5.

Haynes, K. A. (1993, September). How good are women cops? *Ebony*, 48, p. 64.

Heidenshon, F. (1992). *Women in control? The role of women in law enforcement.* Oxford, England: Clarendon.

Herek, G. M. (1984) Beyond "homophobia": A social psychological perspective on attitudes towards lesbians and gay men. *Journal of Homosexuality*, 10, 1–21.

Hiatt, D. & Hargrave, G. E. (1994). Psychological assessment of gay and lesbian law enforcement applicants. *Journal of Personality Assessment*, 63, 80–88.

House, C. H. (1993). The changing role of women in law enforcement. *The Police Chief*, 60, 139–144.

Hudson, M. (1990). Black and blue. *Southern Exposure*, 18, 16–19.

James, G. (1994, June 21). Gay officers get their turn to present a heritage exhibit. *New York Times*, p. B3.

Kaminski, R. J. (1993). Police minority recruitment: Predicting who will say yes to an offer for a job as a cop. *Journal of Criminal Justice*, 21, 395–409.

Katz, J. (1976). *Gay American history: Lesbians and gay men in the USA.* New York: Avon.

Kennedy, E. L. & Davis, M. D. (1993). *Boots of leather, slippers of gold: The history of a lesbian community.* New York: Penguin.

Leinen, S. (1984). *Black police, white society.* New York: New York University.

Leinen, S. (1993). *Gay cops.* New Brunswick, NJ: Rutgers University.

Lewis, N. (1992). Florida bias suit settled. *Black Enterprise*, 23, 20.

Lewis, M., Bundy, W., & Hague, J. L. (1978). *An introduction to the courts and judicial process.* Englewood Cliffs, NJ: Prentice-Hall.

Marks, P. (1995, February 9). Black and Hispanic officers file discrimination charges: Left out of Suffolk's top ranks, suit says. *New York Times*, p. B6.

Marotta, T. (1981). *The politics of homosexuality.* Boston: Houghton Mifflin.

Martin, S. E. (1980). *Breaking and entering: Policewomen on patrol.* Berkeley, CA: University of California.

Martin, S. E. (1994). "Outsider within" the station house: The impact of race and gender on black women police. *Social Problems*, 41, 383–401.

McDowell, J. (1992, February 17). Are women better cops? *Time*, pp. 70–72.

McNaught, B. (1993). *Gay issues in the workplace.* New York: St. Martin's.

Morris, H. (1991, May 1). Meeting with mayor encourages gay activists. *Atlanta Constitution*, p. D1.

Narine, D. (1988, May). Top cops: More and more black police chiefs are calling the shots. *Ebony*, 43, pp. 130, 132, 134, 136.

Pike, D.L. (1991). Women in police academy training: Some aspects of organizational response. In I. Moyer (Ed.), *The Changing Roles of Women in the Criminal Justice System: Offenders, Victims, and Professionals* (2nd ed.). Prospect Heights, IL: Waveland.

San Francisco Police Chief is dismissed. (1992, May 16). *New York Times*, p. A6.

Patton, M. Q. (1990). *Qualitative evaluation and research methods* (2nd ed.). Newbury Park, CA: Sage.

Pharr, S. (1988). *Homophobia: A weapon of sexism.* Inverness, CA: Chardon.

Puerto Rico police accused of harassing a gay group. (1995, February 14). *New York Times*, p. A7.

Rosen, S. A. (1980). Police harassment of homosexual women and men in New York City: 1960–1980. *Columbia Human Rights Law Review*, 12, 159–190.

Serrano, R. A. (1991, November 7). Violence at gay protest examined. *Los Angeles Times*, p. B3.

Serrill, M. S. (1985, February 18). The new Black police chiefs: Updating a long tradition of ethnic groups rising to the top. *Time*, p. 84.

Shilts, R. (1982). *The mayor of Castro Street: The life and times of Harvey Milk*. New York: St. Martin's.

Shilts, R. (1993). *Conduct unbecoming: Gays and lesbians in the U.S. military*. New York: St. Martin's.

Strange justice for Tom Potter. (1994, October). *New York Times*, p. A30.

Sullivan, G. (1990). Discrimination and self-concept of homosexuals before the gay liberation movement: A biographical analysis examining social context and identity. *Biography*, 13, 203–221.

Suraci, P. (1992). *Male sexual armor: Erotic fantasies and sexual realities of the cop on the beat and the man in the street*. New York: Irvington.

Timmins, W. M. & Hainsworth, B. E. (1989). Attracting and retaining females in law enforcement: Sex-based problems of women cops in 1988. *International Journal of Offender Therapy & Comparative Criminology*, 33, 197–205.

Townsey, R. D. (1982). Black women in American policing: An advancement display. *Journal of Criminal Justice*, 10, 455–468.

Turner, W. W. (1993). *Hoover's FBI*. New York: Thunder's Mouth.

Valentine, P. W. (1993, April 29). Md. police drop policy against gays. *Washington Post*, p. C3.

Vincent, C. L. (1990). *Police officer*. Ottawa, Canada: Carleton University.

Watts, E. (1981). Black and blue: Afro-American police officers in twentieth-century St. Louis. *Journal of Urban History*, 7, 131–168.

Wexler, J. G. & Logan, D. D. (1983). Sources of stress among women police officers. *Journal of Police Science and Administration*, 11, 46–53.

Wilhelm, M. (1985). Portland greets its new female police chief with a warm 'may the force be with you!' *People Weekly*, 23, 42–43.

Yarmey, A. D. (1990). *Understanding police and police work: Psychosocial Issues*. New York: New York University.